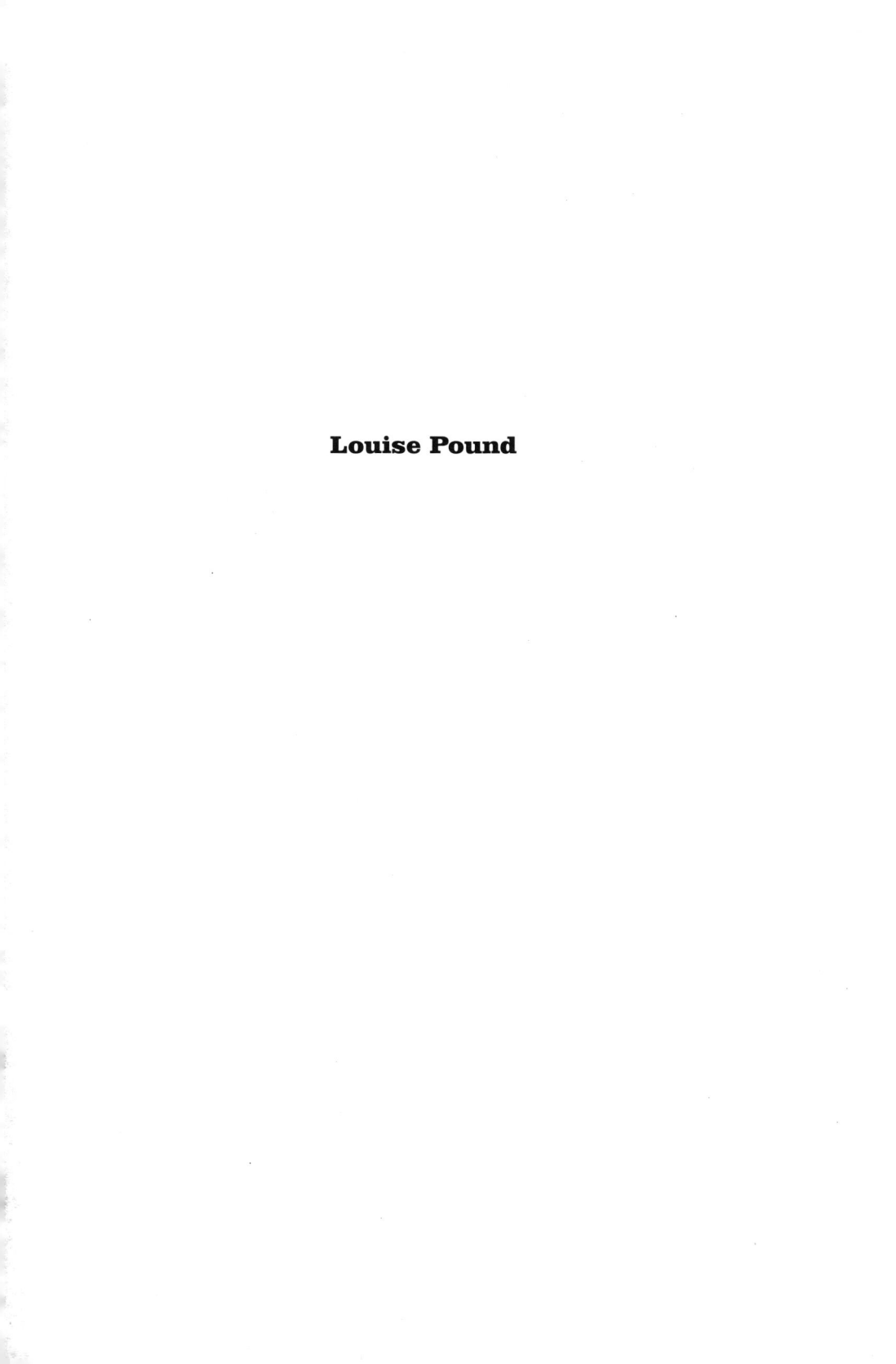

Louise Pound

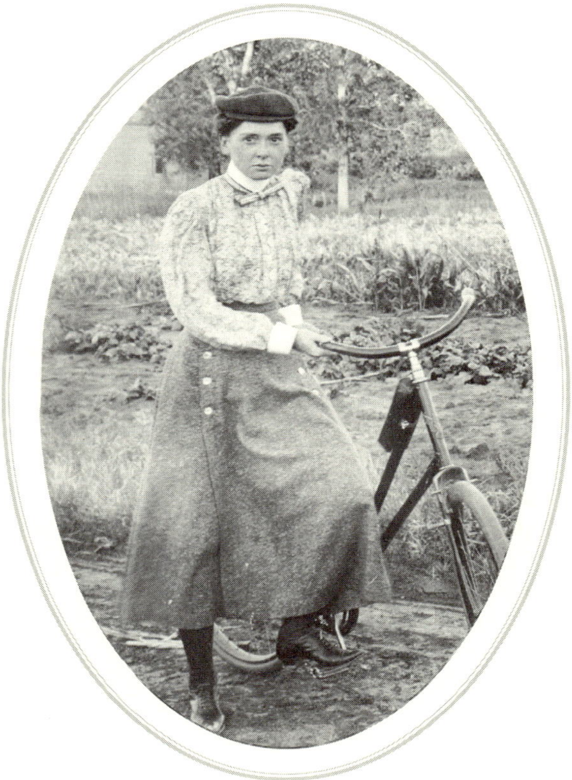

Louise Pound

Scholar, Athlete, Feminist Pioneer

Robert Cochran

University of Nebraska Press
Lincoln and London

© 2009 by the Board of Regents of the University of Nebraska. All rights reserved. Manufactured in the United States of America ∞

Library of Congress Cataloging-in-Publication Data

Cochran, Robert, 1943–
Louise Pound : scholar, athlete, feminist pioneer / Robert Cochran.
   p. cm.
Includes bibliographical references and index.
ISBN 978-0-8032-1546-7 (hardcover : alkaline paper)
1. Pound, Louise, 1872–1958. 2. Women scholars — Nebraska — Biography. 3. Scholars — Nebraska — Biography. 4. Athletes — Nebraska — Biography. 5. Feminists — United States — Biography. 6. Women's rights — United States — History. 7. Folklorists — United States — Biography. 8. College teachers — Nebraska — Biography. 9. University of Nebraska–Lincoln — Faculty — Biography. 10. Nebraska — Biography. I. Title.
CT275.P7525C63 2009
978.2'03092 — dc22   [B]   2008031035

Set in Bitstream Iowan by Kim Essman.
Designed by A. Shahan.

To the memory of John Long

Contents

          List of Illustrations   viii
          Acknowledgments   ix

ONE   "I have always been satisfied with Nebraska"   1

TWO   "The iridescent glamor of life beginning"   33

THREE   "A genuine Nebraska cyclone"   67

FOUR   "She's an athlete; she's a scholar"   119

FIVE   "Incapable of orderly thought"   159

SIX   "There is always zest"   185

SEVEN   "First woman again"   223

          Notes   267
          Index   307

ILLUSTRATIONS

Following page 26

1. Laura Biddlecome Pound
2. Judge Stephen B. Pound
3. Louise Pound as a young child
4. Louise Pound in preparatory school
5. The Pound family home

Following page 110

6. Professor Lucius A. Sherman
7. Louise Pound and Willa Cather
8. Louise Pound in rational costume
9. Louise Pound as a University of Nebraska student
10. Photo of Louise Pound from *Leslie's Weekly*, 1897
11. Ani Königsberger Pfister
12. Louise Pound as an instructor at the University of Nebraska

Following page 216

13. Louise Pound the golf champion
14. Mamie Meredith
15. Ruth Odell
16. Louise Pound at a book signing
17. The Pound siblings
18. Louise Pound, Mari Sandoz, and Olivia Pound
19. Louise Pound

Acknowledgments

First thanks go to Robert Knoll; this project properly got under way when my son Taylor and I spent three hours in his basement study in 2003. I told him I wanted to write a biography of Louise Pound; he told me how to start, loaned books and articles, mentioned many Nebraskans. Over the next four years, he and his wife, Virginia, were constant mentors, sources of assistance and encouragement.

Two Lincoln archives—the Archives and Special Collections, University of Nebraska–Lincoln Libraries, and the Nebraska State Historical Society—provided tireless assistance on repeated visits. The latter holds the major collection of Pound's papers; the former provided copies of her academic transcripts, yearbooks and literary magazines, and microfilm of student newspaper articles. Staff members at both archives were extraordinarily helpful. At the University of Nebraska's Love Library I am especially grateful to Peterson Brink, Mary Ellen Ducey, and Carmella Orosco; at the Nebraska State Historical Society I was assisted by Anne Billesbach, Andrea Faling, Linda Hein, Mary-Jo Miller, and Matt Piersol.

I made even more persistent use of the Interlibrary Loan division of Mullins University Library at the University of Arkansas, where Lisa Little, Robin Roggio, and Michelle Tabor diligently sought out scores of obscure books and articles and microfilm of old newspapers. Many other archives and libraries provided valuable assistance: Chicago History Museum; University of Chicago Library Special Collections Research Center (Julia Gardner); Rare Book, Manuscript, and Special Collections Library, Duke University Perkins Library (Janie Morris); Milton S. Eisenhower Library, Johns Hopkins University (Kelly Spring); Knox College Library Special Collections (Mary Kiolbasa, Matt Norman); Library of Congress (Jeff Bridgers, Todd Harvey); Lincoln City Library; Archives of the University of Missouri (Kris Anstine); Special Collections/College Archives, Shaffer Library, Union College (Marlaine DesChamps); Wayne County (New York) Historical Society.

A special thank-you goes to Harold Davey, Ed Dosek, Barbara Fox, Frank Hallgren, E. A. Kral, Paige Namuth, Michael Shugrue, and Janet Sullivan. In face-to-face interviews, telephone conversations, and e-mail and regular mail exchanges they shared their memories of Louise Pound, putting me in closer touch with a personality who without them would have been approachable by me only by way of her writings. I was put in touch with them by Andrea Cranford, who published my letter of inquiry in the winter 2006 issue of the University of Nebraska alumni journal, Nebraska Magazine.

Several students, former students, and University of Arkansas staff members and administrators also bestirred themselves on my behalf. Kelly Riley's researches on Mari Sandoz turned up a number of references to Pound, and Sarah Fine collected mentions of Pound in Mabel Lee's fulsome memoirs. Anna Klamer sought out biographical information about Ani Königsberger in Heidelberg, and Sarah Fine helped bring order to my photocopies of her letters to Pound. Jesse Cochran cleaned up typos and redundancies in an early draft of the manuscript. Dana Harris, who manages everything connected with the Center for Arkansas and Regional Studies at the University of

Arkansas, arranged my research trips to the archives at Lincoln and elsewhere and assisted with the many tasks connected with preparation and copying of the manuscript at various stages.

I am grateful for the work of the University of Nebraska Press in turning a manuscript and a selection of photographs into a handsome book. Hands-on roles in this process were played by Elaine Jenkins, Jonathan Lawrence, Ladette Randolph, Kristen Elias Rowley, and Sabrina Stellrecht. Thanks to all of you.

This book is dedicated to the memory of my friend John Long. Almost fifty years ago he was by his varied talents and prodigious energy the "universal wonder" for me that Pound was for Henry Marvin Belden. The planet chilled for me when he died, as it had earlier at the loss of my father, Robert Cochran, and my pals Raymond Garrow, Charles Mazer, and Bob Pierle. The warmth it maintains is centered in friends and family—final thanks, deepest gratitude, goes always to you: Carolyn and Charles Allen, Milton and Mimi Burke, Joe and Anne-Marie Candido, Jack and Tess Clarkson, Emily Cochran, Mary Cochran and Garin Wiggins, Ruth Cochran, Sarah Cochran, Steve Cochran and Barbara Adams, Henry Glassie and Pravina Shukla, Jeff Gordon, Tünde Incze and László Bakk, Alison and Chris Little, Julie Long, Mike Luster and Rachel Reynolds, Mattie McCray, John Pickerill. Most of all, I am sustained in everything I do by the company I keep at home: Bob, Shannon and Sam (and now young Robin), Masie and Duncan, Jesse, Taylor. It's all wonderful—the basketball games and the Christmas camping trips to Moab and Big Bend, the pilgrimages to see sharks and my cool new stereo system, the weddings and wonderful photographs, the hilarious videos and the article in Bitch. Few parents are so proud, or so contented. Last, most, always, at the center, sustainer for a quarter century of our whole shebang: Suzanne.

Louise Pound

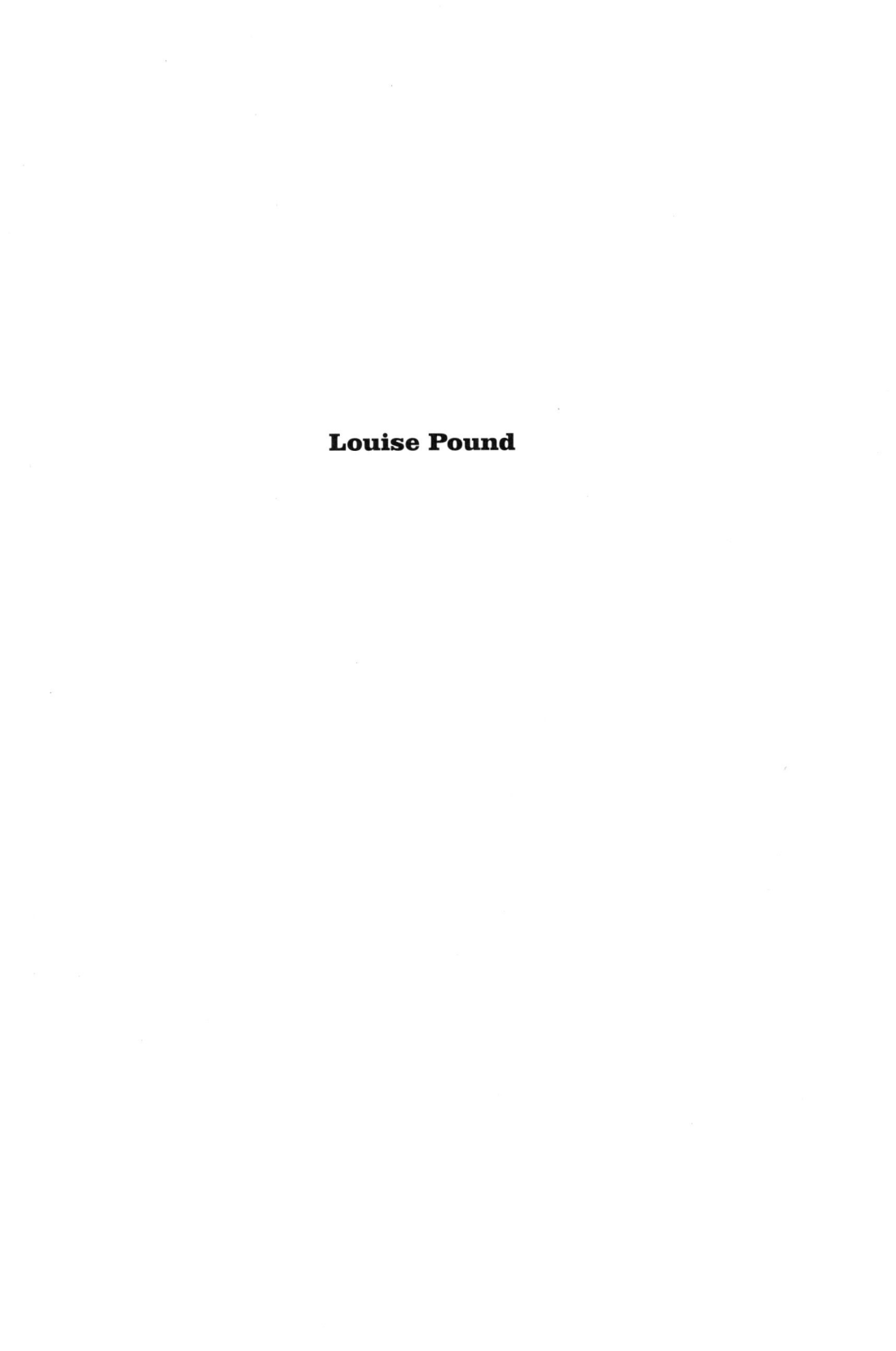

ONE

"I have always been satisfied with Nebraska"

The bride arrived at Lincoln's Atwood House hotel by stagecoach, hungry and spattered with mud, on Friday, February 12, 1869. She had traveled with her new husband for nine days, ridden a midnight mail train from Chicago to Council Bluffs when misdirected baggage made them miss the express, and entered Nebraska by walking a mile and a half across the Missouri River to Plattsmouth guided by a seventeen-year-old boy on ice so thin the stages refused to cross. "It seemed to me a long way," she later wrote. "In many places the water stood in pools, and I would step aside only to be told peremptorily by my guide to 'get back in line.'" With nine others in their party, she had slept the previous night in the single upstairs room of a wayside house. The bride, in short, was an intrepid and determined woman, and with such adventures behind her she was only mildly surprised to find herself, later that evening, the only woman in a crowded dining room. The state legislature, she was told, was in session (the senate, in fact, had approved a bill establishing the University of Nebraska that very day). She had not eaten since the previous afternoon, and was "too hungry," she wrote, "to permit this fact to spoil a good dinner for me."[1]

Thus did Laura Biddlecome Pound, an educated twenty-seven-year-old New Yorker of distinguished Quaker background, come to Nebraska. She would stay for the rest of her life. Beginning in 1876 she would spend two years as a student at the fledgling university, "perfecting herself in the German language," among other studies.[2] Closer attention to her written account of the hard winter journey from Rochester only confirms the initial impression of fortitude and determination. In Plattsmouth, for example, the morning after her dangerous walk across the Missouri's ice, she is introduced to an attorney named Irving, who addresses her confidently, "Mrs. Pound, you won't like Nebraska." Determined to make herself clear, she replies in emphatic terms, "I have burned my bridges behind me," an interesting choice of image in a place then distinguished by the lack of any bridge at all. In the next sentence she notes that Irving returned to the East "when the grasshoppers came," while the Pounds, even in the hard times of the 1870s, "were still content to stay."[3]

When Mrs. Pound recalls the moment of her arrival in Nebraska (she got stuck in the "almost impassable" mud on the riverbank and had to be pulled out), her narrative displays both unruffled composure and a finely understated humor. Told that a group of men she had noticed seated on the bluff above the river were "waiting to see the ice break up," she allows that "this was not very comforting information, considering that my husband was still on the Iowa side" (he had waited with their belongings on a sandbar after the driver of the wagon they had hired in Glenwood refused to go further). After some hours of anxious waiting, wondering if she would be "left a widow on the west bank of the Missouri," Mrs. Pound was relieved to hear "the rumble of a wagon" and look out from the sitting room of the Platte Valley House to see "the rest of our party with my dignified husband perched on top of a trunk in the back of the wagon."[4]

The husband who shared this challenging journey with his dignity intact was Stephen Bosworth Pound, like his wife a Quaker and a New Yorker. Eight years his wife's senior, he was born January 14, 1833, in Farmington, a small upstate town some twenty miles west of Phelps, the even smaller village where Laura Biddlecome was born on May 14, 1841. Both attended the academy in nearby Macedon, about ten miles north of Farmington, he from 1854 to 1855, she from 1856 to 1857. From there Laura went west, to Galesburg, Illinois, where in 1860–61 she studied ancient and modern languages at Lombard College, a Universalist institution that opened its doors in the 1850s, was a hotbed of abolitionist sentiment in the years leading up to the Civil War, and closed for good in 1930. Lombard was also unusual at the time for regularly admitting female and African American students. Plus there was a family connection: "Her uncle, Reverend Daniel Read Biddlecome, was the Universalist minister in Galesburg, and Lombard College itself was a denominational school of the Universalist church." Laura was a fine student, though she never completed her studies: "Her record there was remarkable, however, the faculty approving a plan for her to graduate after only one more year of residence. But the unsettled conditions due to the approaching Civil War caused her parents to think it unwise for her to return to Galesburg."[5]

Stephen Pound also had abolitionist ties in his background—the upstate New York farm of his great-grandfather Hugh Pound "was one of the important stages on the underground railroad for runaway slaves making their way to Canada."[6] From Macedon Academy he went east to Schenectady, where he graduated from Union College with honors in 1859 and also played on the school's baseball team.[7] He then came back to his home county to study law with Judge Lyman H. Sherwood in Lyons, just east of Macedon. He was admitted to the New York Bar in 1863 and worked in partnership with his mentor until Sherwood's death in 1866. At this point he made his move. Before the year was out he was in Wisconsin, where, according to a 1909 interview, "a glowing description of Nebraska" moved him westward again. He apparently went first to Omaha, where a "big lawyer named Poppleton" (Andrew J. Poppleton, in 1866 an unsuccessful candidate for one of Nebraska's first U.S. Senate seats) advised him to try Nebraska City, further south along the Missouri River and then "a lively place and quite a trading point." Though impressed, Stephen did not stay long: "a great many people had their eyes turned toward Lancaster, later called Lincoln. Though the capital had not been located there at this time, it was confidently expected that it would be, and I decided to cast my fortune there."[8]

The "great many people" were right on in their guesses. Lancaster, then a mostly imaginary city, was selected as the new capital in two momentous steps filled with political maneuvering and financial chicanery so egregious that impeachment proceedings against the governor eventually resulted. Political alliances in Nebraska tended to divide along the Platte River, with north-of-the-Platte Omaha, the territorial capital, opposed by a host of south-of-the Platte contenders. In the first step, a bill authorizing relocation of the capital was approved on June 14, 1867, despite a last-ditch move by an Omaha senator to turn south-of-the-Platte Democrats against the measure by changing the name from Capital City to Lincoln. In the second, the three commissioners charged with selecting the new capital met in the attic of W. T. Donovan's home in Lancaster on July 29, 1867, and voted unanimously (on their second ballot) to locate the capital there. Lancaster, then a tiny village less than a decade old with "six or seven houses" and a population of "about 30," was by these decisions renamed Lincoln and established as the capital of Nebraska.[9]

Lincoln's hopes for the future were pinned on the expectation of great wealth to come from development of the area's salt deposits. Governor David Butler addressed the inaugural legislative session in glowing terms just a month before the Pounds' arrival: "we have, within sight of this hall, a rich and apparently inexhaustible supply of pure and easily manufactured article. It will be directly and indirectly a source of wealth to the state whose great value no one can fully estimate."[10] As it happened, while the hopes based on capital relocation endured and eventually prevailed, those founded on the salt deposits were never realized, in the long run producing "nothing but lawsuits, and the only tangible evidence remaining today is a saltwater swimming pool at the west edge of the city."[11] (Actually, the salt flats did leave at least one other lasting legacy—the Lincoln Saltdogs minor league baseball team plays today in the southern division of the Northern League.)

While these tumultuous deals went down, Stephen Pound was a brand-new resident seeking his fortune in the retail sector. For most of 1867 he operated "a small merchandizing shop in the front room of Jacob Dawson's double log cabin," though his neighbors apparently suspected his heart was not in it. "As a merchant," it was said, "he was noted for his application to his law studies."[12] (There is also a report, written much later by his younger daughter, Olivia, of one adventurous voyage westward to Fort Kearney as a "freighter." During this journey he innocently gave a ride to two soldiers who turned out to be deserters, was falsely accused of setting fire to haystacks at a farm where he stayed, and was freed only when a search party hunting the deserters arrived.)[13] In 1868 his legal studies paid off; the thirty-five-year-old New Yorker was admitted to the Nebraska Bar and went into practice with Seth Robinson, another Lincoln attorney. At the end of the year he went back east to claim his bride, having assured her that he would be bringing her to a place not entirely lacking cultural and intellectual attainments. In a letter of 1868, also cited in Olivia Pound's recollection, the suitor reports the formation of "a reading club, the first of the kind over formed here, and of which I have the honor to be president."[14]

But despite these successes, as well as the optimism with which he apparently contemplated the future he would share with his new wife in Nebraska, one moment in Laura's account of their journey reveals that her husband, like attorney Irving in Plattsmouth, worried at least a little about her reaction to a place as raw and undeveloped as Lincoln. On the train, moving west across Iowa, he queries her about her expectations: "Have you any idea what sort of a place you are going to," he asks, and when she replies with a one-word affirmative, he asks her to show him, in the landscape out the window, "a place you think something like Lincoln." When she selects the small town of Tama, then a collection of "a few dingy shops with the regulation low, square fronts" (it is still there, still small, proud of a restored "Lincoln Highway" bridge on U.S. Highway 30), Stephen is impressed and relieved. "You have done pretty well," he replies cheerfully, "only it is better than Lincoln."[15]

The newlyweds, then, had grounds for optimism that February evening as they enjoyed their dinner surrounded by legislators in the crowded dining room of the Atwood House. They had come through their difficult midwinter journey safely, and by virtue of their education and by Stephen's occupation they were members of the new capital's elite on the day they stepped down from the stagecoach. (Their safe journey was itself no small achievement. Fifteen years earlier, the Nebraska Territory's first governor, South Carolinian Francis Burt, had died after just two days in office following the rigors of a similar trip.) Less than a year after that day, the couple had established themselves in their first Lincoln residence (located to the south of the original County Courthouse at what was then the edge of town) and the new husband had been elected judge of the Probate Court of Lancaster County. Stephen Pound, just a year after his admission to the bar, was Judge Pound, a title that would be joined to his name for the rest of his life.

Higher offices and two changes of domicile followed. After occupying a second home at 1542 P Street, the Pounds moved in 1892 to 1632 L Street. From these quarters Judge Pound's career was a steady ascent. He was founder and first president of the Lancaster County Bar Association, a Nebraska state senator for the 1872–73 term, and a delegate to the state constitutional convention in 1875. A solid Republican who would have had no problem with the town's earlier name change, Judge Pound was three times elected (twice unopposed) to four-year terms as judge of Nebraska's Second Judicial District, serving from 1875 through 1887.

Laura Pound also rose quickly to prominence in the new community's affairs. She served a full decade (and a little more) on the board of directors of the Lincoln Public Library. Her report "The Lincoln Public Library, 1875–1892" notes ten years of service by "Mrs. Richards and Mrs. Pound," who are also noted as "members of the present board." Laura was also a charter member of the City Improvement Society, the Nebraska Art Association (originally called the Hayden Art Club), and the Lincoln Women's Club, as well as an early member of the Nebraska State Historical Society. She was most prominent, however, in the Nebraska Daughters of the American Revolution (DAR), where she was a charter member of the state's first local group, the Deborah Avery Chapter, and served four terms as state regent.

Bar associations, public libraries, a state art association, constitutional conventions—it is clear from such a list that Laura and her husband accomplished their climb in a world that was itself very much on the rise. They arrived near the beginning and grew up with the country. On the eve of statehood, in 1867, Nebraska claimed approximately 50,000 residents; just three years later, the 1870 U.S. census reported a population above 122,000. The new capital was at the very center of this boom. If Lincoln could boast only thirty residents and fewer than a dozen homes in 1867, a year later one of two local newspapers was reporting "by actual count 143 homes in Lincoln," and by 1870 the population had increased to 2,500.[16] The same year saw the Burlington Railroad arrive from Plattsmouth, and by 1872 the lines had continued west to Kearney and a connection with the Union Pacific. The new University of Nebraska opened its doors in January 1871, a faculty of five greeting a student body of ninety. Five years later, Laura Pound would enroll to perfect her German.

One of the new city's most prominent citizens, C. H. Gere, was a newspaperman whose pioneering *Nebraska Commonwealth* began as a monthly, grew to a weekly, changed its name to the *Nebraska State Journal* in 1869, and became a morning daily in 1870 on the day the railroad arrived. Another early leader was James Sweet, a banker who gave his name to the Sweet "Block," a stone structure built in 1868 to house Sweet's State Bank of Nebraska and other businesses. Sweet was a major player in the deals that brought the state capital to Lincoln—he nearly got caught in the scandals that brought down the state's first governor, Republican David Butler. Lincoln was from its first days a city of churches—so much so that one of its abundant self-congratulatory nicknames was "The Holy City"—others included "The Hartford of the West" (celebrating insurance companies), "The Athens of the West" (celebrating colleges), and "The Retail Capital of the Midlands" (celebrating commerce). Congregationalists and Methodists were the first to organize, but by 1870 Baptists, Roman Catholics, Episcopalians, Lutherans, Presbyterians, and Universalists were also holding services.

All this is not to suggest that the state or its capital enjoyed smooth, uninterrupted progress from rude frontier to a flourishing and civilized society. The 1870s, especially the years in the decade's middle, were a difficult time for Nebraska, and for Lincoln. Some setbacks were national in scale. The financial panic of 1873 had roots in Europe but was triggered in the United States by the collapse of finance king Jay Cooke's investment empire. The New York Stock Exchange shut down for ten days, farm prices plummeted, banks failed, and foreclosures mounted. Back in Nebraska, the general depression was exacerbated by bad weather. The early and middle 1870s were years of sustained drought, made worse by devastating invasions of grasshoppers. A Lincoln-area report from July 1874 makes clear the biblical scope of the destruction: "The hoppers entered Lancaster County from the northwest. . . . In two hours they were four inches deep on the ground. They ate the onions out of the ground, beets, carrots, and everything. All that was left of the garden was the holes in the ground. . . . They did this job in about two hours."[17] It was this period, presumably, that drove out Irving, the Plattsmouth attorney who had confidently predicted Laura's unhappiness in Nebraska.

Then, as if depression, drought, and grasshoppers were not enough, Lincoln was hit by damaging floods in 1873 and 1874 (two people died in the latter). The city was still reeling from the political and financial scandals of the capital location battles and the first legislative sessions. The "public buildings at Lincoln," according to one modern report, "stood out as stark monuments to the slipshod way" the new state's affairs had been handled. "All had cost more to build than had been appropriated, and all were so poorly built that they began falling apart almost as soon as they were occupied."[18] The machinations of an ill-defined "Lincoln ring" were suspected (not without reason) to be at heart of these failures. Attempts to remove the capital from Lincoln continued to plague the city and undermine investor confidence until the matter was finally laid to rest by the adoption of a new constitution in 1875. It all added up to hard times. In 1873 and 1874, Lincoln experienced its first declines in real estate valuations (this was a statewide pattern—property assessed at $4.79 per acre in 1870 had fallen to $2.86 per acre by the decade's close).

Many of these tribulations, political and climatic, touched the Pound household. Laura, in particular, left vivid accounts of hard times in "The Athens of the West." In September 1869, just seven months after her arrival and four years before the panic, she answered a letter from back east with news from Lincoln. Her tone is resolutely upbeat ("so far we have done well here"). The letter goes on to say that "two railroads" and "better times and more to eat at cheaper rates" are confidently anticipated for the following spring. "Nothing short of a good-sized fortune," the new settler concludes, "would ever tempt me to come back East to live."

But mixed in with all this good news are a few complaints, with rain getting top billing: "I think there has not been a week since the last of April that it has not rained a little at least and generally in torrents." When rain combines with winds out of the south, the water floods under the door "so badly that I have to tear two sides of my carpet unnailed and turn it back." In addition, prices are "exorbitantly high," the house lacks even one "decent pen," and the writer anticipates a "dull winter with nothing much to do." But these are minor quibbles; the dominant tone remains decidedly optimistic. Laura in September is now a settled resident of the Lincoln she first saw in February, and the spirited determination of her responses to her husband's queries on the train in Iowa and attorney Irving's predictions in Plattsmouth is still very much in evidence in her letter to the folks.[19]

Nearly a quarter century later, however, in January 1893, Laura took a very different view when she looked back at Lincoln's early years. The occasion was her address "The Lincoln Public Library, 1875–1892," read at a meeting of the Nebraska State Historical Society. The city's library, she reports, "was organized towards the close of the darkest period in the history of Lincoln, the year 1875." An impressive catalog of disasters follows. In the first place, "the summers of 1873–74 had been dry, the crops were poor, and what the drouth and hail had spared, was taken by the grasshoppers." Then the winter came, with unusual cold, even for the Great Plains, "the thermometer during the months of January and February standing for many days at a time below zero."

A general assessment of this "darkest period" follows, closing the second paragraph of what must have opened as an unusually grim report of a public library's origins: "It was a time most painful to remember. There was the long and constant appeal for help, from the poor and suffering during the winter, and the gloomier prospects of the spring to come."[20] Even the prisoners at the new state penitentiary were tried beyond patience, rising up in January in a violent "mutiny" that ended with the fatal shooting of the rebellion's leader, an inmate named McWatters.[21] The contrast with the letter of 1869 could hardly be stronger. The letter subordinates present difficulties to anticipated future improvements; the report presents hard times aggravated by anticipated future worsenings. (Histories of Nebraska and neighboring states confirm Laura's portrait of Lincoln for the region as a whole. "At first," writes one, "public officials and newspapers, concerned with promoting settlement, minimized the seriousness of the situation. . . . But as reports of destitution began to pile up from all parts of the state, it became apparent that something had to be done." Stopping short of a legislative special session, Governor Robert W. Furnas turned instead to private elites, convening "a number of well-known citizens" in the fall of 1874 "to find a means of dealing with the situation." The citizens responded by incorporating the Nebraska Relief and Aid Society to "collect money, provisions, clothing, seeds, and other supplies for distribution among the needy."[22] Delegations were also dispatched back east to more settled states in search of aid, where they sometimes found themselves competing with similar appeals on behalf of suffering Kansans and South Dakotans.)

It is a poor spring indeed that presents "gloomier" prospects than winter, but the spring of 1875 did arrive with a double-barreled combination of climatic and political worries. It was, Mrs. Pound reported, "cold, backward [i.e., belated], and rainy, but not cold enough to destroy the young grasshoppers or retard their growth." The following summer was "probably the rainiest ever known in the annals of Nebraska . ... Salt Creek was out of its bounds the most of the summer, and once during the month of June, the high water reached nearly to the Metropolitan hotel." But Lincoln residents in 1875 feared other things at least as much as rain and lack of rain, hail and grasshoppers, and economic slumps. According to Mrs. Pound's report, citizens were also "looking ahead with gloom and foreboding at the approaching session of the legislature," for then "stalked forth the grim spectre of Capital Removal." On May 9, in particular, they anticipated "fresh troubles" in connection with "the meeting of the constitutional convention," since these deliberations, too, might very well involve the location of the capital. There were also worries about the new University of Nebraska. Led by an Omaha newspaper, critics were calling for "the closing of the State University for five years, in order to give the high schools of the state a better chance, and to save expenses."[23]

Mrs. Pound's listeners, in 1893, were no doubt properly impressed by this astonishing litany of disasters. As it turned out, however, the hard winter, "backward" spring, and rainy summer were attended before fall by several triumphs. The constitutional convention, adjourning on June 12 after almost exactly a month, at last put to rest the "spectre" of Lincoln losing the capital. Under the new constitution, the capital could be relocated only by popular vote. The movement to shut down the university was also defeated. Even the Lincoln Public Library, whose prospects had looked so bleak in April when the reading room sponsored by "the ladies' library and reading room association" had been closed "on account of hard times," was by the end of the year "practically established." Mrs. Pound, in retrospect, was inclined to see the events of 1875 as "the turning point in the history of Lincoln." Credit, she said, was due to "to the untiring energy of the Lancaster delegation."[24] She did not say so, but Judge Pound was surely a part of that delegation, working to advance the interests of the community where "I decided to cast my fortune" nearly a decade earlier.

It is abundantly clear, then, that despite the hard years and the times "most painful to remember," the new state and the new couple were from the beginning a perfect fit. For his part, Judge Pound's 1909 interview in the *Nebraska State Journal*, just two years before his death, affirms his continuing satisfaction with his decision for Lancaster/Lincoln more than forty years earlier: "I decided to cast my fortune there. I have never been sorry, either."[25] For her part, Laura's wedding journey account, published more than half a century later, makes clear that the bride who "burned her bridges" in 1869 never changed her mind. She ends her reminiscence with a ringing endorsement: "I have always been satisfied with Nebraska. I liked the altitude, the dry climate, the blue skies, the sunny days and gorgeous sunsets, the strange, new flora and the song of the prairie lark."[26] Stephen and Laura Pound, then, helped construct and thereafter lived successfully and contentedly in the highest tier of Lincoln society, and their accomplishments often made both of them visible on a statewide stage. But in addition to all this they did something else that lifted their town and themselves to still wider notice, to national and even international fame: they had children.

And here is a place, less arbitrary than most, to begin the story of Louise Pound. She was by any measure an extraordinary woman. In the academic world she was a pioneering scholar who made important contributions to at least three disciplines. In the world of sports she was an outstanding athlete who would have been at one point the nation's top-ranked woman tennis player had such listings been compiled at the time. She excelled at every sport she attempted, and she attempted them all. She was a passionate supporter, both as a player and as a coach, of high-level athletic competition for women; Title IX legislation, had she lived to see it, would have seemed to her the restoration on a national scale of a golden age for women's athletics at the University of Nebraska in which she played a central role. She fought (and lost, in the short term) her life's bitterest battle in support of women's athletics at the University of Nebraska. But such gender-based commitments extended far beyond the playing fields—Louise Pound was throughout her long career as a teacher and scholar a dedicated advocate of opportunities for women in general and more especially for their educational and professional advancement. No cause—and she was active in many—gained her greater loyalty.

Last, but far from least, she was for all her long life a Nebraskan at home in Lincoln, casting her lot with her community and state every bit as wholeheartedly as her parents had before her. Like her elder brother, she could have gone elsewhere, to more prestigious academic posts (she did accept such appointments, but only for summer terms). Her choice, wholly conscious and fiercely affirmative, was for Nebraska. Nebraska had raised her and bestowed upon her the best it had to offer in the way of material advantages and educational opportunities. She remained grateful to the end of her days, and she worked diligently over a long professional lifetime to return the gift, to chronicle the state's history and more especially its traditional culture in scores of written studies and hundreds of lectures.

Louise Pound was not, however, her parents' first child. That was her brother, Roscoe, born in 1870, himself destined for a career very nearly as remarkable as hers. (Some would say more remarkable, and two of his champions have already written biographies.)

Louise came second, born on June 30, 1872, followed by her sister, Olivia, in 1874. With the arrival of her children, Laura Pound, already a woman of marked independence and resolution, came fully into her own. In retrospect it seems obvious that she was a homegrown pedagogical genius, a sort of Great Plains Maria Montessori, a woman whose own wide learning, combined with public school teaching experience in New York and in Nebraska, provided her not only with strikingly innovative instructional notions of her own but also with the confidence to implement them even in the face of community disapproval. Her first decision was to educate her children at home. The public schools of Lincoln she judged "too stereotyped"; she and her husband would be better pedagogues.[27] To this end, unruffled by neighborhood criticism, Mrs. Pound ordered a large blackboard and had it attached to the wall in her living room.

Her method could not have been more straightforward. Her bedrock principle, from which all good results followed, was to root education in inquiry. The student's innate curiosity, which the instructor was at pains to enlarge and systematize, initiated the adventure of learning. This process could therefore begin at an early age, presumably with the child's first queries. "I believe," she told an interviewer in 1922, "in beginning the training and teaching as soon as they are born, and their inquiries should be answered intelligently; if a parent does not know the correct answer let him [or her, as it was most often in the Pound academy] find out what it is."[28] In the same interview, Mrs. Pound uses Roscoe as an instance of her method in action (despite her obvious commitment to equal educational opportunities for women, and despite the reasonable guess that her branding of the Lincoln public schools as "too stereotyped" referred to a too-limited sense of appropriate educational and occupational goals for women, she invariably uses him as her example): "every child should have a fad. My boy's fad was collecting bugs and butterflies. He began by bringing into the house a cocoon which he just pulled from a tree, and stuck it up to await hatching time. It turned out to be a beautiful Cocropea moth."[29]

This, then, is the beginning. The child's initiative produces a piece of the natural world and a question about it. The well-prepared teacher swings into action—that's a great question, she says, asked before by other inquiring minds. There are answers, and what's more, these answers exist within an organized investigative system. The child is thus introduced to nomenclature, to taxonomy, even to epistemology: that's called a cocoon, that's called a Cocropea moth. And the boy at play is thus hooked, launched into learning. In this instance, young Roscoe finds himself, without ever leaving his living room, taken over the threshold of Natural Science Hall, freed to explore in the entomological and botanical wings. As Mrs. Pound related it: "From studying insects he must study what they fed upon and must study botany to find out: so this took on a new interest for him and he learned it without knowing exactly how or when." From such beginnings, she concludes, the captivated and encouraged mind, trained to systematic inquiry, takes its increasingly independent way: "in the college later, he covered all the work which Dr. Bessey gave."[30]

For Roscoe's sister Louise, one early "fad" was apparently stamp collecting. Her earliest surviving letter, written to a cousin in the summer of 1881, when she had just turned nine, opens with thanks for the gift of several stamps ("three of them I did not have") and goes on to a proud, carefully classified and quantified account of her collecting: "My album now contains 192 stamps. 49 are U.S. 39 are U.S. Rev. One Confederate and 103 foreign. I have only been collecting 3 months, but have some very old and rare stamps." The letter concludes with a description, similarly detailed, of her friend "Lute" Bumstead's coin collection.[31] Like her brother's interest in entomology and botany, Louise's attraction to collecting and arranging, which would lead in her case to significant gatherings of everything from folk songs to dialect, got an early start in the Pound home. Louise was also playing the piano at an early age (did her mother teach her this as well?). Although her brother did not play, he was very fond of listening to his sister: "Almost every evening before the Pound children settled down to their studies, Roscoe would stretch out on the floor and ask for one piece after another."[32] The natural sciences, then, were at the heart of Mrs. Pound's pedagogy, and it is clear from her remarks elsewhere that she was in this area an ideal mentor and guide.

In the Lincoln Women's Club, founded later (in 1894), Laura Pound's expertise was recognized; as the leader of its science department she was responsible for the club's program on January 31, 1898.[33] She listed "the strange new flora and the song of the prairie lark" among Nebraska's abiding attractions, and even her arduous wedding journey is enlivened by the sights of a country that is "monotonous but interesting," offering her discerning eye "acres of dry sun flowers, thickets of sumac and wild plum, and a shrub unknown to me which I later classified as Indian currant."[34] (The oxymoronic phrasing "monotonous but interesting" indicates a spirit with little need for spectacle and speaks to Laura Pound's capacity for untumultuous, ruminative pleasure.) Once settled in her new home, Mrs. Pound encountered other indigenous plants previously "unknown to me" and promptly shipped off specimens to Asa Gray, the nation's foremost botanical scholar.[35] Knowledge, it is clear from such actions, was for her a cooperative and a progressive enterprise. She defined the world of learning as a community of scholars, and she drew its boundaries generously. By sending prairie plants to Gray, she included herself, made her own contribution to the growth of knowledge. From all of this it is clear that Laura Pound was a wonderful teacher in the first place because she was an avid learner. At the heart of her educational enterprise is the simple sharing with her children of her own pleasures in exploring the world around her.

But insects and plants were not the whole of Laura Pound's interests. After all, she did not enroll at the new university to perfect her botany. Languages, to note a second obvious subject, were no less central; and German, as the leading "scientific" lingua franca of the day, was the modern language of choice for the Pound children. Roscoe began his studies at six, in the same year that his mother, practicing what she preached, enrolled at the university for a two-year course of studies (the newspaper account of her "perfecting herself in the German language" refers to this time). The family in fact went all out in its campaign to learn German—a German maid was hired, and no doubt encouraged to use her native language in conversations with the children, while Roscoe was sent to Sunday school in a German Methodist church, where he "often won prizes for reciting the most Bible verses correctly."[36] Louise, just two years younger, may have gotten an even earlier start. There is no record of her reciting Bible verses in a German Sunday school, but a quarter century later she would be completing a PhD in philological studies at the University of Heidelberg.

Meanwhile, along with all the botany and German, the languages of the traditional curriculum were not neglected. And here Judge Pound came to the fore. Roscoe was introduced to Latin at eleven, and his father, "who was quite adept at classical languages, shared the teaching responsibilities with Mrs. Pound."[37] The *Centennial History of the University of Nebraska* offers a wide-angle view of the Pound home as a frontier classics oasis in action: "In the Pound household . . . on Sunday afternoons the Greek Scriptures were read aloud for visitors."[38] The Pound home here shows itself as one of Lincoln's cultural standard-bearers, one of the "houses of brick or wood in chaste or classical lines or spun wonders of Victorian Gothic" (this would describe the longtime Pound residence at 1632 L Street) where the town's elites "moved in, took out their white kid gloves, subscribed to *Century*, shipped in oysters frozen in blocks of ice, and tried to keep life very much as it had been in Ohio, New York, Illinois, or Virginia."[39] As another observer put it, "It may have been mud-flats on the outside, but it was Boston within."[40]

Actually, the "Boston" is misleading, and the "Ohio, New York, Illinois, or Virginia" is much more apt. Certainly, there were New Englanders who played important roles in the settlement and development of Nebraska and its capital, but the majority of the pioneer elites arrived, like the Pounds, from mid-Atlantic and midwestern states. The early leaders of the University of Nebraska had similar backgrounds. The land-grant universities established by the Morrill Act in 1862 looked consciously not to the nation's oldest institutions in New England but to the educational institution most obviously modeled on a Jeffersonian vision: "the grandparent of the state universities was the University of Virginia, not Harvard." In fact, in the case of Nebraska a traceable, three-generation line of descent is strikingly direct. The legislative bill establishing the university in 1869 was written by Augustus Harvey, who used the University of Michigan's charter as a model. The 1837 charter of the Ann Arbor school, in its earlier turn, was based on the prose of U.S. Circuit Judge Augustus Woodward, who in his still earlier turn had met with Jefferson as he was planning the University in Charlottesville. "The University of Michigan can be said to have kindled its fire from Jefferson's university and so, in time, did the University of Nebraska."[41]

Louise probably began her studies in Latin and Greek alongside her brother, just as she may have done with his earlier work in German. In the 1940s she suggests a possible Greek origin (a later consensus describes a nineteenth-century American source) for the American expression "O.K."[42] Later still, on the occasion of her eighty-fifth birthday, her brother recalled that when Louise graduated at the head of her class in 1892 he was "moved to translate the S.P." on her Phi Beta Kappa key (it stands for *societas philosophiae*) with an explicitly feminist Latin motto, "*sedeant pueri*: Let the boys go back and sit down."[43] Louise, presumably, would have appreciated the joke and could have translated it for herself. But despite the impressive accomplishments of Roscoe and Louise, the real classicist in the family was Olivia, the youngest, whose studies carried her to a master's in Greek at the University of Nebraska and a distinguished career as Latin teacher and longtime assistant principal in the Lincoln public schools. No doubt those schools were much improved from the days when Laura Pound found them inadequate, and surely she would have been pleased at her family's signal contribution to their betterment. It seems entirely appropriate that there is today a Pound Middle School in the Lincoln system, though it is a glaring omission that the school's website names Stephen Bosworth Pound and his three illustrious children but omits the mother whose innovative teaching started it all.

But of course the curriculum at Laura Pound's little school on the prairie did not end with ancient and modern languages and natural science. The humanities were by no means shortchanged. In this area, as in the language studies, Mrs. Pound credited her husband's contribution: "Their father was away a large part of the time, but when here, he read with them good books like 'The Iliad' and was very painstaking."[44] Roscoe's biographer provides a wider view of Judge Pound's reading lists: "Judge Pound often read aloud to the children, and Dickens, Scott, Thackeray, and Shakespeare were among the family favorites."[45]

The young Pounds also read, according to Olivia's written remembrance, European fairy tales (Grimm and Laboulage) and history (Froissart's *Chronicles*, Kingsley's *Greek Heroes*, and Macaulay's *History of England*) as well as the American tales of Hawthorne (*Tanglewood Tales* and *The Wonder Book*). "Father and mother were careful about the books they got for us," Olivia recalled. "Father read aloud to us a great deal. . . . Louise never cared much about listening. She would rather have the book herself and read at her own lightning pace. . . . Louise and I found the 'Elsie' books and Louisa Alcott's too slow. I think we used Watson's readers when mother started us out."[46] Toward the end of their home schooling, with Roscoe already dividing his instructional time between his mother and German classes at the university, Mrs. Pound was able to concentrate on her daughters: "While Roscoe was at the University Mother taught Louise and me reading, spelling, arithmetic, and later geography, grammar, and United States history," wrote Olivia.[47] In at least one instance, a parental bribe was offered in support of these ambitious readings. When Roscoe was twelve, "his parents offered him and his younger sister Louise a dollar to read Macaulay's *History of England*. They read together to ensure honesty, and they periodically asked each other questions. Tradition had it that Louise read faster but that Roscoe retained more."[48]

Mrs. Pound inculcated this curriculum (surely she included mathematics as well, though specific mention of algebra, geometry, and trigonometry is missing from the record) via a method that would today would be recognized as supervised independent study. Formal schooling—that is, time spent in face-to-face teacher/student interaction—"covered but one hour of the day," and even this was apparently insisted upon less for its opportunities for direct lecturing or questioning and more for its embodiment of "regularity and system."[49] Mrs. Pound, asked to describe her pedagogy, gives short shrift to instructional technique but devotes painstaking attention to opportunities for the free play of curiosity and "fancy": "A large playground is one of the things all children need. Ours had a big back yard, which they turned into canals, or towns, or whatever their fancy dictated." The children were also liberally provided, neighborly disapproval once again registered and dismissed, with books and other supplies: "One day I bought a rather expensive article for my boy to use in his work with the insects. A rich neighbor told me I was going to ruin the child, and I answered, you would think it all right for me to pay ten dollars for a hat."[50]

Most of all she wanted independent minds capable of directing themselves. And if a given practice served these ends she pursued it unswervingly, even in the face of disapproval: "I was regular and painstaking with them and began early to teach them the wonderful advantage one has who is able to decide and not change his mind."[51] In this emphasis upon individual initiative the parental Pounds were very much of one mind. In 1897, Judge Pound delivered a short, informal address to the Nebraska State Historical Society. Published the next year as "View of Judge S. B. Pound," the piece is a surprisingly flippant exercise, very funny in places, but ending with a serious, almost curmudgeonly defense of "individual effort." He begins by taking issue ("I am not prepared to agree") with previous speakers who have "placed a very high estimate" upon the members of the

Nebraska Territory's first legislative session. Noting that this body simply adopted verbatim the criminal and civil laws of another state, the judge suggests ("that is pretty crude legislation") that its members "lacked the knowledge and ability to frame laws of their own and express them in their own language."[52]

All this sounds straightforward enough, but then the judge goes on to note that this same legislative body incorporated "some fifteen or twenty cities," thereby establishing a state lacking thereafter "any small towns or villages." The explanation he provides can only be tongue in cheek: "the early inhabitants of this state were, at least one-third of them, distinguished and titled persons; they were majors, colonels, generals, judges, and governors, who preferred to live in cities." This ratio, he continues, has endured to the present day: "we are all colonels, or judges, or something of that sort, so that this may be fairly claimed as one of the results of this legislature. We all live in cities. We have the cities of Brownville, Nemaha City, the city of Plattsmouth, Dakota City, the city of Carlisle, the city of Fontanelle, Republican City,—all these are cities."[53]

This is on its face an extraordinary passage, a wholly appealing send-up. Judge Pound, himself one of the "distinguished and titled persons" gently mocked, speaking to an assembly of his fellows inclined, as the tenor of the addresses preceding his own makes clear, to celebration of themselves, quietly deflates the entire occasion. That he seems not to have offended, that his remarks were duly published in the group's *Proceedings and Collections* series, speaks warmly of the esteem and affection his neighbors and fellow citizens held for their judge. But Judge Pound closed his remarks in a more serious vein. That same 1855 inaugural legislative session, with its penchant for incorporation that resulted in so many paper cities, also called into being "some thirty ferry companies" in a society with "little or no travel," and in addition a host of "banks, and railroads, and emigration societies, and seminaries, and insurance companies, and all sorts of corporations." Such actions, the judge concludes, reveal a habit of mind: "people at that time seem to have thought that the great source of wealth and prosperity was in legislation." This overvaluation of legislation and incorporation is accompanied by an undervaluing of the "private individual"—"Nothing could be carried on by individual effort."[54] This attitude, the judge concludes, is persistent: "there is a prevailing sentiment of that kind abroad at the present time, in the minds of people, that individual effort cannot accomplish much." It is also wrong, and harmful, and the judge ends on a monitory note: "I think it is a false opinion—a false idea. Legislation can do something, but not much. Very much depends on the individual and very little on the legislation."[55]

The tone of Judge Pound's remarks, then, is much more bantering and merry than any surviving utterance, public or private, attributed to Mrs. Pound. Stephen Pound was cherished in his family for exactly this impish sense of humor under his judge's robe. As family stories reported by Olivia make clear, Judge Pound was especially fond of stories deflating pomposity and pretense, the antics of the horde of "distinguished and titled people" who crowd the upper echelons of small-town society. One fellow attorney who much amused him was famous for frequent (though often wildly inaccurate) "references to Greek and Roman history or mythology." This gent's rhetorical arsenal featured, among other excesses, the phrase "embossed battlements," only slightly altered to fit particular cases. Thus a stack of railroad ties accused of frightening a team of horses were characterized as offering to the nags "the terrifying aspect of the embossed battlements of a military encampment." In another case the jury itself was described as sitting "as the embossed battlement of civil and religions liberty." Judge Pound took this phony elegance home, where his wife and children soon learned to expect to hear "embossed battlement of a military encampment" employed to describe "any obstruction."[56]

In another case, the same attorney was pleading a case where a set of missing check stubs played a significant evidentiary role. "Embossed battlements" were insufficient to this cause, and the advocate trotted out instead "the funeral cortege of the noble Roman lady

Juno," which passed through the streets of "the eternal city." But when the crowd noticed that one figure was missing from the group of ancestral images carried in the procession, they called out repeatedly, "Where is the bust of Brutus? Where is the bust of Brutus?" The attorney then returned from Rome to the case at hand: "Gentlemen of the jury, I ask you, 'Where are these stubs?'" This gem, too, came home to the Pound household, where "If my father ever missed anything around the house he would usually call out 'Where is the bust of Brutus?'"[57]

On another occasion a family breakfast was enlivened when Judge Pound smiled, chuckled, and finally burst out laughing. "We all joined in," recalled Olivia, "not having the least idea what we were laughing about." Finally, Mrs. Pound asked for an explanation, and the judge recounted a story from a dinner of the bar association the evening before. "You know how pompous M. is," he began, naming a prominent local barrister who had "enjoyed too much port wine" with his dinner. "In the midst of one of the speeches he got up solemnly and to everyone's surprise began to walk up and down, gesticulating with wide sweeps of his arms, and declaiming eloquently—'If anyone tries to haul down the American flag, spot him on the shoot, spot him on the shoot.'"[58]

The preponderance of evidence suggests that, outside the home, Judge Pound usually kept his penchant for such mockeries on a short leash. Accounts of one spectacular murder trial from the 1870s, for example, would suggest that he was himself wholly capable of the same florid oratory he pilloried in more private moments. Sentencing the youthful murderer and horse thief William Henry Dodge "to be hung by the neck until dead on July 21," the judge attempted to satisfy both the requirements of the law and those in the community favoring a life term as more appropriate for such a young and presentable prisoner by making "'touching and pertinent remarks' in passing the sentence 'which brought many tears to the eyes of those who witnessed the scene.'"[59] On at least one occasion, however, when a trial was disrupted by the drunkenness of one attorney, he allowed his sense of humor to peek out even from his judicial robes. After tolerating the inebriated lawyer's incoherencies for a time, Judge Pound brought down his gavel and postponed the case for a week. "The lawyer for the plaintiff," he ruled, "is trying to practice before two bars at the same time. It can't be done."[60]

The point does not need to be overstated—Laura Pound was herself certainly capable of a wry humor, as in her reaction in 1869 to the crowds gathered to watch the ice she has just crossed break up. Another instance would be her response to her son's outraged reaction when he discovered a battered volume of Horace on the family bookshelf. "What vandal" had done such a thing? he asked. "His name was Roscoe Pound," his mother replied—evidently young Roscoe numbered hurling books into pails of water among his "favorite pranks."[61] A third example comes from Mrs. Pound's published account of her efforts in support of a turn-of-the-century DAR campaign to mark "the only point touched in Nebraska by [the Lewis and Clark expedition] which could be positively identified" by placing "a Nebraska boulder upon the site." As committee chair, Laura Pound was obliged "to raise the money and to find the boulder." The money came easily, but finding the boulder proved more difficult, and Mrs. Pound's account brings both the scientist and the dry humorist to the fore: "Finally a boulder of Sioux Falls granite was found in the Marsden farm, north of Lincoln, and it was given to the society by the owner, who remarked that he was 'glad to be rid of it.' Its dimensions were $7\frac{1}{2}$ x $8\frac{1}{3}$ x $3\frac{1}{2}$ feet. Its weight was between seven and eight tons."[62]

On the maternal side of the family, the gift for humor is traced back another generation in one of Louise Pound's articles from 1918, where her discussion of a "negro spiritual" named "Weeping Mary" in a short piece for *Modern Language Notes* is based on a family story originating with her maternal grandmother:

> I learned it from my mother, who caught it from the singing of a white woman, Nancy [last name forgotten], in the village of Ham-

ilton, Madison County, New York. My mother used to repeat it, imitating the original singer. Nancy had just come from a Methodist "protracted meeting," and was singing "Weeping Mary" over and over again, on the occasion when my mother heard her, working herself up to a frenzy and beating incessantly with something in her hands as she sang. Finally she attracted so much attention from passers-by that she had to be stopped. My mother had a tenacious memory, and was a good mime, and she often reproduced for our entertainment Nancy's hysterical singing of her religious song.[63]

Biddlecome women, then, were fully capable of levity, just as Pound men assisting runaway slaves were capable of unmixed earnestness. But a fundamental (and wonderfully complementary) difference of temperament nevertheless seems clear. Both were essentially serious people, widely respected for their accomplishments and admired for their many kindnesses to others, but if Laura Pound was a nearly perfect teacher, just the one to help her children appreciate the importance of their schoolwork, her husband, a fine teacher himself, was perhaps no less perfect as an encourager of their play.

And play they did. The Pound home seems to have served as a neighborhood social club for the children and their friends. Olivia's papers, in particular, preserve a number of brief family history pieces devoted to her parents and siblings. One of these, "Home Life of the Pound Family," includes an account of war games featuring armies of wooden soldiers "whittled out by Louise, dressed by Olivia, and given the proper military designations by Roscoe. They were maneuvered by Roscoe and Louise. Sometimes the battles became so fierce that Mrs. Pound had to interfere and imprison both armies till a truce was declared. Roscoe and Louise composed histories and geographies of the countries of the opposing armies, also the full peerage."[64] Roscoe's biographer notes that the siblings "had many friends in common, and as they grew older, the living room of their home often resounded with the gaiety of dances and parties. Judge Pound, an excellent dancer himself, occasionally joined in the fun."[65]

For Louise in particular, that fun included a striking range of sports and games, and here again her father played a prominent role. By Roscoe's report, his sister "inherited a skill at games" from her father, who "played baseball in college in the formative period of that game and was actively interested in what would now be called athletics."[66] In Nebraska Judge Pound retained his enthusiasm for baseball—he was such a well-known fan of Lincoln's squads in the 1890s that umpires reportedly opened games with a standard declaration: "If both teams are ready and Judge Pound is in the grandstand, the game will begin."[67] His eldest daughter apparently began with croquet—a 1983 study devoted to her distinguished athletic career notes that this genteel lawn sport "was much too tame for Louise, who, by the time she was 14, was a master of the mallet-and-ball game."[68] Many less-tame games and sports would follow—figure skating and roller skating, baseball and softball, riding and rifle shooting, diving and bowling and cycling, and above all basketball, tennis, and golf. Down the road there would be local, regional, and (in tennis) even national acclaim.

The young Pounds, then, as their mother completed their primary education in a home that seemed to offer the finest instruction west of John Stuart Mill's house (and without the stresses), were sent off each in his or her turn to the new University of Nebraska. It may have been new, but Laura Pound had sampled its wares, and if she had confidence in it sufficient to enroll her children, its faculty and administration must have been doing something right.

1. Laura Biddlecome Pound. Nebraska
State Historical Society, RG0909 PH4 5.

2. Judge Stephen B. Pound. Nebraska State Historical Society, RG0909 PH4 3.

3. Louise Pound as a young child. Nebraska State Historical Society, RG0909 PH7 2.

4. Louise Pound as a preparatory school student.
Nebraska State Historical Society, RG0909 PH7 7.

5. The Pound family home at 1632 L Street.
Nebraska State Historical Society, RG0909 PH18 3.

TWO

" The iridescent glamor of life beginning "

As it turned out, the University of Nebraska was making a number of very good moves in the nineteenth century's final decades. From its inception in 1871, in recognition of the widely varying levels of preparation afforded entering students by the frontier school systems scattered across the new state, the university had in place a two-year preparatory school (the Latin School). Louise Pound enrolled in 1885, at the age of thirteen, in the School of Fine Arts, though she first formally registered for graded classes in the 1886–87 school year. After two years in the preparatory school, she entered as a freshman for the 1888–89 year, graduating in 1892.

Fifty years later, asked for written remembrance of her undergraduate experiences for the school's alumni magazine, she took the opportunity, before discussing her college years, to go back even further, to offer particular praise for her preparatory years in the Latin School: "Among my teachers in the preparatory school were the distinguished professors C. E. Bessey in botany and D. B. Brace in physics . . . and the scholarly C. E. Bennett, later head of classics at Cornell University."[1] It might be expected that a high school student, even one as precocious as Pound, would refer to her teachers as "distinguished" or "scholarly" (even when the student, by then a distinguished scholar in her own right, makes the assessment a half century later), but a closer look at the figures she names more than bears out her estimate.

Charles Edwin Bennett (1858–1921), Pound's Latin teacher, came to Lincoln after prior teaching stints in New York and Florida. Born in Rhode Island, he graduated from Brown in 1878 and continued his schooling in Germany and at Harvard. At Cornell he later established a solid scholarly reputation with his studies of Latin syntax and more especially with his studies of the Latin subjunctive—in 1898 the ninth number in Cornell's Studies in Classical Philology series published his monograph, *Critique of Some Recent Subjunctive Theories*. Bennett also wrote, with George P. Bristol, *The Teaching of Greek and Latin in Secondary Schools* (1900), plus a number of school texts. (His edition of Horace's odes and epodes, published in 1914 in the Loeb Classical Library, has only recently been superseded, and the course list for Cornell's classics department for the fall term of 2005 used both his Latin grammar and his edition of Cicero's *De Senectute* for an introductory Latin course). For this promising teacher and scholar on the rise Pound was a star Latin student—in six terms during her time in the preparatory school her lowest mark was a 98, and three times she made a perfect 100. Her course work, in addition to three terms of elementary Latin, included readings in Caesar and Cicero.[2]

Dewitt Bristol Brace (1859–1905) was if anything even more impressive. Arriving in Nebraska from the University of Michigan in 1887, just in time to teach Pound, he carried with him the best education in physics available at the time. After undergraduate work at Boston University he attended MIT and Johns Hopkins before completing a PhD at the University of Berlin with von Helmholtz and Gustav Kirchhoff in 1885. At Nebraska he quickly moved to establish a professional physics curriculum, instituting laboratory work in place of the recitations by students of material memorized from textbooks that were then standard pedagogy not just in physics but in most other fields. Brace also pursued his own studies in optics and optical magnetics, constructing for the purpose a 3,400-pound electromagnet in the university laboratory.

On the practical level, Brace supervised construction of the system that brought electric light to the library and campus sidewalks. In his field he was best known for his experiments in the double refraction of light, which replicated with far greater accuracy the famous 1887 Michelson-Morley "ether drift" experiments. The resulting paper, "Double Refraction in Matter Moving through the Ether," published in 1904, was widely cited and praised. Albert Einstein, some have suggested, may have made it a part of his reading as he prepared his landmark 1905 first essay on relativity. In 1907, just two years after Brace's untimely death, Edward L. Nichols's summary article, "The Scientific Work of Dewitt Bristol Brace," gave Brace high marks as a speaker, as an inventor, and most of all as a meticulous experimenter. His vice-presidential address to the American Association for the Advancement of Science in 1902 is a "lucid and altogether admirable semi-popular presentation," and his experimental measurements come in for even more extravagant praise: "The experimental difficulties of researches of this character are almost undescribably great and the results obtained by Brace although uniformly negative are to be accounted among the greatest achievements in modern physics."[3] Pound completed two terms in Brace's physics classes in 1887–88, her second year in the Latin School, scoring perfect 100s both times.

Charles E. Bessey (1845–1915) was the most distinguished of the lot. His education lacked the glossy credentials of Brace—though he studied at Harvard, he never completed a doctorate. He achieved his greatest renown as the author of the longtime standard text in the field, *Botany for High Schools and Colleges* (1880), written at the suggestion of his mentor, Asa Gray (the same eminent figure who received Nebraska plant specimens from Laura Pound). At the University of Nebraska, Bessey and noted entomologist Lawrence Bruner gathered a cadre of exceptionally able students (Roscoe Pound among them) who by their labors made the university, twenty years after its founding, a leader in a science moving from a purely descriptive taxonomic focus to an explicitly dynamic approach to plant systems. They called themselves the Botanical Seminar, or "Sem. Bot." (in all likelihood another Roscoe Pound Latinism), and what we would call today botany majors included a number of female students sufficient to generate a cartoon showing one of them painting the words "The Fem. Bot. Sem." on a fence. The group undertook field collecting trips throughout the state, and on at least one occasion traveled all the way to Estes Park, Colorado. A fully ecological botany was on the horizon, and no figure played a larger role in its emergence than Bessey's student Frederic Clements. Roscoe Pound also figured prominently in these developments; back in Lincoln as a practicing lawyer after studies at the Harvard Law School (1889–90), he and Clements worked together on *The Phytogeography of Nebraska* (1898), a pioneering study of Nebraska plants in their environmental contexts which earned PhDs for both. A century later, ecologists often recognize it as the first truly "ecological" study done in the United States.

Roscoe Pound went on to glory in the field of law, but Clements stuck with botany, where his studies soon garnered an international reputation despite their Lamarckian orientation. His best-known work is *Plant Succession and Indicators* (1928). Bessey's greatest claim to fame was his students, but a genus of Great Plains cacti (*Neobesseya*, now usually classified as *Escobaria*) was named in his honor, and buildings on three campuses also carried his name (even today there is a Bessey Herbarium and a Bessey Hall at the University of Nebraska). Pound studied botany with Bessey in 1887–88—in that year's winter term she was studying Latin with Bennett, botany with Bessey, and physics with Brace. From Bessey for three terms of study she earned three perfect 100s.[4]

So, a gifted young woman, Louise Pound, completes the eleventh and twelfth grades in Lincoln, Nebraska, at the end of the 1880s. Not only is her early education supervised by the redoubtable Laura

Pound, her mother, who devotes the best of her very considerable talents to the education of her children, but her amazing good fortune continues in the final years of college preparation. Her Latin teacher ends up at one top-flight university and has his translations published by a second's press; her physics teacher accomplishes research that earns him the highest kind of accolades from his academic peers; and her botany teacher trains a group of students (her brother among them) who revolutionize the field. The young Miss Pound, on the face of it, is an extraordinarily fortunate student.

She is also an extraordinarily diligent and successful one. Her classwork was concentrated in Latin (six courses), mathematics (five courses) and the sciences (eight courses, including two in chemistry and one in zoology in addition to her physics and botany classes). She also completed courses in history (three), English (three), essay writing (three), and infantry drill (one). It all added up to twenty-nine grade marks, ranging from a high of perfect 100s (nine) to a low of 85 (two). Her first year was strong (eleven marks averaging just over 94), but her second year was stronger (eighteen marks averaging just under 98).[5]

Here, in microcosm, was the combination (intelligent students, superb teachers, an institutional framework to bring them fruitfully together) that propelled the young university at the end of the 1880s into what its excellent historian labeled "A Golden Era."[6] The University of Nebraska was for a time, and though it came to an end it was not an especially short time, fortunate in nearly its every move, bringing together a series of energetic and able administrative leaders to join a remarkable core of innovative and dedicated faculty with ever-increasing numbers of gifted and determined students eager to seize the new world of opportunities their pioneering ancestors had made available to them.

The university was led from 1884 to 1895 by three chancellors. The first, J. Irving Manatt, a Yale graduate who had previously taught Greek at Marietta College in Ohio, served a stormy four-year term that opened at the beginning of 1884 and closed with his dismissal in the summer of 1888. His manner often offended, but he arrived with the explicitly stated intention of improving the faculty by "removing a bit of dead timber."[7] His record on the hiring front was stellar—Bennett, Brace, and Bessey came to Lincoln during his tenure, and there were other distinguished hires as well, including geologist Lewis Hicks, language scholar A. H. Edgren, and chemist Rachel Lloyd, the second woman appointed to the faculty.

Unfortunately, Manatt was also something of a martinet, prone to sarcasm, disinclined to compromise, and (worst of all) afflicted with too active an interest in the private lives of others. Professor Lloyd, who gained her doctorate from the University of Zurich in 1886 (and still gains notice as the first American woman to earn a PhD in chemistry), attracted the chancellor's particular notice: "Manatt inquired into the religious commitments of the faculty generally and at one time commented on Rachel Lloyd's church attendance." This did not go down well with the men and women of the New West, especially those who appreciated Lloyd's researches into the sucrose content of Nebraska sugar beets, and when Manatt subsequently failed to renew her contract for "causes not for public debate," the debate immediately became very public indeed.[8] The Omaha papers weighed in, and the faculty voted with near unanimity to reinstate her. Finally, in July 1888, spurred on by the alumni association and the student body (including once again the omnipresent Roscoe Pound), the board of regents dismissed their chancellor and would-be beadle and (in September) persuaded Bessey to take over on an interim basis.

The interim lasted three years, but Bessey was a very popular teacher and an able administrator who quickly reestablished harmonious relationships with faculty, students, and regents. The contrast with his predecessor could hardly be stronger. Instead of Yale and the East he was from the Midwest and Michigan Agricultural College (later Michigan State); instead of Greek he taught botany and horticulture in Iowa and served as dean of the Industrial College at the University of Nebraska; in the place of a traditional education conceived as charged with transmitting established cultural traditions he understood the university as leading an ongoing enterprise of discovery and dissemination of knowledge central to the well-being of society. Bessey was a gentle man and a deeply pragmatic figure, but never a mere servant of utilitarian ends. As president of the National Education Association in 1896, he insisted upon the larger benefits of the "scientific" pedagogy he had championed: "Let us hear less in the school of the practical value of science. . . . The proper pursuit of science should develop a judicial state of mind toward all problems."[9]

But Bessey saved his greatest administrative achievement for last, and nothing became his chancellorship so much as his leaving it to the perfect replacement. That was James H. Canfield, lured north from Kansas by Bessey and Charles Gere, the regent and prominent Lincoln newspaperman who had worked with Laura Pound to establish the public library in Lincoln. As the historian of the university's early years tells the story, "Bessey and Regent Gere had a meeting with Canfield in Kansas City, keeping it secret at Canfield's request, and after an all-night conversation in a hotel room, Gere 'virtually tendered him the chancellorship.'"[10]

It was a masterstroke. Canfield was a spellbinding orator, "an egalitarian, a western democrat, an idealist," who understood the state university as the culmination of the state's public education system, grades thirteen through sixteen, as he put it himself. He immediately took his show on the road, crisscrossing the state tirelessly, selling their school to its people: "The University is only the upper grades of this work; the faculty are simply teachers in other rooms from those occupied by the teachers in the graded schools or in the district schools."[11] Canfield logged some ten thousand miles in his first year (and eight thousand in subsequent years), speaking to "any group that would have him" ("I may not know Nebraska from alpha to omega, but I know it from Arapahoe to Omaha," he said). The message itself, combined with the flair of the messenger, proved an irresistible combination: "Nebraska and the Great Plains suffered severely from depression and drought in Canfield's years, but these difficult times he took only as opportunity. 'If you cannot earn,' he told his audiences, 'you can at least learn.' . . . People came through mud and weather to hear his fervent message."[12]

It was an astonishing performance, and it was perfect for that time in that place. Enrollments boomed, despite a depression so severe—the droughts and grasshoppers that were such a trial to Laura Pound in the 1870s had returned with a vengeance twenty years later—that the chancellor's wife joined with other prominent Lincoln women to plan a soup kitchen for the indigent. When Canfield arrived in 1891, enrollment in the collegiate divisions was approximately five hundred; by the time he left in 1895 it had nearly tripled. Conservatives did not appreciate his views on free trade; his enthusiastic support of coeducation was off-putting to some (he taught a course on "The Status of Women in America"); and others were appalled when he "invited a socialist, Iowa professor George D. Herron, to deliver the commencement address" in 1894.[13] But the students and citizens alike loved his informality, his enthusiastic support for the school's football team, his obvious concern for the well-being of his charges. (In 1891 Canfield took an injured freshman football player to his home, nursed him for several days, and wrote a letter to his parents that ended with a sentence any parent would have to love: "Do not worry about him. I will keep you posted if he does not.")[14]

Canfield's enthusiasm was contagious, and somehow everything came together. The ambitious, innovative faculty, the bright, eager students, the charismatic chancellor extolling education's wonders in every far-flung hamlet—their meeting and synergistic interaction struck fire and made light, and Lincoln in Louise Pound's student days was a magical place. Those who were there knew it, too. Willa Cather, one year younger than Pound, remembered the students who arrived "straight from the cornfields with only a summer's wages in their pockets, hung on through the four years, shabby and underfed, and completed the course by really heroic self-sacrifice. There was an atmosphere of endeavor, of expectancy and bright hopefulness about the young college that had lifted its head from the prairie only a few years before."[15]

Will Owen Jones, an earlier student who by the 1890s was teaching a journalism course and editing the *Nebraska State Journal*, recorded a similar response: "The sons and daughters of the pioneers, some of them from the sod houses on the homesteads, were catching their first glimpses of the glories of the ancient and the modern world. It was an enchanting and inspiring time."[16] Dorothy Canfield Fisher, the chancellor's daughter, six years younger than Cather, made the same point more lyrically: "both town and university had the iridescent glamor of life beginning, for which almost anything is possible because little has yet been tried. The very air over the campus was glittering bright with what might be."[17] Writing in 1968, the distinguished historian John D. Hicks, who came to Nebraska in 1923, looked back with pride on the growth that made Lincoln at that time such an attractive place. Under Bessey, Canfield, and Benjamin Andrews (who served from 1900 to 1908), Hicks wrote, "the University of Nebraska shook off the last remnants of frontier provincialism and took its place among the important universities of the nation." Both Roscoe and Louise Pound are noted as "already members of the Nebraska faculty" at the time. Even into the 1920s, Hicks concluded, the University of Nebraska "carried the brightest torch for learning to be found anywhere between the Missouri River and the Pacific Coast."[18]

Pound's prose, addressing only the period of the 1890s, is considerably less purple, perhaps in part because she is writing fifty years after the fact, but it is clear nevertheless that she shares the views of her friends. Members of the class of 1892, she writes, share "the realization that they attended the institution at an especially fortunate time." Chancellor Manatt is praised for "the skill and foresight to select a brilliant faculty," while Chancellor Canfield was "remarkably able, approachable, and stimulating." Twelve faculty members are singled out for notice, along with ten "distinguished" members of the fifty-strong class of 1892. (Pound includes herself, "whom I have been instructed not to overlook," as the tenth and final star.) The piece's close is an extended comparison of the "Victorian" past with a present afflicted with "the influence of Hollywood and the tastes of Walter Winchell," advantageous to the former. In her college days, she says in her penultimate sentence, stating succinctly her agreement with Cather and Dorothy Canfield Fisher, there was in Lincoln a "tonic atmosphere."[19]

By her own report, then, Pound was as fortunate in her undergraduate career as she had been in her preparatory years. She singled out for special praise her professors in English and in French language and literature, Herbert Bates and August Hjalmar Edgren. The latter, "who organized and developed the graduate school at Nebraska and was its earliest dean (1893)," had other admirers in the Pound family—her mother had also been his student in a French class. Louise Pound, despite her deep attachments to Nebraska, shared (and built upon) her mother's interest in self-congratulatory organizations like the DAR. Unlike her father, who found them pompous and comical, she had a lifelong weakness for various honorary societies, offices, and titles, and she could not resist deploying a truly sonorous instance in her description of Edgren—he left Nebraska in 1900, she reports, to become "Rector Magnificus at the newly established University of Gothenburg, Sweden."[20]

And Edgren (1840–1903) was a truly impressive figure, even without the "Magnificus" title. Born in Sweden in 1840 and trained in the Swedish Royal Military Academy, he apparently came to the United States specifically to join the Civil War fight against slavery. He saw action as a lieutenant in the Union army's Ninety-ninth New York Volunteer and was promoted for valor in 1863. After the war he returned to Sweden and then to studying in France and Germany. By 1880, however, he was back in the United States, and in 1885, with degrees from Cornell (1871) and Yale (1874) in hand, he came to Nebraska as professor of modern languages and Sanskrit. Yes, Sanskrit—at Yale he had studied linguistics and Sanskrit with William Dwight Whitney, an internationally renowned student of languages (Chancellor Manatt had also been his student), and there discovered his greatest talent and deepest vocation. In Lincoln the modern languages included not only the French he taught to Laura Pound and her daughter but also German, Italian, Spanish, Italian, "the Scandinavian languages, and of course Sanskrit." The Sanskrit caught on, too—in 1890 the student newspaper bragged that Nebraska had "a larger class in Sanskrit than Yale College."[21] Edgren returned to Sweden in 1891 for his "Rector Magnificus" stint, but by 1893 he was back in Lincoln in time to help establish the new graduate school. He stayed this time until 1900, when he returned for the final time to his homeland to join the newly organized Nobel Institute.

Pound studied French for nine terms, in her sophomore, junior, and senior years, with the final year specified as elective. She also had nine terms of German, in her freshman, sophomore, and junior years, and two of Spanish, specified as elective, in her junior year. In her senior year, 1891–92, she also completed a two-term course in French literature in the winter and spring terms. The focus on language study was especially strong in her sophomore and junior years, 1889–90 and 1890–91, when she completed four terms of Anglo-Saxon and the two of Spanish on top of the French and German. That she impressed her distinguished teacher is clear from a "To whom it may concern" memorandum Edgren wrote for her on Department of Romance Languages and Sanskrit letterhead in the spring of 1895: "Miss Louise Pound, a graduate of the University of Nebraska, had in her undergraduate work in my department (then of Modern Languages) two years of French and three of German. Her record was throughout excellent, her standing among the very highest in her class, and her acquirements thorough."[22]

"My instructor in English," Louise wrote, "was Herbert Bates, writer of fiction, poetry, criticism, and literary history, and author of a notable Charter Day ode, written for the University's quarter-century celebration in 1894, which is found in his *Songs of Exile* of 1896." Bates (1862–1929) is best remembered today as an inspiration for Willa Cather's Gaston Cleric, Jim Burden's classics teacher in *My Ántonia*, but in his own day he was much respected as a poet and essayist. He was in Lincoln only five years, from 1891 to 1896, but he made quite a splash, writing music columns for a local newspaper, composing the celebratory ode for the university's twenty-fifth-anniversary festivities, and impressing students as gifted as Pound and Cather. Another classmate, Annie Prey, writing a "Character Sketch" for a student newspaper, credited Bates with being the first to appreciate the literary talents of his prairie students: "It was Prof. Bates I think who discovered first that there was a chance for real literary work at the University."[23]

The Charter Day ode was printed in the 1895 yearbook, the *Sombrero*, and again another quarter century later, so much did Pound admire it, in the *Semi-Centennial Anniversary Book* she edited for the university's celebration of its first half century. The poem in question is "notable" both for its high-flown expression and its thoroughgoing regional optimism. The "West" is told to rise and shine ("Awake, for the future calls thee! Hear, / Child of the plain, today your limbs are strong, / Your eyes are radiant"), to raise the song of its "new-born soul, / Strenuous and tireless." The university's newly minted graduates are to "spread the gathered wealth abroad / In every dwelling-place of men," including the settled regions to the east, here imaged as "gray hearts of older lands."[24]

Bates published "The Spirit of the Western University" in 1897, after he had left Nebraska (reportedly to be a literature and music critic in Cincinnati), but his continuing admiration for Nebraska (and other upstart western universities) is apparent. Not even Canfield articulated a more enthusiastic vision of its achievements and its potential. If "The Spirit of the Western University" is taken as representative of Bates's prose, it holds up far better today than the poetry, if the Charter Day ode is a typical specimen, though in fact the two pieces differ only in manner—the matter is the same in both cases. The University of Nebraska, Bates writes, boasts at the young age of twenty-seven some twelve hundred collegiate students instructed by a faculty of "over a hundred men [and Rachel Lloyd, among its small cadre of female professors], graduates of the first universities of this country and Europe." It already ranks "ahead of Princeton, Brown, and Amherst," and even with MIT in "all the externals of scholarship." Its entrance requirements, he notes, are more rigorous than Harvard's or Yale's, requiring, as they do not, both trigonometry and solid geometry.[25]

But what about "real culture," the "exposing of the maturing mind to the stimulating influence of the world's best"? Here, echoing Arnold even at the phrasal level, Bates concedes that in their beginning the educational institutions of the western frontier emphasized "applied science": "The west was then plowing its fields, building its railroads, planning its cities. It needed facts to help it, and it had no leisure to seek anything beyond these." But all this has now changed: "There are literary clubs, circles that have ambitions, that compare work, that argue over authors. Finally, there are college papers and magazines." Given these developments, Bates looks confidently to the future: "in the general diffusion of culture, in proportionately widespread appreciation of the best in letters and art, the West will possibly, even probably, surpass us [the East]." What's more, Bates specifically credits the presence of female students for much of this progress. "Coeducation has been a strong influence in the right direction."[26]

The precise sources of his high estimate of female students cannot be known, but the young instructor out of Harvard would not have been alone had his reflections on the developing literary culture in western universities centered on students like Louise Pound and Willa Cather. They were certainly paired in the memories of at least one other first-person observer of the scene, the noted economist Alvin Johnson, who recalled the same twosome as "the two most original persons among our university students."[27] Johnson went even further: when a fellow student expressed doubts as to the worth of "scholarly effort," it was Louise Pound, Johnson remembered, who provided a stirring defense of scholarship's value. "'Scholarship,' she said to Nienhuis, 'is a mission. If you can add just one cubic centimeter to the mass achievement of scholarship, you have not lived in vain.'" Johnson concluded by making an explicit comparison of the two famous siblings: "Louise Pound, modest and extremely talented sister of the great Roscoe—Louise, who doesn't know to this day that at least one person considers her greater still."[28]

Pound also studied literature with the English department's senior scholar, Lucius A. Sherman, who was the major supervisor of her graduate work. Like Edgren over in Romance Languages and Sanskrit, Sherman was much impressed with his young student. In fact, since Pound served as an assistant at one or another level in the English department after taking her master's in 1895, he seems to have regarded her as a sort of junior fellow, even a protégé.[29] His letter of introduction to Professor F. A. Blackburn, written on University of Nebraska "English Literature" letterhead in the summer of 1897, makes clear both his professional and personal approval: "This will introduce Miss Louise Pound, AB and AM of this institution. . . . She has been an invaluable assistant in my department for some time. . . . Miss Pound is a scholar after mine own heart, and I am confident will be disappointing neither in abilities nor attainments to yourself."[30]

Four years before writing these praises, Sherman had published his most ambitious work, *Analytics of Literature*, an attempt to put the study of literature on a "scientific" footing. Just as his colleagues Brace and Bessey aspired to give students hands-on experience with physics and biology by replacing recitations from standard authorities with laboratory exercises, so Sherman planned to involve his students in quantified and schematic examinations of novels, plays, and poems. If scientists proceeded by focusing attention on atoms and cells, understood as basic building blocks of the physical and biological universes, Sherman encouraged his charges to tabulate vocabularies and diagram sentences, the better to comprehend the ground-level elements of literary excellence.

A number of his ablest students were not much impressed: "from the first, some of his students, Willa Cather and Louise Pound among them, said his scientific certainty amounted to little more than word counting. Louise Pound thought his book silly and Willa Cather thought it arid pedantry." Cather, unlike the more circumspect Pound, apparently paid a price for her attitude—"her open contempt for the 'Sherman method' kept her from getting a teaching assistantship in the Department of English in 1896."[31]

A closer look at Sherman's text makes it difficult to quarrel with Pound's and Cather's harsh assessments. Early in their work, for example (in chapter 3), students are given two passages from Browning and Arnold and ordered to pick out "suggestive" words in them "and compute their number." The "suggestions to the teacher" for this exercise offer the sequence "'Glade,' 'grove,' 'woods'" as exhibiting "progressive decrease in suggestive quality." Later chapters move up from vocabulary items to sentences, and by chapter 19 students are learning that Spenser's *View of the Present State of Ireland* averages nearly fifty (49.2) words per sentence over its first five hundred sentences, while a similar computation applied to Emerson's *Address before the Senior Class in Divinity College* manages merely twenty (20.58). Not much space is devoted to what such numbers might indicate, beyond each author's possession of "an individual and unwavering sentence-ideal" and the blithe assertion that "the individual mind is the unit of literary progress," but students are by this time counting their own "sentence-averages," using for the purpose "three hundred sentences from their most recent themes or essays."[32]

In her undergraduate studies, then, as in her Latin School years, Pound impressed her teachers (even the ones she did not wholly admire) and compiled a superlative record. She is listed in the catalog for her freshman year as enrolled in the School of Fine Arts as a "Piano and Sight Reading" student, but as a sophomore she's also listed as a "LIT" student (even as the notices of her study in the School of Fine Arts continue), meaning that she is studying in the "Academic College," described as offering "two courses of study, the Classical and the Literary"). It is worth noting, given this apparent double focus, that Pound's academic transcript shows no music classes. These double listings continue for her junior year, and the 1892 edition lists her degree as a "B.L."[33] Her class record over the four years of her undergraduate study shows a marked emphasis on literature and language courses, three years of history courses, and only a smattering of anything else. Classifying courses is not always a straightforward matter, but it may be useful to note that in what might be termed humanities courses Pound completed a total of forty-one classes in literature, rhetoric, and oratory and another twenty-six in language study. In history she completed nine terms, plus two of political economy for a total of eleven in the social sciences. After that it drops down to three terms of mathematics, three of physical education ("physical culture"), two of psychology, and one of "Infantry Drill" in her freshman year.

The "Infantry Drill" course is an interesting story in itself, and fortunately Pound told it herself, in "Penthesilea Rediviva," a comic essay published in the 1895 *Sombrero*. Framed in the most general and abstracted terms imaginable, Pound's account of "the once notorious Company D" opens with a review of contemporary times as an "Age of Woman," an era when females are so "successfully monopolizing those duties and provinces heretofore deemed particularly man's" that the "man of the future" must soon "find himself professionless and sphereless."[34]

But not to worry: men "should not lightly renounce hope," Pound's essay continues. There is one role, at least, where the initial performance of women was so "sadly inglorious and ephemeral" that "she has since evinced no disposition to redeem herself." Company D was formed in the spring of 1888 (Pound's final term as a Latin prep) with the support of Lieutenant Dudley, "then at the head of the military department." The coeds drilled with enthusiasm for several weeks, worked through the manual of arms, and were "encouraged to master the mysteries of the march."[35] Uniforms were issued, officers were elected (Nettie Clenen was elected captain, and Pound herself was named second sergeant), and photographs were made.

But the first dress parade, before an "unusually large number of spectators," was a disaster. Company D's recruits found the rifles too heavy, "the other companies seemed to take *dreadfully* long steps," and they also "became so interested in us as not to drill with their usual precision." Pound also remembered "the ultra military deportment of Captain Clenen and Lieutenants Alma Benedict and May Tibbles, and the wild applause of the spectators whenever we came within reasonable distance." There was a second dress parade before the term ended, but when the fall term convened Lieutenant Dudley had decamped and the new Lieutenant Griffith was less supportive of Company D, looking "rather dubiously on the reigning company of the year before" and finding it hard to hide "his amazement at many of their movements." Coed cadets were increasingly absent from drill, uniforms fell into disrepair, and soon it was over, "a demise unaccompanied by loud regret or impressive ceremonials." All that was left were the photographs (the *Sombrero* article prints one of Captain Clenen in uniform) — many of them "yet to be seen in several houses of this city, whose daughters, after the lapse of five or six years, look back on their short careers as soldiers with some curiosity and more awe."[36]

Pound closes "Penthesilea Rediviva" with a return to the overarching frame of the alleged "Age of Woman." The cadets of Company D, seen in this light, exhibited "pronounced retrogression." Had the female soldier "done her duty," Pound concludes, she would, "arrayed in epaulets and chevrons, be carrying onward the oriflamme of her progress towards ultimate monopoly."[37]

On style alone it is easy to like this piece, to see in the gentle mockery of "epaulets and chevrons" and the exaggerated sonorousness of "oriflamme" the newly graduated MA who is heir to her father's easy humor. Her gentle send-up of the female cadets with herself at their center is very much of a piece with the no less warmhearted laughter her father, two years later, would direct at himself and other members of Lincoln's newly minted aristocracy of "titled persons." A reader would be deeply mistaken, however, to understand the comedy of "Penthesilea Rediviva" as a conservative endorsement of separate spheres of endeavor for men and women — "the bravest to drill and the fairest to look on," as she put it in her description of campus dress parades following the dissolution of the coed company.[38] It is important to remember that the same Pound who wrote the humorous account of Company D's brief life and inglorious end was throughout that life an active member. She fired her gun on the university shooting ranges, and (of course) she hit her targets impressively enough to set marksmanship records. And two years after she and her sisters in arms returned their weapons to the armory, Pound was defeating all comers, male and female, to claim the university singles championship in tennis. She would not again carry a gun or wear a uniform, but Louise Pound would soldier tirelessly, all her life, in the academy and on the athletic field, in support of wider opportunities for women.

But Company D was a blip on the screen, a fleeting and at the time aberrant episode. At the center, in those years, the crown of undergraduate social and intellectual life, were the literary societies. They are long gone now, worsted and left for dead by the rise of fraternities and sororities, but in Pound's day they dominated the campus. They sported fancy names—Palladian, Adelphian, Philodicean, for example—and convened weekly in their own on-campus meeting rooms for varied programs heavy on edification and uplift but also not lacking in entertainment and opportunities for socializing. Faculty members and people from the Lincoln community often attended these gatherings, and their proceedings were regularly reported in the campus newspapers.

Louise Pound and her siblings were members of the University Union society, founded in 1876 (the Palladian, established in 1871, was the first). Writing the "Organizations" essay for the university's fiftieth-anniversary celebrations, in 1919, Pound described the "varied features" of the programs of the societies at some length: "Staple were the 'essay,' the 'oration,' the 'recitation,' with such musical numbers as were available interspersed, and the program closed normally with a 'debate.'" These formal programs were followed by "social sessions," which sometimes included "the serving of 'light refreshments,' such as doughnuts, apples, popcorn, or more rarely, ice cream; and there were promenades through the long corridors."[39]

In the 1880s and 1890s, according to Pound's recollection, the "more prodigal members" occasionally met for oysters at a local restaurant following the program. There was, however, no dancing: "The recreation of dancing was frowned upon in those days, and was not to be thought of." In Pound's accounting the literary societies come across as playing an important role in undergraduate education: "Not only did they provide social diversion but they gave to the students almost their only training in conducting public meetings, in self-government, and in acquiring self-possession before an audience."[40]

Pound's essay also calls attention to a "classic institution" of the early literary societies, known as the "slate," designed to rectify a situation where "some young women might have had many invitations to attend meetings while others might have found themselves without escorts." The "slate" was "a small book listing the names of the girl members, to be duly 'scratched' for Friday evening by the men members."[41] (It must be remembered that social conventions of the day dictated that female students be accompanied by male "escorts" to lectures, society programs, athletic events, and other public programs. The ongoing and eventually successful fight against such restrictions occupied coeds of the period, and Pound's recollection includes reference to a group called "the G.O.I." or order of "Go Out Independents" who took a stand for the right of female students to attend such events "without first having to acquire individual escorts." She adds that the rebelling coeds had the "encouragement" of Chancellor Canfield, "who was always forward-looking and anxious to promote the welfare of the girl students.")[42]

Writing another quarter century later, in celebration of her class of 1892's fiftieth reunion, Pound opens with personal recollections—longtime family friend D. N. Lehmer, "professor of mathematics, poet, editor, composer of music at the University of California," was a fellow member of the Union Society; "Willa Cather and I were the two 'sergeants-at-arms' in 1892"—before insisting again on the value of the literary societies. "The programs of these societies were genuinely academic and musical. Papers, essays, recitations, stories and poems were presented, and always emphasized were debates. . . . Activities were of a pretty serious nature." The 1942 account is noteworthy for a truculent comparative note absent from the 1919 version. The intellectual substance of the old literary society programs contrasts sharply, says the seventy-year-old observer, with "what seems to be the most absorbing phase of the present-day college life of men students: that is (according to the news reports in the college paper), the assembling of groups of girls from whom may be 'judged' 'beauty queens,' 'sweethearts,' 'glamour girls,' 'prom girls,' 'dream girls,' 'ideal coeds,' 'goddesses of agriculture,' and others on the same order." Even worse than the cloddishness of the men, Pound concludes, is the compliance of the women: "And the girls of today stand for it, or think they have to do so."[43]

This is pretty astringent material for an alumni magazine piece on a class's fiftieth reunion. The dismissal of contemporary collegians seems especially harsh when one remembers that "present-day college life" in 1942, for men and women alike, had World War II as part of its immediate future. (The most sobering experience of preparing this biography, for an author born in 1943, was the perusal of the *Cornhusker* yearbooks for the war years, the seemingly endless pages memorializing those who went from the campus to die in uniform.)

But Pound has a cold eye on a major cultural shift; she is perfectly aware that "Victorian" has become a "term of disparagement" and is having none of it. From the gloomy assessment of the contemporary campus, of men who would patronize and women who would collude in their own diminishment, the peppery essay moves in its final paragraph to panoptic survey: "On the whole one looks back with gratitude half a century later on the Victorian period, with its optimism, regard for peace and order, and its serene expectation of a world which was to grow consciously better and better." The unjust "disparagement" will pass, for "it was perhaps the most highly civilized period that the world has known or may know for a long time to come." The final sentences, still blasting away at the failings of the contemporary world, stress again the blessings enjoyed by the class of 1892: "Campus life, though somewhat Spartan, was stimulating, unaffected as yet by the influence of Hollywood and Walter Winchell. There was a fine faculty and a tonic atmosphere. Members of the class of 1892, suppressing a faint nostalgia, may well feel fortunate to have attended the institution then."[44]

In addition to classes and the weekly literary society meetings, Pound's college years were filled with a varied mix of social and athletic activities. Both Roscoe and Louise were also active during these years in the meetings of a Carroll Club apparently formed as a seriocomic "literary society" patterned on the Browning societies popular at the time. Roscoe Pound's biographer notes that Roscoe, "with mock solemnity, read a learned paper on the philosophy of the Bellman," while Louise, apparently at the same meeting, "enlightened the gathering on Lewis Carroll's theory of portmanteau words."[45] D. N. Lehmer, friend since childhood and fellow member of the Union Society, is remembered in Olivia's memoir as an enthusiastic Carroll Club member whose contributions to meetings especially delighted her father:

> Lehmer . . . set "Jabberwocky" to music and sang it with all the gusto of a metropolitan opera singer. It was the only piece of music that Judge Pound could ever recognize. As soon as Derrick Lehmer started the opening recitative, "Twas brillig," explosive chuckles could be heard somewhere in the more remote rooms of the house. By the time the cadenzas of burbling reached their full fortissimo Judge Pound's hearty laugh would ring out as a resounding accompaniment. Derrick Lehmer set other of Lewis Carroll's nonsense verses to music. One of the best was the plaintive "There was a pig that sat alone beside a ruined pump."[46]

Years later, in scholarly articles on American speech and dialect, Pound would make repeated reference to Carroll's coinages. Pound's pleasure in Carroll's play with language was clearly a durable one—her extensively researched 1914 article on word fusions or blends, for example, calls attention in a footnote to a translation of *Jabberwocky* into Latin elegiacs with Latin neologisms to match Carroll's.[47]

In addition to this already daunting academic and social schedule, Pound managed to find time outside classes to really make her mark as an athlete. In her junior year she won the university's mixed singles and ladies' doubles tennis championships, and earned a varsity men's "N" letter in intercollegiate competition, playing male opponents in singles matches and pairing with teammate Emory Hardy in doubles. She was also the Lincoln city champion in 1890 and the Nebraska state champion in ladies' singles in 1891 and 1892. During the same period she played by invitation in the men's division of three Nebraska state tournaments, twice in Lincoln and once in Hastings, losing each time to the eventual winner. She was during this time the sole female member of Lincoln Tennis Club, and here too she was often the best player: "S. L. Geisthardt was the best player," Pound told an interviewer in 1945, but he was mysteriously disarmed in matches against her: "Somehow, when he played me he became nervous and hit most of the balls into the net. Later, when Donald Raymond returned from Yale and joined the club, he was too much for me."[48] Pound, in short, achieved her first real athletic fame as a tennis player. Her greatest triumphs on the court were still to come, but by the early 1890s she was already recognized as the best her town and state had to offer.

And tennis was not her only sport. The *Hesperian* for November 11, 1892, carried a brief seriocomic notice beneath a story about the donation of Peruvian mummies to the university: "Miss Louise Pound now comes and goes mysteriously with red ink upon her hands. . . . [W]e heard that she had ordered a bicycle for the purpose of averdupoise."[49] The truth, of course, is that Pound put her new bicycle to uses far more demanding than anything contemplated by the newspaper's patronizing suggestion of a weight-loss regimen. She turned herself into a formidable cyclist, achieving on the roads around Lincoln a reputation very nearly as daunting as the one she had managed on the tennis courts. By 1895 she had earned her first Century Road Club bar for riding "100 continuous miles in a single day." Evidently she enjoyed the experience, because she did it again in 1896 and went on to pick up a "Rambler Gold Medal for riding 5,000 miles" the same year.[50]

And even this does not end the list of athletic triumphs. The *Nebraskan* for January 18, 1895, carried in the "Local" column a brief snippet to the effect that "Miss Pound is acknowledged the finest skater of the young ladies of the city."[51] The reference is to figure skating on ice, though Pound would be recognized as a skilled roller skater as well. According to Nellie Yost's 1983 survey of Pound's athletic career, "Louise was one of the first women to swish her long skirts on Lincoln rinks and ponds."[52] In a 1945 interview, the seventy-two-year-old Professor Pound described her figure-skating adventures in detail, even demonstrating the "On-to-Richmond" figure in her dining room. "I learned to do the Maltese Cross backwards, the double Philadelphia grapevine, the On-to-Richmond, knitting, waltz, and two-steps, mostly out of a book. Racing was impossible on such tiny areas, so I had to cut figures."[53] If her competitive nature is nearly audible in her regret at the lack of opportunities for racing, there is another point in the same interview where Pound stresses Lincoln's social constraints: "Of course I was no Sonja Heinie; my skirts were too long and cumbersome. But I had fun even though I was the only girl figure skater." (In fact, as she recalled later in the interview, there were at least some times when she had company in her skating: "I remember when Dorothy Canfield Fisher was just a little girl in prep school she sometimes skated with me.")[54]

In the classroom, on the tennis court, in the literary society, in the music hall, even on the drilling field—in every venue Louise Pound was a winner. She subjected the female drilling team to comic treatment in "Penthesilea Rediviva," but even in that endeavor Pound was elected "second sergeant." A prominent family's beautiful daughter with every material and educational advantage, she had the intelligence and diligence, the athletic skills and the musical talent, to excel in every arena. She was a star. The *Sombrero* for 1892 lists her as a senior in the "Literary" degree program and publishes beneath her name an imposing list of academic, social, and (especially) athletic accomplishments. It's worth reproducing in full, if only for its glimpse at the wide range of her interests and activities: "Union, all offices in the society; class poet and orator; second prize Union oratorical contest '91; associate editor *Lasso*; secretary French Club; state tennis champion ladies' singles '91; University champion mixed singles and ladies' doubles '90–'91; second prize inter-collegiate gentlemen's singles, '90–'91; vice president Tennis Association; captain Co-ed. Skating Club."[55]

Even this list leaves out her election to Phi Beta Kappa membership and the diploma in music she was awarded with her academic BA. A less official assessment appeared in the *Hesperian*, in an alphabetically ordered story devoted to thumbnail sketches of the members of that year's graduating class: "Miss Louise Pound, a favorite in society and the classroom, is the next to engage our attention. She has been thought by many to be cold-hearted. This is due, perhaps, to the fact that many have not become well acquainted with her. She has many admirable traits of character and will be successful in anything she undertakes."[56]

The "class orator" designation apparently obliged Pound to prepare and present a speech for Class Day Exercises, held on June 14, 1892, with the senior class staging their program at Funcke's Opera House. The proceedings, as reported in the *Hesperian*, must have occupied a substantial chunk of the day, as they included several musical performances, a class history detailed enough to require two narrators, the reading of a comic essay on "Mrs. Socrates," the "recitation" of a short story, and at least two "orations." The first of these, titled "The Apotheosis of the Common," was Pound's. This address, said the *Hesperian*, was "well prepared" and "delivered in a clear and forcible manner," though the speaker "showed nervousness."[57] The *Nebraska State Journal*, in its notice, was more alert to the address's content:

"'The Apotheosis of the Common' was the title of a most scholarly oration by Miss Louise Pound. As the title indicates her principal thought was the modern tendency toward indiscriminate elevation of the common and the dangers thereof. Whether or not the auditors agreed with her assertions none could question the strength of her argument. Then, too, it appealed to that feeling possessed by so many that they are endowed with certain qualities entitling them to a place higher than that deserved by their fellow men."[58]

The full typescript of this address makes for interesting if sometimes puzzling reading. It is in the first place a surprisingly darkminded piece for a graduation celebration. There is next to nothing of the customary "Look out world, we now go forth to make our mark" note, and even less of urging one's classmates onward and upward. Exhortation in fact takes a backseat to resignation. Pound takes her departure from the opening lines of Matthew Arnold's 1888 Westminster address (just two months before his death) at the unveiling of a memorial honoring Catherine Woodcock, Milton's second wife. First printed in the posthumous *Essays in Criticism, Second Series*, "Milton" opens by citing an unidentified "most eloquent voice of our century" for a prophetic "warning cry" against the threat to "the saving ideal of a high and rare excellence" represented by the "view of life and the social economy of the ever-multiplying and spreading Anglo-Saxon race."[59]

Pound, citing Arnold's entire opening paragraph for her own introduction, continues in a vein that at last exceeds her original in its disparagement of the American veneration of the common. Where Arnold soon moves on to a celebration of Milton as the great native model of a "master in the great style of the ancients" available as a standard of true excellence to English readers unversed in Greek and Latin, Pound stays with his opening fears of the United States as the world's leading example of a society dominated by the "Anglo-Saxon contagion," where "the *average man* is too much a religion," his virtues "unduly magnified" and his flaws not clearly perceived.[60]

The collegiate orator, off and running with Arnold's alarm, is by the end of her first paragraph lamenting the tarnishing of "Excellence and Genius, the essence of which is rarity," by the pretense of their widespread occurrence: "Here the commonplace is a god. The average man and his average performance are the measure of all things." This contagion is especially obvious in the political sphere, with "the demagogue, seeking by flattery the votes of what is significantly called the community," but it extends as well to "thinkers and writers"—with them too the "average man, the common man, is the Procrustean bed to which all must be fitted."[61]

What may be surprising to contemporary readers is the persistent rhetorical dimension of the argument, the association of the threatened "Excellence and Genius" with poetry and the menacing apotheosis of the common with prose. This is in her source—for Arnold it is a given that the powers of verse exceed those of prose. But where this contrast is a passing note in "Milton," Pound gives it repeated stress and makes an attempt at a historically based explanation. In what may be the most overheated passages in her speech, Pound imagines a vaguely druidic prior world where "man might at any time withdraw from the monotonous contact of his fellows, and live his own life in forest or wilderness." With no civil authority in place, "he was the avenger of his own wrongs, the defender of his own home." With no ecclesiastical authority present, "he worshipped in the grove or by the spring." When he met with his fellow home defenders, "his assemblies were held with clash of arms under the open sky." In this splendid if unlikely scene, "All his surroundings were poetic" and "man could but speak in verse."[62]

All this versifying is now threatened: "The advance of civilization has of necessity robbed life of these poetic elements. Machinery is replacing the individual on every hand. His surroundings are made prosaic and monotonous." Pound goes on to castigate a good many contemporary agents of this increasing prosiness—not only machines themselves but the commerce machines serve, the newspapers and novels and stories of "realism" they print. Here she is on the newspaper, the "oracle of the common man": its "chief aim is to make everything common. . . . The obscure are raised from their insignificance; the well known are systematically depreciated. . . . [E]ach village points out its Gladstone and its Bismarck, and has its Milton, no longer 'mute' and 'inglorious.'" Now for "realism": "For realism, philosophy and eloquence must be made common, and easy of attainment to all." The orator's disdain for these developments could hardly be clearer: "It is this kind of realism which dwells upon Washington's false teeth, which rehearses the gossip of great men's kitchens as biography, which even tells the story of the Redeemer of Mankind in the form and style of a paper-covered novel."[63]

At the very heart of Pound's critique of the modern is the presumed devaluation of the individual. Individualism, in fact, though she suspects it as doomed, is understood as opposed in every way to the apotheosis of the common, and if the latter is somehow English in origin (and by extension and intensification American), the former is understood as essentially German: "It is this great development of machinery and the deference paid to it by the Englishman, which, fastening upon and perverting the Teutonic character of individuality, has enthroned the commonplace." This contrast between the potentially excellent individual and the necessarily mediocre group thus highlighted, the oration moves to its dystopian peroration: "No freedom on the part of the individual is permitted to exceed the limitations of the average. Where the individual must be common, he loses that identity which makes him an individual. All is one dead level—a lifeless, soulless average."[64]

In its denunciations, as in its (infrequent) enthusiasms, this utterance of a twenty-year-old daughter of small-town privilege may not be so surprising, after all, even if one misses the leavening comic note that Judge Pound would surely have suggested if asked. The basic thrust of her argument, however, is remarkably similar to "View of Judge S. B. Pound," delivered five years later—Louise got more than her athletic talent from her father. His central belief—"much depends on the individual"—was hers as well. Delivering her "class orator" address at the triumphant close of her undergraduate career, then, Pound presents herself as one out of step with her times, a proud adherent of an undeservedly outworn creed. She seems determined above all upon the pursuit of excellence, of a life anchored not in one or another variety of commercial or material success, but in the service of private, even solitary pursuits.

Much that is callow, even priggish, in "The Apotheosis of the Common" will soon be jettisoned—indeed, Pound will make her biggest mark in the world of scholarship by a scathing critique of the assumptions about the allegedly "poetic" utterance of the folks she celebrated thirty years earlier for avenging their own wrongs and conducting al fresco worship services. Some elements, however, will persist. Fifty years later, in her 1942 piece for her class's fiftieth reunion, the now-distinguished member of the faculty is as starchy as ever in her dismissal of newspapers and all they stand for. The apotheosis of the common will always seem to her a thing to be regretted. The manor, in the Lincoln of the late nineteenth century, may have been newly built, but Louise Pound was born to it. And she never left. In her "oration" of 1892, the new graduate takes her first steps in the shoes of the faculty matriarch who a half century later will use the occasion of a fiftieth class reunion to pen a spirited defense of the Victorian era coupled with a highbrow sneer at Hollywood and Walter Winchell.

Willa Cather, in any discussion of Louise Pound's life as an undergraduate and MA student in Lincoln, demands a section of her own. No contemporary of Pound's at the University of Nebraska, not even the great Roscoe, went on to so make so large a name, and no discussion of Pound's collegiate years can be complete without a closer look at the relationship of these two young women. They were close friends, fellow members of the Union Literary Society, associated in everything from editing student magazines to amateur dramatic productions. Cather was many times a guest in the Pound home; a studio photographic portrait shows the two women together.

It took scholars interested in Cather a long time to notice her association with Pound. E. K. Brown's *Willa Cather: A Critical Biography*

(1953), the earliest full-scale biographical treatment, mentions Pound only in passing, and Mildred Bennett's *The World of Willa Cather* (1951) omits her entirely.[65] More recent scholarship, however, has more than made up for this early neglect. By 1983 Pound had been recognized in print as the "most serious romantic attachment of Willa's college life," the focus of a two-year "infatuation" amounting to "obsession."[66] By 1987, with the publication of Sharon O'Brien's influential study *Willa Cather: The Emerging Voice*, the relationship was getting even more attention, with two letters from Cather to Pound (one from 1892, the other from 1893) serving to demonstrate to the scholar's satisfaction that Cather "viewed herself as a lesbian."[67] The friendship with Pound, given the passion brought to it by at least one party, is in O'Brien's treatment intensified to an "affair."[68] Other scholars have resisted O'Brien's certitude—for James Woodress, for example, in his *Willa Cather: A Literary Life*, a full-length biography published the same year as O'Brien's study, to "call this a lesbian relationship, as some critics have done, is to give it undue importance. Pound did not return the affection with anything like the fervor with which it was given."[69]

This summary barely touches the surface of what has been a very busy focal point in recent studies of Cather. Few points are uncontested. The debate is at times silly, rooted in social environments and scholarly fashions remote from both Pound's and Cather's experience, and it is often overheated as only scholarly debates with little in the way of real information at hand can be overheated.[70] But two things, amid all the controversies, are clear. One is that Pound's voice is entirely absent from the discussion—all the surviving letters are Cather's. Another is the sad fact that Pound's important contributions to both scholarship and increased opportunities for women have been almost wholly obscured. She has been much more prominently mentioned in recent years as a bit player in an ongoing debate over Cather's sexuality than for any achievement of her own. Strikingly divergent paraphrases of the now famous letters have been printed—the provisions of Cather's will prohibiting their publication or quotation have only stimulated greater curiosity. Yet another examination results first of all in a strengthened sense of both their suggestiveness and their ultimate indeterminacy. O'Brien is clearly right in her sense of Cather's overwrought infatuation; Woodress is no less correct in his sense of Pound's much lower temperature.

Willa Cather came to Lincoln in the fall of 1890 from her hometown of Red Cloud, some one hundred miles west. She was not quite seventeen, she was accompanied by her mother, and she planned to be a surgeon. Cather was just a year and a half younger than Pound, but was three years behind her in school—she graduated in a class of three in Red Cloud but needed one year as a "second prep" student in Lincoln before enrolling as a freshman in the 1891–92 school year. She quickly made a name for herself, not as a surgeon in training but as a writer—her first article (on Carlyle) appeared in the *Nebraska State Journal* (in March 1891) while she was still a preparatory student, and the same newspaper published a second, two-part article ("Shakespeare and Hamlet") in November, during the first semester of her freshman year. By the end of the year, Cather and Pound are listed together as editorial "Associates" on the masthead of the December issue of a Lincoln literary magazine, the *Lasso*. By 1892 Cather was on the staff of the *Hesperian*, the campus literary journal, where she published four stories and a short play in a single semester. By her junior year she was the managing editor, and later added work on the class yearbook, the *Sombrero*, to her undergraduate writing and editing résumé. By 1893, in addition to these campus responsibilities, she was turning out regular columns and reviews for the *Nebraska State Journal* and other Lincoln newspapers.

Despite all this mainstream activity—writing, editing, acting in plays, visiting in the homes of prominent citizens—Cather often stood out as an unconventional and sometimes openly controversial figure. She was outspoken in her opinions, even when she expressed them in print, and seemed "mannish" in dress and deportment to many of her classmates. A habit of signing her name as "William" went back to her Red Cloud days, but she continued it in Lincoln.

It took the gentle intervention of Mrs. Charles Gere, the mother of her close college friend and longtime correspondent Mariel Gere, to persuade her to let her hair grow. On several occasions her reviews and commentaries were so caustic that aggrieved parties felt obliged to respond. Flavia Canfield, for example, wife of the university president, wrote a "sharp reply to an attack she [Cather] had made on women's clubs in the *Journal*."[71] A similar attack, this one aimed at none other than Roscoe Pound, made Cather no longer welcome in the Pound home.

Critics have been much interested in this last little piece, one in a series of "Theophrastian characters" published in the *Hesperian* on March 10, 1894, under the title "Pastels in Prose." Attention has focused more upon Cather's motives in writing it than upon the item itself, a description of a university graduate inordinately proud of his academic accomplishments and either unwilling or unable to take them off campus into a larger world. Roscoe Pound, who had returned to Lincoln in 1890 from a year at the Harvard Law School, was the clear target—Cather's college man is proud of his Latin and his knowledge of botany. "He called everything by its longest and most Latin name, and the less his victim knows about botany the more confidential he becomes and the more copiously he empties forth Latin words upon him."[72]

The attack is nasty enough—it looks backward to the Latinizing botanist's childhood as a "notorious bully" and closes with the breezy prediction of an insignificant future. "He is a University graduate, and that's all he ever will be in this world or that to come."[73] Events, of course, also proved it spectacularly in error, at least with regard to the future, even if, as at least one critic has suggested, Roscoe Pound might have been "a truly disagreeable young man."[74] Roscoe Pound, in fact, had every good reason to be on campus in 1894 (studying with Bessey while practicing law in Lincoln, he received his PhD in botany in 1897), and he went on to a thoroughly distinguished law career—by 1915 he was dean of the Harvard Law School. It would be hard to name a more highly regarded figure in American jurisprudence for the first half of the twentieth century. It is easy to sympathize with the reaction of the Pound family—given their nearly four years of extending hospitality to Cather, they must have found the attack nearly incomprehensible.

Scholars, of course, have rushed in with explanations. The most detailed may be that offered by Phyllis Robinson, whose 1983 *Willa: The Life of Willa Cather* runs through a wide range of possible injuries "she could not forgive." First, Robinson considers that Pound may have been a rejected suitor—"had he found himself attracted to her and been rebuffed"—who then "lashed out and bullied her for preferring his sister to himself."[75] Other possibilities do not depend on a spurned romantic attraction. Woodress describes Roscoe as "the soul of propriety and convention" and suggests that he may have found the "aggressive nonconformity" of his sister's friend irritating.[76] Exploring this line of reasoning further, Robinson wonders if Roscoe made disparaging remarks about Cather's attachment to his sister—Robinson describes her infatuation with Louise as "common knowledge." Did he "say ugly things about her to Louise?" she asks, and then arrives at the end of this speculative line: "He may even have used the term 'lesbian' to describe her."[77]

Having reached this point, Robinson wisely notes its lack of solid footing: "We do not know" is her very next line.[78] What is certain, however, and for the student of Pound and her work it is a saddening certitude, is that Louise Pound's many stellar accomplishments, very nearly as impressive in their own sphere as Cather's were in hers, have in recent years received scant attention. What she was actually doing, in the years of parrying Cather's overwrought attachment, was picking up an master's degree, teaching her first classes at the University of Nebraska, making a spectacular splash as a tennis player, and taking her first steps toward a thoroughly professional postgraduate training in philology. She would ultimately return, and stay for the rest of her life, but these steps would initially take her away from Lincoln, first to Chicago and then to Germany. Cather, her eccentricities and importunities tolerated out of appreciation for her evident gifts (at least until she lashed out at brother Roscoe), was a blip on the screen. Louise Pound, class of 1892, was a young woman just into her twenties with so strong a sense of purpose and direction in life that she was "thought by many to be coldhearted."[79] (It is tempting, given the similar laments in Cather's letters, to wonder if the *Hesperian* sketch's author might not even be Cather.) In any event, that purposiveness had its eyes on prizes far beyond Lincoln's city limits. The daughter of Judge and Laura Pound, seeing herself as marching against the apotheosis of the common, would always place her strongest reliance upon "individual effort." That would stand her in good stead, as big efforts and big adventures were just around the corner.

THREE

"A genuine Nebraska cyclone"

When she picked up her BA (along with a Phi Beta Kappa key and a diploma in music) in the spring of 1892, Louise Pound had lived in Lincoln for all of her twenty years. The University of Nebraska campus had been her home, as a preparatory student and as an undergraduate, for six years. She had acted in plays, marched with a rifle, spoken French, skated on local ponds, lectured on Lewis Carroll, and starred on the tennis courts. Her life in Lincoln was a rich one—she was born to the town's emergent elite, the fortunate child of capable and generous parents, and she possessed in full measure the intelligence to seize every given opportunity and the energy necessary to create others.

But the time was coming for a bigger stage. By the decade's end she would be in Germany as a PhD student at the University of Heidelberg. Before that, in the summers of 1897 and 1898, she would enroll in classes at the University of Chicago. And before that, concentrating her work in the English department, she would earn an MA in 1895. Her studies were apparently both literary and linguistic, what in the day would have been termed philological. In 1896, after the MA but before the classes in Chicago, these would bear fruit in the form of her first scholarly publication. The summers in Chicago would also bring her greatest athletic triumphs—glorious victories in major tennis tournaments that were chronicled in vivid detail in the Chicago papers and reported as far away as New York City. Louise Pound would go on to make her greatest name as a scholar, of course, but for her first appearance in the national spotlight she chose a tennis racquet.

In the same years, in what must have been the biggest change from her undergraduate routines, Pound began teaching classes. As early as the 1893–94 school year, her first as a graduate student, she was employed, according to the memory of H. M. Belden, then a newly hired instructor who would later encourage her initial efforts in folksong collecting, as "one of the theme readers for the English department."[1] The *Hesperian* for September 27, 1893, two years before she would complete her MA and just over a year after the awarding of her BA, carried a brief snippet: "Miss Louise Pound has been ill with malarial fever. When she recovers she will resume her duties in the department of English."[2] In 1895, the year she earned her MA, she is listed in the *Sombrero* as an "Assistant" in the English department.[3] Professor Sherman's 1897 letter to University of Chicago professor F. A. Blackburn explicitly notes that Pound "carried last year all the Anglo-Saxon work given in the University."[4] By very good evidence, then, Pound was teaching classes by 1895 (or even a year earlier), and by 1896 she was carrying a heavy pedagogical load indeed—the course in Anglo-Saxon was required of all English majors at this period.

In a 1945 interview, Pound recalled that she taught her first classes during James Canfield's tenure as chancellor (he left in 1895)—"I was broken in as a teacher of Anglo-Saxon to 80 sophomore students."[5] Finally, the vita assembled by Mamie Meredith and Ruth Odell and included on the last page of the 1949 *Selected Writings of Louise Pound* lists Pound as an "Assistant" in the Department of English in 1893 and as an "Assistant Instructor" beginning in 1894.[6] Adding all this together would suggest the 1894–95 academic year as the first in which Pound had real instructional responsibilities, as distinct from reading and grading themes. Retiring in 1945, the date also given in the vita of the *Selected Writings*, she had dedicated a full half century, with only the 1899–1900 academic year away for work on her doctorate, to the teaching of Nebraska students.

In its initial stages, however, the shift to graduate study was surely softened by many routines familiar from undergraduate days. In her first semester as a graduate student, Pound appeared in two dramatic productions, both times in association with Willa Cather. The first was a two-part dramatic presentation in November 1892 by the "Union Branch of the University Dramatic club." It made a big splash, gaining coverage in the *Nebraskan*. The "curtain raiser" was a "laughable farce" called "The Fatal Pin," followed by "Shakespeare Up to Date," which starred Pound as Juliet, her sister, Olivia, as Ophelia, and Cather as Lady Macbeth in an "emotional drama" featuring an Ophelia who has married Hamlet and cites him ("as Ham says") in her every speech, a Juliet who has married Romeo and regrets it, and a Lady Macbeth enraged by Shakespeare's treatment of her. The women agree upon vengeance, and the play closes upon a mad scene with Ophelia insane, Lady Macbeth invoking dark powers, and Juliet replaying her balcony scene. "All are raving and shouting together," according to the *Nebraskan*'s reviewer, who adds that all roles "were well played and showed study and ability." A later note in the same issue describes the two performances (on November 22 and 29) as "successful, from both a dramatic point of view and in a financial way."[7]

One month later, according to a much briefer report in the *Hesperian*, the Dramatic Club mounted another triumphant "entertainment." "The effort was a most successful one," notes the reviewer, "and merited the patronage of every student in the University." The notice, so brief that even the title of the production is omitted, then closes with praise for two actresses in particular: "Especial notice should be made of the excellent work of Misses Pound and Cather."[8]

Fortunately, the *Nebraska State Journal* provided fuller coverage of this event. The "entertainment" presented, like the earlier updated Shakespeare, a comic romp with music titled "A Perjured Padulion," featuring numerous spoofs of "noticeable features of university life" within a frame of over-the-top melodrama. Pound played the role of Sophomorista Saltonstall, described as "A Co-ed—'Varium et Mutabile,'" whose new beau, Enrico Watkins, dies in a duel with a former admirer, Leonidas Rebenhorst, described as "Out of school for a year." Sophomorista, of course, then takes her own life at the side of her "devoted Enrico." But even this is not all. Diamond Witherspoon, played by none other than Willa Cather, a cutting-edge feminist who has "been endeavoring to have Sophomorista join the G.O.Gs," feels responsible for friend's death and ends the play by adding her own body to the pile.[9] ("G.O.G." stands for "Go Out Girls," also sometimes known as "G.O.I.," or "Go Out Independents," the same group praised by Pound in her 1942 recollections as having Chancellor Canfield's support in their demand for the right to attend campus lectures, concerts, and dramatic presentations without male escorts.)[10] Had they noticed the details of this performance, Cather scholars of the 1980s and 1990s would surely have made much of it—the lovelorn Cather, six months after her first smoking-gun love note to Louise and only fifteen months before her poison-pen attack upon Roscoe, here manages to die on stage in fealty to her friend.

The *Nebraskan* also noticed the production of "A Perjured Padulion," included its description of itself as an "emotional tragedy in five acts," lamented the small size of the crowd, and explicitly credited it as having been "written by Miss Louise Pound."[11] Meanwhile, the same issue of the *Hesperian* that carried the brief notice of "A Perjured Padulion" also carried a fuller notice of a meeting of "Le cercle Francais" on Tuesday, December 6, hosted by "Miss Pound." The group focused on the work of La Fontaine—Miss Covel read a paper, and Mr. Guilmette gave a reading from "Les Fables." General discussion followed, in French of course: "Needless to say 'on parlait Francais tout le temps.'"[12]

If the just-graduated Pound found her "duties in the department of English" increased by grading and teaching responsibilities in the years between 1892 and 1895, she surely also found her schedules lightened by the absence of regular classes. A standardized curriculum for graduate study at Nebraska, or anywhere else for that matter, had not yet been formulated in this period. Although graduate degrees had been awarded for some time—the University of Nebraska catalogs from the 1870s allowed for a master's degree to be awarded to students who studied an additional year under the supervision of the faculty, and in 1886 the university awarded its "first 'real' master's degree—the first earned by pursuing a systematic course of graduate study."[13] The great proponent and organizer of graduate study at Nebraska was none other than August Hjalmar Edgren, he of the Sanskrit classes and teacher of French to Louise Pound—but he was away in Sweden on his "Rector Magnificus" stint from 1891 to 1893. By the time he returned and got the graduate school organized in 1896, Pound already had her MA.

She earned it, then, between 1892 and 1895, in what would soon be the old-fashioned way, doing supervised research under the direction of the English chair, Lucius A. Sherman, of *Analytics of Literature* fame and infamy. Pound's first significant work of scholarship, published in *Modern Language Notes* in the spring of 1896 but no doubt the product of her studies in the previous years, shows every sign of his mentoring. Pound and Cather may have come to share a low opinion of Sherman's approaches to literature, but *"The Romaunt of the Rose*: Additional Evidence That It Is Chaucer's" shows Pound applying his lessons with considerable diligence and impressive results. As the title makes clear, Pound's essay consciously participates in an ongoing scholarly controversy: the poet's role in an English translation of the popular thirteenth-century French *Le roman de la rose*, a matter, we learn in the opening paragraph, that "is now the subject of much dispute." Pound proceeds to cite opinions on both sides, beginning with that of W. W. Skeat (1835–1912), a renowned British Chaucerian who had just edited a six-volume complete works for Oxford's Clarendon Press (published in 1894 and referred to as "his recent edition"). Skeat's view is that most of the translation (the exception being the section known as Fragment A) "cannot be Chaucer's," and Pound notes that Skeat "rests his proof mainly on internal, philological grounds, relating to the vocabulary, to the dialect, to the grammar, and to the rime."[14]

The opposing view, which Pound summarizes in the next two paragraphs, is represented by Thomas Raynesford Lounsbury (1838–1915), a Yale professor and well-known Chaucerian whose 1892, *Studies in Chaucer: His Life and Writings* is described by Pound as disputing Skeat's conclusions "at the length of more than one hundred and fifty pages." Pound is sufficiently impressed by these pages to basically align herself with his position: "Professor Lounsbury has put forth a strong array of arguments, and believes he has shown that henceforth the burden of proof should rest as much with those who deny Chaucerian authorship as with those who affirm it."[15]

Having opened her essay with summaries of the controversy's two opposed positions, Pound moves to a straightforward statement of her own contribution: "There remain other tests which it may be interesting to apply, the tests of sentence-length and sentence-structure." The body of the essay then follows. Mostly it is tables. Stage one is an analysis of five works acknowledged as Chaucer's. Pound first divides each into groups of one hundred sentences, then lists word counts, predications (i.e., number of verbs), number of simple sentences, number of initial conjunctions, and number of interior conjunctions for each group. Following these five tables is a summary for "All Chaucer" which shows the average Chaucerian sentence as containing 22.02 words and 2.76 verbs. Very nearly a quarter of these sentences are "simple," about a third open with conjunctions, and the typical sentence contains almost 1.5 interior conjunctions. More important for Pound's purposes than the numbers themselves is the minute variation from text to text—the longest average sentence length (22.81 words in *The Legend of Good Women*) varies by fewer than 2.1 words from the shortest (20.73 in *The Deth of Blaunche*).

A similar consistency is revealed in the "predications" column, with the Chaucerian sentence always averaging some fraction of two verbs (the range runs upward from an average of 2.54 in the "Prologue" to *The Canterbury Tales* to 2.89 in *The Legend of Good Women*).

Step two applies the same analysis to five texts once attributed to Chaucer but now "generally recognized as not his." These results are much more varied, "as one would expect in poems coming from different hands." The sentences of *Chaucer's Dream*, for example, average more than twice as many words (53.27) and verbs (6.58) as those of *Court of Love* (24.73 and 3.08).[16]

All this just sets the table for Pound's real purpose: "Now to see with which of these two groups belongs the *Romaunt of the Rose*." Another table follows, this one representing a truly mind-boggling computational labor. Pound examines the *Romaunt*'s total of 2,205 sentences made up of some 48,359 words, counts up the verbs, the simple sentences, the initial and interior conjunctions, and presents her numbers in the article's largest single table. These results, given Pound's already announced leaning toward Professor Lounsbury's position, are most gratifying, and are highlighted by the essay's shortest table, which compares the *Romaunt of the Rose* averages with the Chaucerian ones. Pound summarizes her data: "The average sentence-length for Chaucer is 22.02, for the *Romaunt of the Rose* 21.93, a remarkably close correspondence. The *Romaunt* shows 2.88 predications and 1.49 interior conjunctions, Chaucer 2.76 predications and 1.47 interior conjunctions a sentence."[17]

This is the heart of the essay, though Pound goes on to analyze three separate sections of the *Romaunt*, since even Skeat had by this time conceded that one portion of the poem was likely Chaucer's. Her internal analysis works against this division, the three sections showing no more variation "than in Chaucer's recognized works." Her conclusion is a sweeping one, a suggestion that her researches have shifted the onus of proof in this controversy: it now lies with "those who have pronounced the translation spurious, not those who believe it genuine."[18]

In her first published article, then, the novice scholar exhibits a strikingly high confidence level. She tells a world-famous Chaucer scholar that his positions rest on sand—they are based upon "vague theorizing or speculations, or on the uncertain foundations of personal opinion." What is worse, he is guilty of tilting the very data that drive his conclusions: "it is the judgment of Skeat that the translator wrote, not in the East Midland dialect, like Chaucer, but in the dialect of the North. If this were a fair statement of the case, the presence of these forms might prove significant, but it is not." If the translation employs a "sprinkling" of Northern forms, Pound goes on to note, it also contains occasional Southern usages. Skeat's evidence is especially misleading, she notes, in regard to the presence of Northern participles ending in *-and* in place of the Midland *-ing*: "When you consider," she concludes, again summarizing Lounsbury, "that in the 7700 lines of the poem, there are no more than five cases of the participle in *-and*, which Skeat would lead you to consider the usual form, and scores and scores of cases of the Midland participle in *-ing*, you see which way the test really points. . . . Add the consideration that this *-and* ending is to be found frequently in manuscripts of poems unquestionably Chaucer's, and you have the matter fairly stated."

Pound's conclusions, by contrast, are more solid, based upon "tests," "figures," and "calculations." Citing the equally quantitative work of her mentor Sherman ("Some Observations on Sentence-Length in English Prose") and her Nebraska colleague W. S. Gerwig ("On the Decrease of Predication and Sentence-Weight in English"), both published in the University of Nebraska journal *University Studies*, the newly minted MA sets the Cambridge don straight.[19] Even at a century's remove, this comes across as a remarkably cheeky performance, both in its serene reliance on Nebraska scholarship (other than the citations of Skeat and the paraphrases of Lounsbury, Sherman and Gerwig are the only authors cited) and in its aggressive phrasing (two direct assertions of "unfair" presentation of evidence).

There is no evidence that Skeat ever responded, directly or indirectly to Pound's article, though even now it can be found in Chaucer studies bibliographies.[20] It is possible that he never saw it, but even if he did a host of factors invited his disinterest. The study of Chaucer at the end of the nineteenth century was already concentrating itself in universities, where it was carried on as a civil if sometimes arch conversation between gentlemen. Even if Pound's piece came to his notice, Skeat would have been encouraged by national, class, gender, and even stylistic and methodological considerations to regard it as an impertinence, the better to disregard it altogether. An unknown Miss Pound, from a semifabulous Boeotia called Nebraska, citing other unknown Nebraskans, attaching a harangue about "fair statement" to a collection of tables based on nothing more than a madly industrious word counting—this was not something Reverend Skeat and his gentleman colleagues would easily recognize as philological or literary study, let alone feel obliged to consider. When Helen Waddell, thirty years later, published her groundbreaking study in medieval literature, *The Wandering Scholars,* her book, unlike Pound's article, was too popular to ignore. But it was resented. Ruffled dons, most famously G. G. Coulton, issued petulant reviews. Recent scholarship has addressed in considerable detail this clubby "old boys" atmosphere with direct reference to Chaucer studies.[21]

Given such a social context, it is hardly surprising that Pound's first foray into the world of scholarly publication elicited little response. It is fair to note, however, that even now her position supporting Chaucer's authorship of the entire *Romaunt of the Rose* translation does not prevail. Sentence length also seems not to have proved convincing as a generally useful litmus test for authorship, and most contemporary Chaucerians still accept a division of the *Romaunt of the Rose* translation into three "fragments," with only Fragment A achieving something like a consensus as the work of Chaucer's hand.[22] Twenty-five years later, however, in a very different controversy, this one dealing not with questions of literary authorship but with ballad origins, Pound would repeat the performance, once again taking on the heavyweights of the field.

And this time the heavyweights would notice. One in particular would not be pleased, and he would respond. It would be the biggest controversy of her career, but she would not be even a little cowed or intimidated. The daughter of Laura Biddlecome Pound, taught nearly from the cradle "the wonderful advantage one has who is able to decide and not change his mind," was clearly ready, even at the opening of her academic career, to hold tenaciously to her views even in the face of disagreement and disapproval from figures of great reputation and authority associated with prestigious institutions. Her Chaucer study sets a tone—civil, laced here and there with a humor rooted in understatement, careful in avoidance of overstatement and painstaking in its rooting of speculation in empirical data, but also confident within its boundaries nearly to the point of brashness. As a voice for her scholarship it must have suited her; she used it again and again for the next fifty years.

It might be added that Laura Pound's pedagogy seems to have made Louise's brother no less capable of holding to his positions in the teeth of powerfully placed opposition. In what became the most celebrated speech of his career, Roscoe addressed the American Bar Association in St. Paul, Minnesota, on August 29, 1906. His topic—"The Causes of Popular Dissatisfaction with the Administration of Justice"—was itself inflammatory, especially in a setting customarily devoted almost entirely to professional self-praise. "The audience was stunned but courteous," reports his biographer.[23] Afterward, a storm of protest erupted. Motions to omit the speech from the meeting's proceedings and the association's annual report were offered; Pound's attempt to defend himself was denied the floor. In the short term, at the St. Paul meeting and in its immediate aftermath, Pound took a thorough drubbing. But he held his ground, young attorneys rallied to his side, and the speech has long been recognized as a pivotal moment in the history of American legal philosophy.

Back in Lincoln, in the 1890s, Louise Pound was not restricting her writing to the academic sphere. On January 27, 1895, two years after "A Perjured Padulion" and a bit more than a year before the Chaucer article, a very different piece appeared in the *Nebraska State Jour-*

nal. It was a short story titled "By Homeopathic Treatment," and if it was a light enough piece it nevertheless exhibits the young scholar trying on a different role, just to check the fit. Like playing the piano and drawing (which Pound also did with some skill—several of her sketches survive in her papers), the writing and publishing of short stories was in the 1890s a popular pastime for educated young women in Lincoln. The obvious direct model for such an effort, however, was Willa Cather, who would go on to make her major name in literature, just as Pound would make hers in scholarship. Cather was at the time churning out scores of articles and stories in various local papers—she has a piece expressing dismay at the just-announced nuptials of an opera singer in the same issue that carried Pound's story.

"By Homeopathic Treatment" tells of an attempt by her circle of friends to "cure" the intemperate monomania of a newly "emancipated" young woman named Matilda. She has become insufferable; she never talks about "ordinary things" anymore, "like new fiction, or the fashions, or the last party that some of our set had given." Instead, she "discoursed about suffrage and the ballot" and insists that her friends study with "gravity" the many "tracts" and other "interminable printed things" she presses upon them. The scene opens upon a meeting of these harried companions, who come through "a dreadful wind" to discuss the "case" over tea. At last they decide upon the treatment indicated by the story's title: they'll host a party where Matilda will be introduced to Clementine, a "social amelioration woman" who is every bit as focused upon her own class-based hobbyhorse as Matilda is upon "the rights of woman." "What we must do is bring them together," suggests an unnamed member of the circle. "Then let them talk each other stiff with their hobbies. The homeopathic treatment will be our salvation. Let like cure like."[24]

The result, of course, is a disaster. The two activists at first mistake each other for soul mates, but a simple query from Berthe, the hostess, soon sets them at odds. "But how is this ennobling of society to be brought about?" she asks, which is more than enough to launch Matilda. "In woman is the salvation of the race," she cries. "The ballot for her is the crying lack of the age." And this in turn is more than enough to light Clementine's fires. "Never mind the ballot for women," she replies. "It is an empty privilege, not worth the gaining. The duty of woman is not to work selfishly for the honors of politics, but to go out among the masses and render herself useful by doing what she can for the amelioration of crying evils." Things go downhill rapidly, and soon Matilda and Clementine are in separate rooms, the latter still holding forth and Matilda "tolerating our half remorseful efforts to placate her with cold indifference." At the story's end she is "more confirmed in her ways than ever."[25]

Such nuance as this little story possesses may be in its close, where the women clearly regard their tea as a success, despite its signal failure to achieve its purposes. "In spite of the failure of the cure," they decide, "we could not help feeling that the afternoon had been its own reward." Even during the tea, they had been "too absorbed to notice each other or to realize adequately the scene which was the consummation of our plans." It seems even possible to read the story as a vindication of sorts for Matilda and Clementine—an afternoon listening to their debates is sufficiently absorbing to be "its own reward," and perhaps that reward is understood as being even more substantial than "the fashions or the last party that some of our set had given." After all, even as they lament Matilda's withdrawal from their customary discussions of new books, fashions, and parties, it is clear that the "girls" are an impressively learned group. At their initial meeting, for example, they compare their gathering to "Spartan Ephors sitting in council over the fortunes of the republic, to Vehumgerichts, or conclaves of Nicean elders."[26] Given such a "set" of friends, a capacity for absorption in the pronouncements of Matilda and Clementine is not so surprising, and the story might in the final analysis be understood as reflecting credit upon all parties.

Pound produced at least two other short stories, though she may not have published either. Typescripts of "Miss Adelaide and Miss Amy" and "The Passenger from Metropolis" have been preserved in

Pound's papers at the Nebraska State Historical Society. The first, set in England and narrated in a dialect so pronounced that it obstructs reading, tells a spectacular, melodramatic tale of sisterly rivalry, psychosomatic illness, and family ruin. Amy reacts to her sister's engagement by taking to her bed, but recovers sufficiently at its breaking off to eventually marry the gentleman herself, with Adelaide at her side as bridesmaid. All too soon, however, Amy sickens again and this time dies, leaving her sister to a lonely spinsterhood and the family line extinguished.[27]

"The Passenger from Metropolis" is much more accessible. The passenger of the title is Mary Barton, who tells a friend on the train of her obsessive interest in a woman known to her only through brief snippets in the "From Our Local Correspondents" sections of newspapers. Barton's curiosity leads her at last on a journey to Metropolis, where she attends an "elocutionary recital" by a Mrs. Etta Baxter, who may also be, in her unmarried state, the Ingalletta Pritchard who has interested her for so long. The denouement surprises Mary Barton but not readers—Mrs. Baxter is on the same train, of course, and in the story's final line she confirms her identity as the mystery woman: "If the information will afford you relief, Mrs. John Phillips Baxter's first name *was* once Ingalletta."[28]

"The Passenger from Metropolis" is an altogether slighter and less compelling story than "By Homeopathic Treatment," but the two share several features. Both, for starters, are Great Plains stories—where "By Homeopathic Treatment" opens with the young women so concerned about their friend Matilda's "case" that they journey undeterred through "a dreadful wind" to meet, the opening paragraph of "The Passenger from Metropolis" features a description of the town itself, seen from the window of a railroad car: "All that can be seen of Metropolis from the car window is the inevitable low red 'depot' of western stations, a three-story frame structure just across the street labeled in large letters, The Cosmopolitan Hotel, and several brick store buildings that catch and reflect the rays of the afternoon sun. The main business and residence parts of the village straggle away out of view behind hills and clumps of trees."[29] More striking than these conventional features, however, is the exclusive focus on women in both stories (and in fact in all three). In neither is a male voice heard; every character is female, and Clementine's extravagant praise for the "great seer" Ralph Waldo Emerson is the only mention of men or their activities in either story. Both stories also feature "best-laid plans" endings—where the "afternoon tea" of "By Homeopathic Treatment" fails of its purpose, the trip to Metropolis, in achieving its goal, embarrasses the narrator.

The same years of graduate study that saw these apprentice efforts at literary and dramatic art featured a parallel expansion of Pound's reputation as an athlete. In the spring of 1894, just a month after Cather's attack upon Roscoe had estranged the two friends and fellow thespians, Louise made the local papers with an astonishing 111-mile one-day bicycle ride. Under the heading "This Takes the Championship," one local account described both the ride itself and the rider's equipment: "Miss Pound wore the rational bicycle costume and rode a twenty-five pound Rambler." The route took her almost directly south out of Lincoln to Beatrice, where she then headed north and east to the smaller town of Ashland: "She first went to Beatrice and her main ride was one of seventy consecutive miles from there to Ashland. At 4:30 she had finished ninety-four miles. Then the rain made progress slow, but she reached Ashland without trouble." (One hundred miles in a single day is an impressive ride today, even with paved roads and multi-gear lightweight bicycles. Pound's ride in 1894, over unimproved roads on a much heavier bicycle with a single gear, was a much more demanding feat.) The lead paragraph frames the achievement in more than local terms, suggesting that the young townswoman's feat is a matter for civic pride: "The friends of Miss Louise Pound of this city are anxious to gather all the records made by young women who ride bicycles in the west, as they are satisfied that she won by her ride on Saturday the championship of several states besides Nebraska."[30]

The phrase "rational bicycle costume" makes little sense today, but both the costume and the act of riding a bicycle would have been understood in the 1890s as political statements. Cycling was quite fashionable among emancipated women, who celebrated the opportunities for physical exercise and social mobility introduced by the invention of the new "safety bicycle" (by which was meant a machine with equally sized front and rear wheels with the rear connected to the pedals by a geared chain). No less a figure than Susan B. Anthony believed that access to bicycles had "done more to emancipate women than anything else in the world," and Maria Ward, author of the popular *Bicycling for Ladies* (1896), noted a more generalized sense of freedom associated with riding: "Riding the wheel, our own powers are revealed to us."[31]

Such views were opposed in other quarters, where cycling for women was feared for its potential to disrupt "the delicate sphere of the family unit" by permitting women to range outside "previous limits without the surveillance of a knowing husband." Young women were considered especially vulnerable, since the bicycle "allowed her to stray farther afield with members of the opposite sex during courtship."[32] Even more far-fetched, not to mention downright prurient, objections were raised: one critic "claimed that bicycling ruined the 'feminine organs of matrimonial necessity,'" while another "believed that bicycle seats were shaped in such a way as might stimulate a woman's sexual excitement."[33] Across the Atlantic things were no less bizarre. In 1897, three years after Pound's celebrated ride, a group of Cambridge men expressed their disapproval of feminist petitions for educational equality by hanging a woman in effigy over a public street. Photographs were taken. Even a casual look shows the woman astride a bicycle, soaring above a crowd of gaping men. Closer examination reveals more — she is wearing bloomers, her own rational bicycle costume.[34]

As all this idiocy makes clear, there was a marked political dimension not only to cycling itself but to the "rational bicycle costume" in particular, which was allied with a more general "rational dress" movement originating in the 1850s with the adoption of flared trousers ("Bloomers") gathered at the ankles by Elizabeth Cady Stanton, Amelia Bloomer, and other women seeking an escape from corsets, stays, bustles, hoopskirts, and other impediments to movement and comfort imposed by the fashion standards of the day. The story has myriad bizarre twists, but the main narrative line is clear enough: Louise Pound on her Rambler, dressed in her rational bicycle costume, is more than an impressive athlete, champion of Nebraska and the West; she is also, for all the next year's portrayal of the "emancipated" Matilda in "By Homeopathic Treatment" as a "case" in need of intervention by her friends, very much an emancipated woman herself. Pound did not hand out "interminable printed things" or organize activist clubs; what she did instead was march with Company D, practice marksmanship, and win a varsity letter playing against men in intercollegiate matches. Riding 111 miles on that Saturday in April 1894, she gave the lie to the patronizing *Hesperian* snippet from 1892, where her acquisition of a bicycle was attributed to "the purpose of reducing averdupoise."[35]

The "twenty-five pound Rambler" also played a prominent role in a wonderful story featuring Louise pedaling furiously to her brother's rescue. According to Roger Welsch's introduction to a 2006 reissue of *Nebraska Folklore*, Pound once "got wind of an impending police raid on a downtown Lincoln sporting club where drinking, carousing, and gambling [were] known to take place." Knowing that her brother was in attendance at the club that day, "probably engaging in some of those illegal activities," Louise hopped on her bicycle and made it to the "den of iniquity" ahead of the law. Roscoe had already left, but as Welsch tells the story, Pound was herself briefly detained when "amazed and even scandalized" officers arrived and found "a woman present at such a gathering of lowlifes."[36]

Pound's appetite for long-distance bicycle riding was apparently only whetted by her 1894 feat—ahead were other daily rides of one hundred or more miles in 1895 and 1896, and a "Rambler Gold Medal for riding 5000 miles in one year" in 1897.[37] And in 1894 she was also playing tennis at an impressive level, finishing second in the men's singles division and winning the doubles competition in a summer tournament in upstate New York as the partner of Charles Foster Kent, who went on to fame as a prominent Old Testament scholar and teacher of biblical literature at the University of Chicago, Brown, and Yale.[38]

Louise Pound's primary focus in these years, however, remained thoroughly academic. If she wrote plays and stories, acted in plays, and played the piano well enough to earn a music diploma, she was nevertheless no Willa Cather, preparing for a career as a writer of fiction. If she rode her bicycle over long distances and played in tennis tournaments, she was for all that no Tillie Anderson, a professional cyclist of the 1890s who once covered one hundred miles in less than seven hours. The 1896 Chaucer study is clearly the major result of her graduate study, but there were other evidences of scholarly activity as well. A short newspaper clipping from April 28, 1897, reports the reading of her paper "English Pronunciation in Shakespeare's Time" to a meeting of graduate students. The emphasis here, as in the Chaucer study, is clearly linguistic; the young scholar is doing philology, not literary criticism. One year later, according to her own memory of almost sixty years later, she participated in her first professional meeting. Her paper "The Relation of the Finnsburg Fragment to the Finn Episode in *Beowulf*" was one of sixteen presented at the fourth session of the Central Division of the Modern Language Association, held that year in Lincoln.[39] Pound's next big step, the first one to take her away from Lincoln, would intensify this focus and eventually lead her all the way to Germany and a PhD.

But the first stop would be Chicago, where Pound enrolled in courses at the University of Chicago in the summers of 1897 and 1898. The focus of her studies there was if anything more purely philological—in 1897 her schedule included two classes offered by the Department of Sanskrit and Indo-European Comparative Philology ("Outline of the Comparative Grammar of Greek and Latin" and "Exercises in Greek and Latin Comparative Grammar") and two in the Department of Germanic Languages and Literatures ("Phonology" and "Morphology"); in 1898 she took two more classes in the latter Department ("Gothic" and "Old High German"). All these were apparently taken on a pass/fail basis—she received a passing mark in every case. Her record in more strictly literary courses given by the English department was much spottier—in 1897 she made an A in "Studies in Lyric Poetry" but earned a B- in "Wordsworth and the Romantic Movement" and dropped out of "Tennyson and 19th Century Literature." In 1898 the studies in Gothic and Old High German were Pound's sole academic focus; she registered for "English Special Readings" in the English department, but the transcript notes that she "did not attend." The same document lists her as a PhD candidate under "Degree sought" and as "Assistant Instructor, English, Univ. of Neb." under "University Appointments."[40]

Several important inclinations already apparent in the focus of her graduate study at Nebraska appear to find confirmation in Pound's Chicago studies. She may have considered enrolling as a PhD candidate, but it seems clear that her supervisors at the University of Nebraska and her hosts at the University of Chicago understood her studies as directed primarily to the improvement of her grounding in the philological and language history skills useful in the courses she was teaching in Lincoln. Professor Sherman, her mentor in the English department there, had stressed these responsibilities in his letter to Professor Blackburn. He referred tentatively to the possibility that Pound will work toward the PhD in Chicago ("perhaps with reference to candidacy for the degree of Ph.D."); the emphasis is on her work at Nebraska.[41] The primacy of this purpose is further indicated by the publication in 1898 by the University of Chicago Press of Pound's "A List of Strong Verbs and Preterite Present Verbs in Anglo-Saxon," a nineteen-page pamphlet described by the author's introductory note as "intended for use in elementary classes in the University of Nebraska."[42]

Louise Pound, then, spent the summers of 1897 and 1898 working diligently at her philological studies. But she also found time for sports, just as she had in Lincoln, and her performances on Chicago tennis courts, especially in 1897, earned her a new level of renown. The high point was her winning of the third annual Women's Tournament for the Western Championship, held in September at Chicago's Kenwood Country Club. Pound played a total of six matches, winning easily (in straight sets) in the early rounds, surviving a tough match against M. E. Wimer (where she lost her only set), and winning handily (6–4, 6–1, 6–3) against a heavily favored Juliette Atkinson. Then, in a final match on September 8, Pound defeated the previous year's champion, hometown (Evanston) favorite Jennie Craven, also in straight sets, 6–0, 6–3, 7–5.

The Chicago papers provided detailed coverage of the matches, presenting Pound as an "unknown girl from the West" whose "terrific drives" and "cyclone style of playing" were something new to Kenwood Country Club crowds. Most vivid is the *Chicago Tribune*'s account of September 7, 1897. Under a headline trumpeting the event as a regional showdown—"West Beats the East"—and a subhead declaring a "Great Sensation in the Overthrow of the National Champion" in a match exhibiting "Play the Best Ever Seen in This Part of the Country," the story opens with an almost gloating account of Atkinson's defeat: "Miss Juliette Atkinson of Brooklyn, N.Y., national, international, and Canadian lawn tennis champion, will not add to her triple title the far greater honor of champion of the west." Only then does the story turn to Pound: "[Atkinson] struck a genuine Nebraska cyclone yesterday . . . and when she recovered from the engagement all hopes of this year's tennis glory in Chicago were gone a glimmering. Miss Louise Pound was the cause. The result, to put it mildly, was a tremendous sensation."[43]

The article continues in a similar vein, stressing the quality of play and the unprecedented crowds. The writer simply lacks a vocabulary to describe the former; again and again the only recourse seems to be comparison to the men's game or to male athletes generally. "It was far and away the greatest exhibition of women's tennis ever seen around about Chicago" is offered for openers, followed by another nearly gloating statement of regional pride: "And it goes without saying, moreover, that it was better than any shown in the East, since the pride of the Atlantic coast was more than outplayed—almost outclassed." The close attempts a more technical description, only to fall back on a generalized comparison to the game as played by men: "Such driving, volleying, and smashing from two young women has never been developed up to this season, if at all. It was men's tennis, and a high quality of that."

In an attempt to capture the fierceness with which Pound rallied from a 2–4 deficit to capture the first set with a run of four straight games, the story has recourse again to similar comparisons: "Up to that point Miss Atkinson was playing most beautiful, aggressive tennis, which it seemed impossible for any woman player to successfully combat. But when a look almost exactly like that of Fitzsimmons came into Miss Pound's face it was a different story. Almost before anyone noticed the change the West was the aggressor, and while the crowd stared in amazement the phenomenal Nebraska player took four straight games and the set."[44] (Robert James "Bob" Fitzsimmons had his own comeback victory just three months earlier, overcoming an early pummeling in a March 17 title fight to defeat Jim Corbett in a fourteenth-round knockout to gain the Heavyweight boxing championship.)

The Lincoln papers were even more enthusiastic, reprinting the Chicago stories and adding a generous dollop of regional pride: "certainly the self-complacent east must begin to awake to the fact that some things are 'riz' beyond Chicago besides corn and hogs."[45] Individual Lincoln residents and other Nebraskans had also followed Pound's triumphs and sent their congratulations directly. One telegram from Lincoln with the news "Your neighbors are with you," signed by Mrs. N. S. Harwood, Mrs. S. Schwab, and Mrs. A. R. Mitchell, arrived at Beecher Hall at the University of Chicago. J. B. McDonald's message from North Platte, sent directly to the Kenwood Country Club, elevated the tournament to an international level (Atkinson was the Canadian champion): "A world's championship nobly won. Accept my heartiest congratulations."[46]

Just ten days later, the *Hesperian* published a front-page poem celebrating the local champion's victory. Taking his title, first line, couplet rhyme scheme, many rhyme words, length, and basic narrative structure from Walter Scott's immensely popular poem, Hal Ryoner's "The New Lochinvar" compares Pound's surprising triumph to Scott's knight spiriting "the lost bride of Netherby" away from her hostile clansmen and intended marriage to a "laggard in love and a dastard in war." Regional pride is again prominent, with the tournament director's "surly" inquiry, "Have ye come from Nebraska, from Lincoln afar, to be downed by our skilled-ones?" answered in a ringing affirmative: "'There are cups in your cupboards I'd carry afar to a new home in Lincoln,' said young Lochinvar." It is clear that the poet had paid close attention to the newspaper accounts, since he puns lamely on Jennie Craven's name ("no laggard in skill, or Craven in war") and includes Craven, Atkinson, and Wimer in the list of "Kenwood Club Clan" left mournful by their defeat.[47]

A month after the event, news of Pound's surprising triumph had reached the east coast, where the October 7 issue of *Leslie's Weekly* ran a short notice accompanied by a photograph of a racquet-wielding Pound looking sharp in a high-collar white dress and plaid cap. The story, delivered in an astonishing flurry of commas, came directly from the Chicago papers: "Miss Louise Pound, of Lincoln, Nebraska, who, by her defeat of Miss Craven, of Evanston, in the recent tournament on the courts of the Kenwood Country Club, became the woman tennis champion of the West, was, until that event, unknown in Chicago." Craven, as defending champion, was a heavy favorite, "regarded by her friends as the sure winner," at least until Pound's defeat of Atkinson in the final round of bracket play: "When, however, they saw this unknown girl from the West defeat Miss Atkinson, holder of a triple championship, they began to fear that their favorite would have to struggle desperately to retain her honors. Their fears were well grounded, as the event proved." Pound's earlier triumphs in Nebraska were mentioned—as "early as 1890 she held the championship of her state"—and the story concluded with a glance at her accomplishments in other sports: "Miss Pound has hardly a rival in her native place in the art of skating, and has won many prizes in bicycling."[48]

Pound, amidst all this celebration of herself, was having a wonderful time. No published account of the tournament is as vivid as the nearly play-by-play account in her own letters home, which are of particular interest for their description of the social milieu surrounding the tournament. On Saturday evening, September 4, she reports on her fourth-round match with M. E. Wimer, the one that turned out to be the sternest test of the tournament for her, the only one where she lost a set. After relatively brief summaries of the first two sets—she worked "fearfully hard" for the first, winning 6–1, and lost the second by the same score, despite playing "just as hard as I know how"—Pound turns to the deciding third:

> Well, the next set—that girl got me three love. Every game was deuce. . . . She took my hardest drives on the half volley and got them every time. . . . I was trying to follow Mr. Gardner's advice, and place, not send them swift, which is what suits her. She's swifter. On the fourth game, I succeeded. I placed down the sideline, and managed to get to the net. I won. Score 1–3. Then the girl gave out, while I was fresher and fresher. She served doubles and grew wild. I persisted and took the net. Score 3–all. Then we fought, and I got the game. We fought again harder, and she won. Score 4–all. Was there suspense? The match hung in the next two games, and the crowd stopped cheering us and was breathless. I never played such tennis as in those last two games in my life. Luck was with me, and helped me down the side lines, on the base line. I don't know just how I got those last two games, but I did. And the match was mine. And I was given a regular ovation.[49]

The letter then immediately moves from the match itself to the socializing that followed. After being carried off the court to the cheers of the no longer breathless crowd by none other than the defending champion, Jennie Craven (who, as it turned out, would be her opponent in the following Wednesday's grand finale), she is invited to dinner at the home of Mr. James P. Gardner, the tournament director. Unlike the ogre of "Young Lochinvar," the actual director is described as "so much for me that—the prizes are not selected yet—it would be just like him to make the second prize nicer than the first."

The dinner, as described in Pound's letter, featured several elements that would strike contemporary partygoers as bizarre, but her tone makes clear that Louise enjoyed the evening immensely and saw nothing unusual in any of its activities. First there is a listing of guests—Juliette Atkinson was staying with the Gardners, as were Jennie Craven, a "Miss Sadie Hudson of Oak Park," and "Misses Mary and Sarah Gardner," the tournament director's nieces. First up, apparently, was a footrace, with Pound anticipating victory, especially as she was dressed in "tennis skirts and shoes" while Atkinson was hampered by a "long skirt and ordinary shoes." But Atkinson won anyway: "Think of it! I always expect to beat in a race, but that tiny thing, in a long dress too, ran fairly away from me."

Next up was wrestling, where Pound had her revenge: "Here I laid her [Atkinson] out at once. Then they put me up against Miss Craven, the giant, and we had no end of fun when I got her—I can hardly reach around her, I told how she picked up and carried me the whole length of the tennis field—flat on the floor!" Things settled down a bit after the running and wrestling. Pound played the piano, Sadie Hudson danced a jig ("the best jig I ever saw"), and Atkinson sang. "Oh it was a jolly evening."

The letter then turns to an extended description, at once admiring and spiteful, of Juliette Atkinson, who would be Pound's opponent in the final round. Atkinson was the most famous player in the tournament, eventually a three-time (1895, 1897, 1898) U.S. Open singles champion, and by Pound's report a "tireless" athlete: "If you feel her arm it's like feeling a board, or a piece of iron, I'm cotton batting beside her." What's more, Atkinson was graceful, petite, and lovely, winning her matches easily, "without growing even flushed," and she "looks like a fashion plate on the court, wears a different colored ribbon belt . . . around her 17-inch waist each day, and a tie to match." Atkinson, on top of everything else, was from the East, plus she had won the running match. It was all too much, and resentment takes over the narrative: "The Gardner girls are wild to have me win from Miss Atkinson. They don't like her. . . . She's told everyone already how she's going to beat me. I know I'm bristling with weak points, I play in bad form, and can make no strokes, and have never known good coaching, but she might say less about it."

At this point Pound shifts back to a grudging admiration: "We're good friends though, great friends. . . . She's a wonder and a whirlwind." From beginning to end Pound's letter makes explicit her expectation of losing to Atkinson in the upcoming final—it runs from the first page's anticipation of Mr. Gardner liking her enough to make the second prize better than the first to the third page's self-consoling conclusion. "It will have taken an international champion to win from me though, bad form and all. No, I can't play tennis like that girl. No man in Nebraska can either."[50]

All in all, the meditation on Atkinson reads like nothing so much as an athlete working herself up to face a top-notch opponent. The event would seem to bear out such a reading, as Pound handled Atkinson easily the next afternoon, winning in straight sets. Read in its entirety, Pound's letter reveals most of all a young woman much pleased to be testing her skills against high-level competition and finding them adequate to the occasion. "I've made a name for myself now and won a prize and am content," she writes in a Sunday-morning addendum, adding, "Who could do better—do as well—with my experience?"[51] In another passage she adds a no less generalized summary: "I'm having the fun of my life these days. I'm petted and coached, and my class work is lost sight of. I'm invited to a grand luncheon out at Hinsdale at a suburban home, et cetera."[52]

The University of Chicago was also quick to claim Pound's successes on the court as its own—the 1898 edition of the school yearbook, *Cap and Gown*, closed the section devoted to the exploits of the men's tennis squad with a report of her victory in the Women's Western Championship, followed by a complete listing of her matches. The section's headnote ended with an optimism based in part upon her exploits: "With the uniformly victorious team, with Mr. Neel, Mr. Bond, and Miss Pound to speak for our interest in tennis and its result, we look for continuous success."[53]

It is clear too that Pound on the courts of the Kenwood Country Club occupied, perhaps for the first time, a strange liminal ground between insider complacency and outsider aspiration and resentment. Born to the manor in Lincoln, she was nevertheless, once transported to Chicago, "the unknown girl from the West" who charmed an urban country club set at least in part as an "artless" (the word is used to describe her in at least one newspaper account) naïf. These same Chicagoans were, however, quick to give their allegiance to a fellow westerner when the opposition was from even further east, where Chicago itself was looked upon as provincial.

The social currents on the Kenwood courts were, in short, richly complex, if composed at last of petty vanities, and Pound's letter makes clear that she was well aware of her position. If the Lincoln papers crowed over her victories as evidence that "corn and hogs" were not Nebraska's only claims to fame, Pound herself was in no way blind to the tournament's regional rivalries, and was ready to fill in the details for her family. Explaining that the whole Kenwood crowd in the Wimer match "was for me, and were heartbroken when I seemed to have the match lost," she goes on to spell out their motives. "You see when Miss Atkinson trampled on Miss Neely, the West sank before the East, and when I was being laid out, too, people felt badly. Those Eastern girls say the West can't play tennis at all. I was a last hope, else two Eastern girls would play off the finals in the Western tournament. Disgrace."[54]

Contrasted to this note, where Pound sees herself, and is seen by the spectators in Chicago, as representing the upstart West against a patronizing East, are those passages in the same letter where Pound takes a very different tone, subjecting at least two players to sniffy dismissal as "not liked" for vague reasons seemingly based on ineffable class distinctions. Neely, for example, is simply "not liked," while Wimer, who also "isn't liked," is faulted because she "has not cordial manners" and "is not attractive in her ways."[55] Here the positions are sharply reversed, with Pound speaking as an insider, a young woman born to the "cordial manners" and "attractive ways" of country clubs. Almost exactly two years later, writing again to her parents but this time from Germany, she carries this note to a yet more unsavory level. Complaining oxymoronically about "spoiled insolent street children" who "chase balls for the men for 20 pfennigs apiece," Pound writes that she has "explained that in no American club would such children be allowed near the courts."[56] From any perspective but one whose access to the courts has never been questioned, of course, the spoiled party in this situation is not the street children.

This note of class and family pride would remain with Pound for the rest of her life. In a 2004 interview, retired University of Nebraska English professor and University historian Robert Knoll, who had been her student, recalled a rash moment when, in response to congratulations from Pound on honors received by both Knoll and his sister, he jokingly suggested that the two of them might turn out to be another celebrated Lincoln pair, just like Pound and her celebrated brother. "Miss Pound did not appreciate the comparison," he recalled, adding that he learned his lesson well and never again compared his own or any other local family to the Pounds.[57] But the point to be stressed here is not the snobbishness of such moments but the psychological advantages conferred by Pound's betwixt-and-between position, the ability to have it both ways, moving easily between insider and outsider stances as the moment dictated. After all, in two passages on adjacent pages in her 1897 letter from Chicago she moves from patrician dismissal of Neely and Wimer to consolation of herself for the anticipated loss to Atkinson by recollecting the disadvantages of never having known good coaching.

The point is a straightforward one, for all its elusiveness. Pound facing Atkinson, "holder of the triple championship," on the courts of the Kenwood Country Club in 1897 occupies a ground similar to that of Pound taking on Reverend Skeat in her Chaucer study, or that of her later scholarly rivalry with Princeton's Gordon Hall Gerould. The same note also sounds in her letters home from Germany during her time as a PhD candidate. As a Nebraskan playing tennis in Chicago, as a female American PhD candidate in Germany, as a woman in Nebraska playing tennis against men and then seeking a life in an academic world dominated by other men, as a faculty member at a midwestern state university engaged in scholarly controversy with an opponent from a distinguished Ivy League institution—in all of these situations Pound found herself on a middle ground with ever-shifting borders. If she would sometimes, as in the Chicago letter, be defensive, insisting in detail on the well-established forces arrayed against her—that would be the outsider, the determined petitioner at the gate. If she would also exhibit an unfailing confidence and a fierce tenacity that allowed her to prevail again and again over just those forces—that would be the insider, the daughter of DAR stalwart Laura Biddlecome and Judge Stephen B. Pound, raised at the top of social order she knew and taught to regard her aspirations and her ideas, once decided upon, as things not easily given up.

In 1898 there was more high-level tennis, though this time the outcomes were less favorable to Pound and the West. As defending champion, she did not play in the Women's Western Championship until September 7, when she again faced Atkinson, who had returned to Chicago determined to avenge her surprise defeat of the previous year. And avenge it she did. The *Chicago Tribune* headlines say it all, giving the news in the main head and offering the partisan rationales in a subhead. "Miss Pound Is Beaten" said the first, while the second noted the inclement weather—the match had been rained out the previous day—and the subpar performance of the defending champion: "Nebraska Player Not in Her Usual Form—Weather Conditions Interfere with the Play."[58] The full report makes clear that Atkinson dominated the match, winning in straight sets (6–4, 6–3, 7–5) and finishing with a flourish, coming back from a 3–5 deficit in the final set to win the last four games, taking the last two at love. In retrospect, it is clear that the 1898 final was the end of Pound's engagement with tennis at the highest level. There would be no more matches with nationally ranked players like Atkinson, Craven (who would herself soon retire), or Wimer. There would be other tournaments and other championships in her future—Pound would win one at the University of Heidelberg in 1900—but the glorious upset victory of the unheralded "Nebraska cyclone" over Atkinson in the 1897 Women's Western Championship would be the high point, the single most spectacular triumph of Pound's distinguished athletic career.

But Pound was playing more than tennis in the 1898, and her new sporting interest would once again bring her to the attention of the Chicago newspapers. The new game was basketball. According to a 1906 "decennial souvenir" pamphlet, "Girls' Basket Ball in the University of Nebraska," it was introduced to Lincoln in 1896 when Anne Barr organized teams in her second-year gymnasium classes. Pound, by the same pamphlet's account, "was persuaded to interest herself in the game" in 1897, and "with characteristic initiative soon had strong first and second teams regularly organized."[59] The 1900 *Sombrero* pictures her in a seven-member team photograph and lists her as center and captain of both the 1897–98 and 1898–99 squads.[60] For the next decade she would be a central figure, first as player and captain, later as manager or coach, in a golden era of women's basketball at Nebraska. "Miss Pound," the pamphlet concludes, "occupies the unique position of having earned two 'N's, the girls', as member of the basket ball team, and the men's, as former university champion, in men's as well as women's tennis, and university representative in intercollegiate singles and doubles."[61]

The *Hesperian* for February 25, 1898, announcing an upcoming match between the "varsity" university squad and an Iowa team from Council Bluffs, makes clear in its lead paragraph the significance of the occasion: "For the first time in the history of the University of Nebraska, or for that matter, in the history of the west, there is to be a formal match between girls' teams at basket ball."[62] The event was at least as much a social event as an athletic contest, and as such was surrounded by community support—much higher billing than went to any player was accorded to seven "patronesses," including the wife of the university chancellor ("Mrs. Chancellor MacLean"), the wife of Lincoln's most prominent political figure ("Mrs. W. J. Bryan"), and the wife of the town's leading newspaper publisher ("Mrs. C. H. Gere"). Five other "Lincoln ladies" are listed by name as providing lodging for the visiting Iowans. The players for both teams are listed almost as an afterthought, in the story's final paragraph, where Pound appears as one of two Nebraska centers, and also as captain. In between, after the patronesses but before the players, the whole matter of admission of spectators was accorded extensive treatment. According to the *Hesperian* pre-game story, the very "style" of the game of basketball—the spectacle, that is, of women exerting themselves in head-to-head athletic competition, in contrast to more restrained gymnasium exhibitions—made the composition of the crowd a delicate issue: "the authorities have to exercise care about the kind of audience present, and have sent out this announcement: Any lady may come, and any gentleman who is accompanied by a lady. About the case of 'single gentlemen' they have not yet decided. Tickets will probably be one remedy. Demands for reserved seats have been received already, and many from out of town have sent word that they are coming in for the match. University colors will be worn and a yell is being made for the occasion."[63]

Two weeks later, the results were printed under a "University Girls Victorious" head. Much attention was again given to social matters—"Tasteful decorations of the different society and fraternity colors ornamented the windows," and Chancellor MacLean showed up along with his patroness spouse. The event was a huge success—even though tickets were priced at the same rate as football games, "the gymnasium was well filled long before the hour by a large and enthusiastic audience."[64] The game itself, this time, got equal billing; the 15–7 final score made the opening paragraph, and Captain Pound's efforts were accorded a detailed account. She was the game's star, leading her team in scoring with eleven points: "The players on the Varsity team deserving special mention are Louise Pound, Harriet Cook and Marie Beach. Miss Pound threw three goals from the field, five on field toss."[65]

In Chicago that summer, Pound played in a basketball exhibition at the University of Chicago which a *Times-Herald* piece described as "the most unique and exciting bit of athletics that this summer has yielded." Pound played for an all-university team made up of "captains from basket-ball teams belonging to other western colleges" against a University of Chicago squad. Rules varied enormously at the time, especially in the women's game (e.g., teams were often made up of four players), so part of the appeal of the Chicago match was its closer approximation to the game as played by men. No point is stressed more in the published account—the subhead, entirely in caps, reads "NO WEAKLINGS ARE ALLOWED," while beneath that a third caption describes the resulting game as "a little like Football." The story itself continues in this vein: "Tackles, rushes, touchdowns were mild in comparison. The big ball would purl through the air like a cannon ball, and with a swirling impetus half a dozen bloomered forms would shoot after. . . . Free of limb, unimpeded by stays or stiffness, these young amazons were quicker than lightning and eager as ever their brothers could be in any of the manly sports."[66]

The "bloomered forms" were attired in what had been previously described as "strict gymnasium dress," the better to play (oxymoronically) with "proper abandon." All this, of course, recalls the "rational bicycle costume" of Pound's cycling exploits and suggests once again the ways in which something as apparently straightforward as a basketball game was also a politically charged event, a bit of activist feminism. The spectators (entirely women; the only male present was the referee) were unused to such abandon, however proper. They "cowered in their seats" and met at halftime break to discuss what they were seeing:

"Isn't it horribly interesting?" shivered a spectator.
"Horribly! Yes, that's exactly the word!"

"I call it worse than football."

"Certainly it's quite as bad, especially when played on this hard floor. I can imagine it might be endurable played on the soft grass."

"There ought to be a physician here, just as at football games."

"Well, I wouldn't play it unless my life were insured. I should be thinking of the 'wife and children at home.' Wouldn't you, girls?"[67]

As captain of the victorious all-university team (the final score was 8–4), Pound is a prominent figure in this account. Both she and University of Chicago captain Clara Tilton are featured in portrait drawings, and her comments as recorded in the article have a studied casualness that stands in vivid contrast to the breathless rhetorical extravagance of the narrative voice. "'Oh, nothing much happens, as a rule,' said Captain Pound, easily. 'Sometimes there's a dislocated wrist or collar-bone, a black eye, a cut on the lip, a broken finger or some little thing like that, but I never saw anything serious happen.'"[68]

Pound's two summers in Chicago, then, were filled with study, tennis, and basketball. Tennis and basketball, especially the former, took her name to a much wider world, but it was the study that took her to her future. The University of Chicago transcript, in a handwritten entry from May 1899, makes explicit the next step toward that future: "Statement of credits delivered in person to be taken to Germany." A passport giving Miss Emma Louise Pound's height as five feet, five inches and describing her face as "oval" was issued on the same day.[69] She was headed for the University of Heidelberg, where she would impress and astonish her mentors, fellow students, family and friends back in Lincoln, and even herself by successfully completing the PhD in just one year. Forty-five years later she told a former student interviewing her for a newspaper profile that gaining "that degree in two semesters was the hardest thing I ever did."[70] (By at least one report, Heidelberg was itself a second choice: "Her application to Leipzic was flatly refused, and even at Heidelberg, where she was admitted, she was warned about the nature of her wearing apparel, 'lest it distract the attention of the Herren.'")[71]

Pound's work in Heidelberg was, if anything, even more strictly philological than anything she had pursued in her MA years. All emphasis on particular literary figures was gone—no more questions of Shakespearean pronunciation or Chaucerian authorship. There was of course a regimen of lectures and examinations—it is clear from her letters that she attended courses in Old French and continued her studies in Old High German that she had begun in Chicago. She felt she was behind most of her classmates in these subjects, though her much stronger background in Old English gave her great confidence in that class. Pound's major professor at Heidelberg was Johannes Hoops, who supervised the dissertation that was her major work of 1899–1900, and seems as well to have encouraged her work at several critical junctures. Pound's letters from Germany make clear her sense of good fortune in having Hoops as her mentor, and her appreciation for his help proved so durable that a half century later she dedicated her *Selected Writings* to his memory, listing his several academic titles and visiting professorships in the United States and eulogizing him as an "internationalist and friend of American students."[72] Pound and Hoops became lifelong friends. He visited her in Lincoln in 1933 when he was a visiting professor in the United States, and after the war she helped him by shipping what Hoops gratefully called a "CARE package" to Heidelberg at a time when conditions in postwar Germany made its contents precious. "You have no idea," he wrote, "what these fine things mean for us in the present time of distress." (The value of the package is made clear by Hoops's itemization of its contents—"flour, sugar, coffee, chocolate, apricots and raisins, whole milk and eggs, margarine and canned meat—all groceries we can't get here.")[73]

Pound's work in Germany reversed what would now be the usual (and in most programs required) order. She worked first on her dissertation, hoping to hand it in even before her first semester got under way. Her earliest extant letter from Germany, dated September 26, 1899, opens on a confident note: "I'm only waiting till Professor Hoops comes back to Heidelberg to show him my dissertation. I have to see whether I'll have to do it all over. I can't see any more to be done with it, myself. That will be fine—to have my dissertation out of the way before the semester begins—and to have done the whole thing in August and September, with some weeks of sickness thrown in."[74]

The dissertation she is describing, *The Comparison of Adjectives in English in the XV and XVI Century*, though it lacks the computational tables of her earlier Chaucer piece, is at bottom a similar if more sweeping undertaking, a data-based, "systematic survey of the morphological and syntactical facts connected with the history of adjective comparison in these centuries," with "fullness though not of course completeness of illustration" as its goal. The preface also puts on record a "strong sense of indebtedness to Prof. Dr. Johannes Hoops," adding that the "investigation which follows was made at his inspiration."[75] The dissertation proper is organized into eight sections in addition to an introduction, which sets the stage for the period to be examined, provides a historical review of prior opinion on the subject, and closes with an ordered list of briefly stated general conclusions. Running through the entire dissertation is a straightforwardly numerical ordering system, which sequences the whole under ninety-seven distinct headings. If the overall presentation is formal and impersonal nearly to the point of monotone, the impression is nevertheless one of systematic address to a carefully delimited topic.

The introduction opens with straightforward statement of fact, buttressed by a blizzard of known and hypothetical forms, on the ground where Pound felt strongest: "Old English, like all Teutonic languages, shows organic or terminational comparison. The comparative degree is formed by the addition of the suffix *-ra* and the superlative by the addition of the suffix *-ost* (*-ust, -ast, -est*) to the positive, representing the Teutonic *-ozan-, *-osta-, *-izan-, *-ista." Additional details of Old English follow, ending with citations given for "full particulars."[76]

This is followed by discussion of developments in late Old English and Middle English, appropriate scholarly terminology, the introduction of periphrastic comparison (by "more" and "most") in the thirteenth century, and a review of prior attempts to establish rules for the use of both terminational and periphrastic forms. The next four headings are given over to conclusions, the first of which is a surrender of the attempts at system just summarized. It seems best, Pound writes, to "admit that literary English is likely to break any rules that can be given," such breaking of rules being "especially common in poetry." Comparison depends most of all upon the length of the adjective, with monosyllables given terminational comparison and words "of more than two syllables" compared periphrastically. Maximum variation occurs with disyllables, and here "the mode of comparison is governed to a certain extent by the ending," though "familiarity of the word" and even "author's preference" also play roles. Following the observation that the centuries under review exhibited "even greater freedom than exists today," the introduction closes with a second description of the dissertation's goals: "In the citation of examples in the following, as suggested elsewhere, fullness and variety of illustration have been the aim."[77]

The first section of the dissertation's main body is then devoted to terminational comparison, with "Formal Elements" getting the first part and "Use" the second. The presentation is straightforward throughout: under each heading a general observation is followed by a list of instances keyed to a wide-ranging "List of Texts examined." The sixteenth heading in this section provides a relatively brief instance. The general observation comes first: "After a short vowel, a final consonant is often doubled in the comparative and superlative. So generally in present English." This is followed immediately by eight confirming instances and three exceptions: "*byggar*, Morte D. 656, 32. *biggest*, ib. 814, 21. *doolfuller*, ib. 846, 5. *gladder*, York

Pl. 425, 135. *maddest*, Four PP. 382. *fitter*, Ascham Tox. 124. *thinner*, ib. 132. *welcommest*, Lyly End. 41. But *trymest, meryest, Þynest*, Heywood Love 171. etc."[78]

Other sections follow, devoted in turn to "Periphrastic Comparison," "The Comparison of Participles," "Irregular Comparison," "Double and Intensified Comparison," "Elative (absolute) Use of the Comparative and Superlative," "The Substantivation of Comparatives and Superlatives," and "Some Syntactical Peculiarities." A one-page appendix is then followed by a bibliography listing thirty-one scholarly sources and reference works ("Literature consulted"), most of them in German, and a much longer "Lists of Texts examined, with Abbreviations." The dissertation then closes with an alphabetical "Partial Index of Forms." He is omitted from the "Literature consulted" section, but Charles E. Bennett, Pound's Latin teacher from her days at the University of Nebraska preparatory school, came to her aid at least once—his *Latin Grammar* is cited on page 3.

All in all, the dissertation presents itself as the summary of an astonishing regimen of carefully focused reading. Imagine, just for starters, reading all the plays of Marlowe, Malory's *Le morte Darthur*, and the first book of *The Faerie Queene* with an eye resolutely directed not to narrative, imagery, or allegory but to the noting and cataloging of comparative and superlative adjectives. The meticulous care Pound brought to this daunting work is at times reflected in astonishingly detailed passages within a given section—what sort of attention, for example, produces in support of the notion that in the early sixteenth century "elative use is most common with periphrastic superlatives" the fact that Sir Thomas Elyot's *The Boke named the Gouernour* "uses about 160 *most* superlatives, 124 being elatives, and 20 superlatives in *-est*"? (Pound uses "elative" not in today's more common sense of a locative case indicating movement away from, but as a not strictly comparative use of the superlative indicating "a quality in a person or thing or idea in an especially high degree.")[79]

The overwhelming sense conveyed by the dissertation, then, as by the earlier Chaucer article, is of a scholarship deeply rooted in painstaking tabulation, a proto-scientific buttressing of carefully moderated general statements with "fullness and variety of illustration." There is in both works a nearly complete absence of what might be called an aesthetic response—the closest thing to a note of "appreciation" in either comes when Chaucer is described in the shorter article as possessing a more advanced "sentence-sense" (because he "wrote a shorter sentence than any Englishman of his time") and is credited with "richness of language and freedom of form" in the dissertation.[80] Pound would go on to a scholarly career deeply centered in the humanities, but she got her training and her start in that career as a researcher deeply respectful of the "tests," "figures," and "calculations" she deploys in both efforts, and suspicious to the point of dismissiveness of conclusions based upon "vague theorizing or speculations, or on the uncertain foundations of personal opinion" she had scolded in Professor Skeat.[81] The nine-year-old girl who describes and categorizes her stamp collection so precisely in 1881 is already a scholar of this sort in the bud, celebrating the rarity and antiquity of certain items and carefully noting the exact number in each category but wholly omitting any mention of personal favorites.

Given the sheer quantity of painstaking work required for the dissertation, not to mention attending lectures and preparing for examinations in Old English, Old French, and High German, it is hardly surprising that Pound later remembered her hurried pursuit of the PhD in Heidelberg as the most difficult challenge of her life. As her letters home make clear, she was often unsure of her success. During the fall semester of the 1899–1900 academic year, she worried that both her nationality and her gender might work against her after a faculty member's daughter told her specifically that *"Americans* were never allowed to come up for examination after two semesters, and that all possible obstacles were thrown in the way of a woman's taking a degree. A friend of hers had got one, but with a lot of trouble, and they gave her a much severer examination than they give men." The same letter, however, goes on to stress more positive aspects of her own experience: "The professors are nice to me, and I'll be ready, all right, but I'm much afraid about getting permission. If I can't at Heidelberg, I can't any where, for the examinations are easiest here. My dissertation, in its present state, is as good or better than half of those they accept—some are *very* thin. . . . In the meantime, I must say that no one in America could have been kinder or more courteous in every way than the German professors and the German students I have met, have been."[82] In another letter, written just as her first semester's work closed, she lets her family in on the line she is taking in describing her studies to others: "I'm telling people at home, in the university, etc, when I write, that I'm *trying* for a degree, but *do not expect to get one.*" Several reasons follow: "It's a fact that a degree after two semesters' residence is said to be quite impossible. I have Prof. Hoops with me though, and *may* do it."[83] Accompanying this mixed fear of discrimination and gratitude for fair and even generous treatment are more personal worries about the adequacy of her preparation. Other foreign students have been in Germany longer and have better backgrounds.

As late as February 1900, waiting for Professor Hoops to finish his reading of her dissertation, Pound was lamenting her relative lack of "credentials": "I wish I had a 'record' like the other people working in English. Of the other women who will take degrees, one is entering on her fifth year in German universities, one is on her fourth, and the other has made the Honor examination at Oxford." Like its October predecessor, however, this letter continues in more hopeful tones: "In any case, if I am not examined, it will not be because I am not a man. No one could have been more fairly treated. The American men who came here, with better credentials than mine, hoping to get degrees in two semesters, gave up long ago."[84]

By the end of February, Pound's worries were at a crisis point. She had long ago handed in a revised version of her dissertation, but she had also learned that she would be required to "make the examinations *entirely* in German, can't use English even to Professor Hoops, who speaks English as well as he does German." She is self-conscious about her spoken German: "I don't blame Professor [Wilhelm] Braune for telling me I'd 'have to speak better German' (he was nice about it)." And she is inclined to think she had made a mistake in spending so much time in Heidelberg, "wishing I had stayed here only in the summer, been at Leipzic in the winter semester, then the third semester at Paris."

But then, on March 1, in the same letter reporting her doubts, she exuberantly reports a fundamental shift—she has just that day been urged by both Professor Hoops and Professor Braune to stay the course; and she has been told that she will, after all, be admitted to examinations in July. "It's the dissertation," she writes. "Professor Hoops *likes* it." Hoops liked it so much, in fact, that he told her he wanted to include it in "a series of philological publications" he is editing. "Isn't this great?" she asks. "It will be quite an honor. . . . If you knew how many people here had told me it was 'absolutely impossible,' you'd know how glad I am to know that there's this chance. Of course I shall have five months of awfully hard work before me, shall withdraw from the world, except for an occasional game of tennis, but I'll like *that*."[85]

In their structuring of experience, Pound's extant letters home from Germany are remarkably similar to the long letter from Chicago before her 1897 match with Juliette Atkinson. Pound casts herself in both instances as entering into a difficult struggle where any reasonable estimator of odds would be hesitant to wager on her success. In Germany her quest often seems "quite impossible": American men attempting to obtain degrees in shorter than usual times have gone home defeated; other women in the program have been in residence for four or even five years; European professors are hard on Americans and harder on women. In Chicago, Juliette Atkinson, holder of multiple championships, with all the advantages of expert coaching, better form, experience playing top-notch competition, superior speed, can be expected to "walk through me as she has walked through the rest of the West, with unruffled hair, an unwilted high collar, a spick and span dress, and a gay smile on her face."[86] In both instances Pound's self-presentation is vividly dramatic; she is David up against Goliath.

Goliath of course tumbles. If "West Beats East" was the 1897 headline celebrating Pound's Women's Western Championship triumph, the story out of Heidelberg in 1900 was no less impressive. Pound returned home in the late summer of 1900 as Dr. Pound, a magna cum laude graduate of a distinguished European philology program with her dissertation headed into print in a prestigious series. It was indeed "quite an honor," yet another astonishing performance, this one in the academic arena, by the "Nebraska cyclone." And if Pound acknowledges it as a year of especially intense work in referring to it afterward as the most difficult thing she ever did, it was for all that not a time of unrelenting toil.

In particular, mixed in with a running account of high and low points in her academic pursuits, Pound's letters make repeated reference both to athletic activities and to dances, in addition to reports on the difficulties and rewards of living abroad. As an athlete, Pound found her tennis and skating skills especially helpful, as her letter of October 15, 1899, makes explicit: "My 'athletics' have helped me a lot here, in making friends and having a pleasant time. So much is made of tennis, and especially by the nobility. I expect it to be the same with skating."[87] The following summer she would be playing in a university tennis tournament (some biographical sketches mention her winning two tournaments during her time in Germany), and her expectations about the skating were proven correct even sooner. "The town is simply crazy over skating," she writes in December, adding that the whole town is out on frozen sections of the Neckar River, "in the afternoon, or in the morning, off in corners, 'practicing.'" Competitive as ever, she notes that she has checked out the skater advertised as "the best in town," and gives her a lukewarm review: "She skates nicely, too, though she doesn't do very difficult figures."[88]

The dances, and there were so many of them that she assures her family she will be skipping some, also come in for detailed description. "I've been to two dances in the last week and am invited to three more in the next two weeks, one a 'masked ball,'" she writes on December 24, 1899, adding with some pride that she has been greatly sought after as a partner: "At the last there was a regular jam, and I had everything taken to a '13th extra' in a few minutes, breaking the record on extras!" At a dance called a Herren Frei-Kür (Men's Free Choice), "where each man has a chance to waltz each lady once around, there was a row of men ten deep waiting to grab me when my partner released me!" No doubt this was also a record, and Pound goes on to describe the delaying tactics her partners used to prolong their time with her: "I didn't have a chance to dance with very many though. Most of my partners found they 'couldn't get by a certain corner' or else danced so outrageously slowly that it took *forever* to get around the hall."[89] In all of this it is clear that despite the strictures on her dress imposed by university administrators, the American from Nebraska nevertheless delighted in distracting the Herren.

A little more than a month after the flurry of Christmas dances, a letter home (filled with that almost obsessive quantification and ranking by now recognizable as a Pound signature—she even ranks actresses!) gives an account of another entertainment: "I have been in a German theatre at last. . . . Four of us went over to Mannheim to hear the greatest actress in Germany (said to be the third in Europe—next to Bernhardt and Duse) in the *Doll's House*. She was stunning." The letter goes on to marvel at the low prices and reports on a coffeehouse stop on the return trip:

> We had splendid seats (price one dollar)—went over at six and got back at eleven (the performance was from seven till ten). This was my first trip to Mannheim. The fare there is a little less than a quarter. It's something to hear the greatest actress in Germany for less than a dollar and a half. . . .
>
> Coming back we stopped—the party of us, at the Wirtschaft "Germanie" at the foot of Landhaus-strasse, for coffee and Schinkenbrödchen [ham rolls], and to chew the rag more or less with one of the Kellerinnen [waitresses]. It was fun![90]

With all this dancing and tennis playing, studying and theatergoing, Pound made a number of friends during her year in Germany. In particular, two gentlemen seem to have boarded with Pound at the home of a family named Leitz at Landhausstrasse 22. One, an American student named Mellinger Henry, who went on to accomplish significant work as a folk-song collector, sent a letter of extraordinary length (eighty-nine pages) from his bookstore job in Providence, Rhode Island, to "Miss Pound" in Heidelberg in January 1900, describing his tramping adventures in the fall of 1899 (including a trying period in two prisons in Milan). Despite the letter's length, Henry's tone is formal throughout—it is "Miss Pound" not only at the beginning but also in the body of the letter—and he closes "yours sincerely" and signs his full name, including middle initial.[91] The other gentleman, a man named Harding, was mentioned so frequently in her letters home that her family inquired about a romance. Pound's reply is emphatic: there is no cause for worry "about Mr. Harding. I'm not living there any more, where he is [at Landhausstrasse 22], and haven't time to make expeditions with him. And *besides*—I didn't know I had mentioned his name so often. I suppose it was because he lived at Landhausstrasse, too. I might have written of several others, instead, if I had thought. But I haven't time now to do anything but work."[92]

Far more significant than either gentleman, however, was Ani Königsberger, the daughter of a Heidelberg professor, who is mentioned in Pound's letters far more frequently, and at much greater length, than Harding. Moreover, the two women corresponded regularly for more than half a century; letters dated from 1900 through 1958 are preserved in Pound's papers. The two shared a love of athletics and the outdoors—Pound writes home of teaching Königsberger "the net game" on the tennis courts, while Königsberger delighted in taking the American on hikes and climbs. The surviving letters are all Königsberger's, every one written after Pound had returned to Nebraska, but there are pages and pages of them. Pound took the trouble to preserve them for half a century, and clearly she responded regularly, as Königsberger's letters are filled with thanks for photographs and letters she has received and with her responses to news of Nebraska basketball teams. Even a cursory reading (they are handwritten, sometimes jumbled in their order, in places difficult to decipher) makes clear that in their year together the two women formed a close, emotionally intense, intimate friendship and that each found in the other a sympathetic and understanding companion. To Mellinger Henry she remained "Miss Pound," but to Ani Königsberger she was "Maid" and "Louise."

The obvious comparison, of course, is to the earlier, equally one-sided, though much less voluminous correspondence with Willa Cather. There are obvious similarities—with Königsberger, as with Cather, Pound would seem the cooler, more reserved party (though much less so with Königsberger). Her letters home emphatically present Königsberger as a "character," an almost mythic child of nature, regarded by all as "half barbaric." "It is said to be one of the 'sights of the century' to see her take a walk on snow shoes," she writes. Pound even lapses briefly into German in reporting community attitudes, describing Königsberger as "ganz toll" (entirely mad) and "verrükt" (crazy).

But, no less clearly, there are also great differences. Pound responded to Königsberger, met her on her own ground, and over a period of many years carried on her side of their correspondence in terms that pleased Königsberger. In the same letter reporting astonished local reaction to Königsberger's walking on snow shoes, Pound raises the possibility of buying a pair for herself. "I should love to send for them to Switzerland," she writes. "Later I could sell them again, of course. It would be quite impossible to take them home with me!"[93] Most telling, perhaps, is the intensely retrospective nature of their later correspondence. As their times together receded, the two women went over them together, carefully and repeatedly, examining the moments they had shared, exploring what they had been thinking or expecting on this or that occasion. One does not so carefully revisit one's casual encounters or acquaintances.

Various readers, should they one day bring to Königsberger's letters the same wide-ranging perspectives and ideological enthusiasms focused upon the vastly slimmer Cather-to-Pound correspondence, would no doubt arrive at similarly disparate readings. There are several passages to warm the hearts of eavesdroppers eager for signs of romance, just as there are others to offer refuge to readers happier with a reserved Pound keeping yet another fervent admirer at arm's length. From such responses one would learn rather more about the responders than about Pound or Königsberger. What would be noted by all, however, would be the significance, this time unmistakably for both parties, of their relationship. Pound found in Königsberger a woman after her own heart, a personality as powerful as her own, though decidedly more eccentric. They met as class equals—both had unchallenged access to the tennis courts—and spoke intimately to each other, sustaining that speaking over many years. That they cared deeply for one another as intimate friends cannot be doubted.[94]

But even here, in what may have been the most intense relationship of a long lifetime seemingly marked by the conspicuous absence of intense relationships, Pound seems not to have even momentarily lost sight of the purpose that brought her to Germany in the first place. She came to get a degree, worked with astonishing diligence to get it, and worried almost to the point of despair when she thought she might not succeed. "I didn't come here to know people," she wrote, "or for social things, or dances &c. Now it's hard to keep out of them. But I shall."[95] Pound may have distracted the Herren, but she would be distracted by neither Herren nor Dammen.

Ani Königsberger's letters ask Pound repeatedly to return, and on one occasion at least Pound seems to have given serious thought to a four-month summer visit centered on hiking in the Alps. But finally it did not happen. Pound's future was back in Nebraska, and it was a future centered in professional life, in teaching and in scholarship. She had planned that life for a long time—the impassioned endorsement of the scholar's service that so impressed the young Alvin Johnson may be its earliest recorded articulation, and the classmates back in Lincoln who had found her "cold-hearted" may have been the first to encounter her singular purposiveness. In Heidelberg, as the century turned and she completed the "hardest thing I ever did," Pound stood at the very threshold of the academy's open gate, her dreams within her grasp. Nothing would stand in the way of that future—not trips to the theater, not dances, not "expeditions" with Mr. Harding, not even Ani Königsberger. Pound's letters from Germany are filled with references to the situation at the university in Lincoln, to the need to keep Professor Sherman apprised of her progress, to his assurances to her of a job awaiting her return. At one point she makes her loyalties explicitly comparative, in the strongest imaginable terms: "All Heidelberg isn't worth a square inch of Nebraska."[96] By September 1900, PhD in hand, she was on her way home.[97]

6. Professor Lucius A. Sherman. Nebraska State Historical Society, RG2411 PHO O.

7. Louise Pound and Willa Cather as University of Nebraska students. Bernice Slote Collection, Archives and Special Collections, University of Nebraska–Lincoln Libraries.

8. Louise Pound in rational costume with a Rambler bicycle. Nebraska State Historical Society, RG0909 PH10 6.

9. Louise Pound as a University of Nebraska student, wearing a Phi Beta Kappa key. Mari Sandoz Collection, Archives and Special Collections, University of Nebraska–Lincoln Libraries.

10. Louise Pound in a photo from *Leslie's Weekly* (New York), October 7, 1897. Nebraska State Historical Society, RG0909 PH57 1.

11. Ani Königsberger Pfister. Nebraska State Historical Society, RG0909 PH16 10.

12. Louise Pound as a young instructor at the University of Nebraska. Nebraska State Historical Society, RG0909 PH8 12.

FOUR

" She's an athlete; she's a scholar "

Home in the fall of 1900 was, of course, 1632 L Street, where the Pound family waited. Judge Pound was sixty-seven, retired from the bench but busy with private law practice in association with his son. Laura Pound was fifty-nine, no longer serving on the public library board but still active in DAR affairs. Roscoe, who would turn thirty in October, had married the previous year, but the couple then resided in the Pound home.[1] Louise returned home as the second Dr. Pound in town, as Roscoe had earned his PhD in botany in 1897. Both had their dissertations published, too, with Roscoe once again preceding his sister. *The Phytogeography of Nebraska*, the Bessey-inspired study he coauthored with Frederic Clements, had been published in 1898, while Louise's dissertation in the Anglistische Forschungen series appeared in 1901. Olivia, the family's youngest, would complete work on her MA in classics in 1897 and (after a brief stint teaching school in the nearby town of Seward) begin her long career as a teacher and administrator in the Lincoln schools.

The house on 1632 L Street would be Pound's home for the rest of her life. She would never marry—in fact, the brief (and summarily repudiated) epistolary query about her association with Mr. Harding in Heidelberg would stand out as the only reference connecting her (despite the record-setting dance cards) to a specific gentleman caller or potential suitor. This alone would in all likelihood account for the "thought by many to be cold-hearted" quip in her *Hesperian* "Last Seniors" entry in 1892—a young woman so accomplished, attractive, and socially prominent surely kept a small army of male suitors at arm's length (perfect for dancing) just as adroitly as she managed Willa Cather's impassioned attachment. There is a jealous mention of an unnamed male companion in a dress coat in one of Cather's overheated letters, but here there is no suggestion of a particular attachment between the two. "It would seem," writes Lynn C. Hattendorf Westney in a *Who Was Who in North American Name Study* profile, "that she lived a celibate, albeit cheerful, complex, and unconventional life for a woman of that era."[2]

That life would be entirely lived within her family, and for its final thirty years, following Stephen Pound's death in 1911 and Laura Pound's in 1928, that family would be her sister, Olivia. Given all the attention later focused upon her undergraduate friendship with Cather, Pound would no doubt be grateful for the almost complete lack of comment addressed to the personal side of her adult life. Robert Knoll, writing in 1983, recounts a story told by his flamboyant colleague Orin Stepanek in 1930s: "Orin said that once in talking to her [Pound], he made some reference to the way young women respond to masculinity—referring of course to the sexual attraction between the sexes. The next day, Louise looked him up and said, 'I've never felt anything like what you were talking about. And I went home and asked Olivia, and she hasn't either.' Orin thought this hilarious and told it often, behind her back of course."[3]

There is also a bleak little Weldon Kees short story, "Every Summer They Came Out," first published in 1943, "featuring two unmarried sisters from Nebraska" and carrying an undercurrent of "repressed incestuous lesbianism."[4] Any reference to the Pound sisters (there may be none, of course) is certainly oblique—though the story does specify that "their father was a judge."[5] Kees would certainly have known about the Pounds—he took classes from Wimberly and submitted stories to *Prairie Schooner*; his close friend Maurice Johnson was one of Pound's students. In any event, both narratives certainly speak mostly to the interests of their authors. Stepanek was famous in his genteel day for risqué remarks—his joking reference to the state capitol building's tower as a phallic symbol got him in trouble with straitlaced administrators—and various forms of uneasy sexual orientation are regular features of Kees's stories.[6]

To the extent that any discussion of Pound's sexual leanings or attitudes is called for, then, the summary from Westney's profile seems appropriate. Joan Acocella's similar description of Cather ("homosexual in her feelings and celibate in her actions"), whatever its adequacy for Cather, might appear to fit Pound almost perfectly.[7] Pound herself, however, in addition to finding the whole subject yet another instance of the reprehensible "influence of Hollywood and the tastes of Walter Winchell," would surely have been puzzled (as puzzled as she was at Stepanek's remark) at the use of "homosexual" in the phrasing.[8] She got on very well with many men (she considered Hartley Alexander in particular a close friend), but there can be no doubt that her deepest feelings were for women—Dorothy Canfield Fisher and Ani Königsberger had no male counterparts as her most intimate correspondents, just as her sister had no counterpart as her closest companion. Her social life was centered in women's professional, literary, and social groups. All this she would have doubtless recognized as obvious. Substituting "homosocial," awkward as it is, for "homosexual" in Acocella's label—homosocial in her feelings and celibate in her actions—might capture her temperament more precisely. In any event, Pound herself is silent on the whole matter, and it is others who identify and measure from her behavior (or think they do) an underlying and determining sexual component.[9]

After 1632 L Street, Pound's second home was the Department of English at the University of Nebraska, where she had been employed as a graduate assistant and instructor since 1893. Her old mentor Professor Sherman was good on his word, too, installing his protégé in a University Hall office at the elevated rank of adjunct professor for the 1900–1901 term. Pound's letters from Germany had expressed confidence in her secure "place" even when the news from home was conveyed with some apprehension. "Do stop worrying about the 'regents,'" she writes her family in October 1899, "they can't do anything, and the 'pops' are as good friends of the institution, really, as any are. I'll be all right as long as Dr. Sherman is there. And if not—Professor [Laurence] Fossler is a good friend."[10] As it turned out, her faith was well placed—the last extant letter from Germany, written in July 1900, ends with another reference to her future employment: "I had a nice letter from Dr. Sherman. He will let me teach about what I want."[11]

Sherman, astonishingly, was not only Pound's teacher and the supervisor of her MA work but also her chair for the first thirty years of her career, supervising her ascent through the ranks from adjunct to full professor in a twelve-year span. He did not retire as chair of the Department of English until 1929, at the age of eighty-two. For Pound he must have seemed a campus fixture every bit as durable as the buildings. More durable, in fact—Sherman was still there when University Hall was torn down in 1927; the English department then moved its offices to Andrews Hall, where they are today. "Louise Pound's office was right by the west door," recalled university historian and former student Robert Knoll:

> I think the number was 101, but they may have changed. It was a big, pleasant office. She was always available to students, eager to help. She had a very firm sense of her own accomplishments and importance, but she was never pompous. She would sometimes tell classes what was going on in the department. She told us all, for example, that Kenneth Forward, the director of freshman composition, was the best writer in the department.
>
> After she retired, I went to her house once with Jim Miller—he

was the chair then—to fix curtains. She laughed about our high rank, and made a joke that she must still be an important figure, if chairs and professors were showing up to work on her house.[12]

In the fall of 1900, then, having returned from her diligent and sometimes stressful year in Germany, Louise Pound found much that was familiar. But one thing at least was strikingly new. After years of a training focused almost entirely upon philological studies rooted in medieval and early modern English and European materials, she would turn in her research to decidedly American topics. There would also be a marked branching out, most notably into folk music and American speech, but also into literary research and analysis devoted to more modern figures. By 1905 the first of scores of studies devoted to American dialect would be in print, and even earlier, in 1902, her first article on folk music would appear. In these two areas, new to her in 1900, she would make her greatest name.

Hindsight is certainly susceptible to seeing deliberate program where accident and chance may have prevailed, but such a widely cast net at the very beginning of a career looks very much like a conscious staking out of spacious ground. There may also be something of a declaration of independence, a taking of Professor Sherman's license with regard to her teaching into the world of scholarship as well. The two literary studies are, to be sure, closely argued source studies, sharply limited in their focus, and almost wholly devoid of anything that could be called aesthetic response. But there are no tables, and there is nothing whatsoever of sentence length. Although Pound would continue to produce literary studies, they would occupy a distant third place in a ranking of her research interests, well behind her work in folklore and American speech.

From the very beginning, too, Pound saw herself as belonging to a community of scholars, engaged in what was at last a shared enterprise she continued to regard as noble, just as she had in her undergraduate days when she thrilled Alvin Johnson with her ringing endorsement of the scholarly life as a "mission" where one who could "add just one cubic centimeter to the mass achievement of scholarship" would not have lived in vain.[13] In service to this view she devoted herself to a voluminous and wide-ranging scholarly correspondence and to truly heroic editorial labors, initiated early and long sustained, where her already apparent organizational skills served her well and proved of inestimable benefit to the disciplines she championed. As it happened, she would be one of the winners in mortal life's health and longevity lottery—and she would make the most of her generous allotment of days. Back in Lincoln as a newly appointed adjunct professor, she had forty-five years at her chosen "mission" ahead of her. In the judgment of her colleagues, especially those not from the University of Nebraska, who over those years rewarded her often with both high offices and honors, her contributions were impressive indeed, far surpassing the "one cubic centimeter" that would have sufficed.

Approaches and procedures close to the practices of her Chaucer article and her dissertation are evident in the two essays on English literature Pound published during this period, the first on Tennyson's *Lancelot and Elaine* in 1904, the second on Arnold's *Sohrab and Rustum*. Both pieces appeared in *Modern Language Notes*, the same journal where she had placed the Chaucer study nearly a decade earlier. The Tennyson essay is in three sections: the first argues that Tennyson's use of an already recognized source was more extensive than previously supposed and then provides four numbered "possible cases, not hitherto noted"; the second suggests Tennyson's possible use of an 1825 collection of Italian novellas as a source for *The Lady of Shalott*; the third offers Tennyson's spelling of "Guinevere" as "an arbitrary modification of Malory's Guenever."[14] The article on Arnold does for *Sohrab and Rustum* what the first section of the Tennyson piece does for *Lancelot and Elaine*—argue that an already recognized source was more significant than had been appreciated. Here too Pound makes her claim first and follows up with observations and citations ordered under numbered headings. The patient amassing of detail that produced in her dissertation an ordering of the more than 180 superlatives in Sir Thomas Elyot's *The Boke named the Gouernour* shows up here in the listing of some fifteen spellings of "Guinevere," ranging across French, German, English, and Italian sources.

But even here, where she hews closest to the style and address of her graduate student work, at least one new note is sounded. The earlier works stand out for their rigorously impersonal tone, though in the Chaucer article this is combined with an openly controversial polemic. The first person is sedulously avoided, occurring only in two paragraphs describing method in the Chaucer piece and suppressed altogether in the dissertation. Even in expressing gratitude to her mentor, Pound appears as "the author." The new pieces, for all their listings and citations, are almost chatty by comparison. The Tennyson essay, from 1904, contains not only a first-person anecdote ("In 1900, I noticed, in the Library of Columbia University") but also a report of her thinking: "I remember my impression, at the time, that Tennyson may well have known this collection."[15] The Arnold article features Pound taking a position of her own ("To the present writer it seems") rather than (as in the Chaucer study) supporting another's. There is even, for what may be the first time, a hint of aesthetic response: "Atkinson's heroic couplets are not very good reading, and the story as given by him from Firdawsí, is relatively tedious."[16]

But earlier than either of these—in fact it was Pound's first post-PhD publication—was a very short article, also published in *Modern Language Notes*, titled "Another Version of the Ballad of *Lord Randal*." It is a slight enough item, running less than a page and devoted almost entirely to a text of an old Anglo-American ballad reported as "sung in a railroad camp at Geary, Colorado" and brought to her notice by "Mr. H. C. House, of Kingfisher College, Oklahoma."[17] But it is an entirely new note—the closest thing to a prior indication of interest in ballads is the citation of a collection of sixteenth-century music, *Ancient Ballads and Broadsides*, in the dissertation—and it would lead to great things. In the next twenty years Pound would establish herself as a major voice in the collection and discussion not only of American traditional music but of balladry and folk song generally. She would assemble, and publish in 1915, one of the pioneering collections of such music from a single state (the first one from the Great Plains), and in 1921 the book that would be the most famous single work of her career would be devoted to ballads and their making. *Poetic Origins and the Ballad,* mostly a collection of previously published articles, would take her scholarly reputation to the national and international level, just as her 1897 victory over Juliette Atkinson brought the "Nebraska cyclone" to the attention of the New York papers.

As it turns out, the genesis of Pound's researches is easily summarized. Henry Marvin Belden, according to Pound's own written acknowledgment, "first encouraged her to interest herself in the study of folk-song."[18] Belden was a major figure in American folk-song research—from his post at the University of Missouri he was one of the first not only to recognize that Anglo-American ballads were in active circulation in the United States but also (and even more influentially) to urge their systematic collection and publication. His major work, *Ballads and Songs Collected by the Missouri Folk-Lore Society,* was not published until 1940, but its collection had been mostly completed before 1920, and Belden had been urging the importance of collecting folk songs in public since at least 1903. His 1905 *Modern Philology* article, "The Study of Folk-Song in America," remains a landmark piece for its presentation of a fully articulated plan for university-centered research. Citing early results from collecting efforts of the English Club at the University of Missouri beginning in 1903—in eighteen months of looking by four primary collectors, "versions have been found of eleven of the British ballads recorded in Professor Child's volumes"—Belden urged that other universities undertake similar labors. "In many of our colleges and in most of our universities there is, among the teachers, at least one who knows and cares something about folk-song. Among the students there are probably several who have direct knowledge of some traditional folk-song, and access to much more."[19]

By 1902, it seems, Louise Pound was the teacher at the University of Nebraska who best fit Belden's description of one who "knows and cares something about folk-song." And there is good reason for that. Prior to his arrival in Missouri (in 1895), Belden spent a year in Lincoln as an instructor in the English department, where he was much impressed by Pound:

> Nebraska was significant to me for two things: here I first came into personal touch with the coeducational system, and here I came to know certain significant people. Of these people the most significant was Louise Pound. She had graduated the year before, and that year of 1893–4 she was one of the theme readers for the English department. She was a remarkable girl: intellectually alive, keen about literary movements. . . . [I]t was she that introduced me to Meredith's *Modern Love*. She was also a beautiful dancer, a prize swimmer, and a champion tennis player. Her father—he came from New York state somewhere—was a judge. Many an evening I spent at their house, dancing and talking.[20]

Perhaps those talks included traditional music, in addition to the then-scandalous Meredith. At any rate, in this instance it was Belden who did the introducing, and by 1902, three years before Belden's ambitious program for the collection of folk song had been fully articulated, Pound was already putting it into action. This is even more readily apparent when the fruits of her labors saw more complete publication a decade later. "Traditional Ballads in Nebraska," her first piece for the *Journal of American Folklore*, appeared in 1913, the year after she had read a paper of the same title for the annual meeting of the Nebraska Academy of Sciences. Two years later, the same organization published her "syllabus," *Folk-Song of Nebraska and the Central West*. In both of these Pound's dual role as collector and editor is explicit—the earlier article's opening paragraph affirms that "the present writer has tried to recover what she could, and to learn what she could, of traditional balladry in her home state," but also makes clear that "the reports and contributions of students and friends who happened to be interested have been relied upon."[21] The larger collection carries an "Editor's Preface" by Addison E. Sheldon, which both credits Belden for encouraging Pound's initial efforts and emphasizes the ongoing nature of her work: "Send at once to Miss Louise Pound, University of Nebraska, Lincoln, the text of any additions known to you, with exact information of the circumstances regarding their use in Nebraska."[22]

Collecting, these descriptions make clear, was in those pioneering days an enterprise rooted first of all in textual recovery. One would certainly welcome opportunities to hear traditional songs performed or in some other way obtain the tune, but in more typical instances the collector would be content with words alone. "The recording of the tunes of songs is of special value but difficult," Pound wrote in *Folk-Song of Nebraska and the Central West*. "For most of those cited here the words only have been obtained."[23] The nation's greatest era of traditional music collecting was just around the decade's corner in the 1920s, with newly established commercial recording companies, not academic folklorists, leading the way. Child ballads, blues, and cowboy songs would be hits, and soon enough folk-song collectors would be visiting mountain cabins and southern prisons with tape recorders. But Pound would mostly miss this; she accomplished most of her folk-song study in the earliest period of systematic collecting, according to the model elaborated by Belden. Many of her songs arrived by mail, sent by the "students and friends" thanked in her prefaces, and her work was largely given over to collating, organizing, and annotating.

It is worth noting, too, that women play a prominent role in Pound's collecting ventures. "Traditional Ballads in Nebraska" singles out six named contributors, of whom five are women (one is Willa Cather's younger sister Elsie, who taught with Olivia Pound at Lincoln High School and was a good family friend), while *Folk-Song of Nebraska and the Central West* names twenty (four for the second time), of whom seventeen are women. Women were also centrally involved in the Belden-directed group of Missouri collectors—of eight original English Club members who gathered material for *Ballads and Songs*

Collected by the Missouri Folk-Lore Society, five were women.[24] Louise Pound was a new PhD in a new state, at work in an emergent discipline too new to own a standard name. The male-dominated networks that ruled more settled lands and more established academic fiefdoms were not yet fully in place. There was room to work.

And she was not alone. Even as Pound collected her folk songs, a young Constance Rourke (to pick an especially prominent example), recently back from her own year of study in Europe (she went to France, not Germany), was commencing the work, even more concentrated in American topics than Pound's, that would eventually lead to her groundbreaking *American Humor* and the establishment of the discipline of American Studies. Her first article, on Paul Bunyan, was published in the *New Republic* in 1918, just three years after Pound's folk-song collection. By 1938, William Carlos Williams was speaking of Rourke in nearly messianic terms: "She seems on the way to becoming our Moses."[25]

In the world of Chaucer scholarship a young woman from Nebraska had little access to Professor Skeat, but in the nascent world of American folk-music study her first major article was annotated by George Lyman Kittredge, and when in 1914 she published her note on "The Little Old Sod Shanty on My Claim," she was able to refer to personal correspondence with John Lomax, whose *Cowboy Songs and Other Frontier Ballads*, published in 1910, is often cited as establishing the field.[26] They were two very different academic environments, and the second one had much to recommend it. The Chaucerians might ignore her work, but the folk-music scholars would not. Kittredge and Lomax were lords of a new realm in 1914, and it must have been a heady and somehow welcoming experience to have the one doing your footnotes and the other answering your mail. Here too a "new Moses" might emerge wearing skirts, or some other rational costume.

"Traditional Ballads in Nebraska" presents a total of thirty-seven items under three headings. First comes "English and Scottish Popular Ballads," echoing in its very heading Harvard professor Francis

James Child's hugely influential collection, *The English and Scottish Popular Ballads*, completed in 1898. All but one of the eight ballads included are variants of those included in Child, and are cited by the numbers assigned by him (the exception is "The Colleen Bawn," identified as originating in Ulster). No Child ballads are placed in other sections. According to D. K. Wilgus's painstaking survey, *Anglo-American Folksong Scholarship since 1898*, this sort of "Child-and-other arrangement" would soon become standard in American collections, having been "firmly established" by Child's protégé and Harvard successor George Lyman Kittredge's "editing of Katherine Pettit's Kentucky collection of 1907."[27] Pound's usual practice is to print for each item a title, a brief synopsis, a single stanza, and in some cases a discussion of other variants or an account of the piece's appearance in Nebraska. Five of the eight ballads are printed this way, while full texts are provided for "The House Carpenter" (Child 243) and "Two Little Boys" (Child 49, where it's called "The Twa Brothers"). Only "Lord Randal" (Child 12) is discussed without textual citation, though here Pound provides the reference for its printing in her 1902 article.

The second section, "Sentimental and Other Pieces of British Origin," presents thirteen pieces in much the same way—nine with some sort of stanza excerpt, three with full texts printed, and one ("The Rich Young Farmer") with just a title and a synopsis. This section also features, in addition to Pound's notes, bibliographic information in notes supplied by "G.L.K."—that is, George Lyman Kittredge himself. The future president of the American Folklore Society, in her first *Journal of American Folklore* article, was appearing in very good company. Even more interesting is the article's third and final section, "American Ballads." It comes last, deferring in placement to the English and Scottish ballads, for no piece is a full text printed, nearly half the songs have no text at all, and for no American song does Kittredge supply an additional note. But it is also the article's largest section, containing sixteen songs, and its range is broad, covering everything from cowboy songs ("The Lone Prairie") and political ballads ("The Death of James A. Garfield"), to outlaw songs ("Jesse James") and religious pieces ("The Model Church"), to temperance numbers ("Father, Dear Father, Come Home with Me Now") and popular parlor ballads ("Lorena," "Rosie Nell").

Pound's brief editorial remarks make clear her acceptance of the then-standard evaluative criteria that drive the article's organizational scheme—the English and Scottish ballads in the first section are the "most interesting group," and the process of oral transmission of ballads is understood as degenerative (e.g., she is happy to report that with just two exceptions "these English and Scottish ballads have, as yet at least, suffered few essential modifications").[28] But she is nevertheless prepared to include the mixed lot of "American Ballads" on the simple principle that people are singing them. *Folk-Song of Nebraska and the Central West* makes this same criterion not only explicit but determinative: "the main essential of a folk-song is that people sing it."[29]

Not every collector subscribed to such notions. C. Alphonso Smith, to pick one example, kept vigilant watch over the collections of the Virginia Folklore Society, lest they be overrun with "all sorts of popular stuff."[30] Pound's more generous standard of inclusion resulted in a collection so heterogeneous that its classification and arrangement proved difficult—at last she opts for thirty-two headings, described as "provisional" and leading off once again with the Child ballads. But even here, in the most stable of categories, one untitled fragment is listed twice—Pound's note calls attention to a possible "slight relationship" to "Captain Wedderburn's Courtship" (Child 46), but the six-line text is actually printed in a catchall section 27, "Miscellaneous Songs and Fragments."[31]

Pound also credits "the syllabus of Professor Shearin" for guidance on "some points of arrangement and presentation"—the work she is citing is *A Syllabus of Kentucky Folk-Songs*, produced by Hubert G. Shearin and Josiah H. Combs in 1911 and one of Pound's few predecessors in the publication of collections from a single state. Shearin and Combs, however, arrange their Kentucky material under eighteen headings, not thirty-two, and their final section is at least as miscellaneous as Pound's section 27, described as "paralipomena which baffle individual description" and containing only a list of fifty-three titles in no discernible order.[32] The collections are of comparable size—Shearin and Combs count theirs as containing "333 items, exclusive of 114 variants"; Pound (uncharacteristically) provides no exact total, though a footnote in "Traditional Ballads in Nebraska" claims "several hundred pieces" in 1913. A count of *Folk-Song of Nebraska and the Central West* yielded a total of 331 entries, excluding cross listings. (It should be stressed that there is ample room for error and disagreement, the text itself being imperfectly numbered—for example, there is no item number 11 in section 31, "Nursery Rhymes and Fragments.")[33]

Surveying early folk-music collections for their inclusion of popular music from 1880 to 1910, Norm Cohen (using Wilgus's very large Western Kentucky Folklore Archive as his standard) concludes that "any representative collection will contain about three times as many TPA [Tin Pan Alley] songs as Child ballad texts." Of course, given the assumptions made by most collectors—C. Alphonso Smith may have been unusually vigilant, but his views were close to the norm—few collections exhibit anything like such proportions. "An analysis of two dozen primary collections of various types indicated that in only three instances do the figures approach these predictions." But Pound's is one of the three, with 11 percent of its total ascribed to Tin Pan Alley as compared to 4 percent from the Child canon.[34] It is also by far the earliest—the other two, including the *Songs Sung in the Southern Appalachians* assembled by Pound's old Heidelberg correspondent Mellinger Henry, are from the 1930s.

Of particular interest in the Nebraska collection is section 7, "Pioneer and Western Songs," which in some ways parallels the "American Ballads" section of "Traditional Ballads in Nebraska." But here the practice of the earlier article is neatly reversed, with the American materials instead of the English and Scottish ballads getting the full-text presentation. This is quite a surprise. Pound had from the beginning concerned herself with songs actually being sung in Nebraska, and her 1913 article in *Modern Philology*, "The Southwestern Cowboy Songs and the English and Scottish Popular Ballads," while most important as her initial foray into the controversies over ballad origins that would make her famous, nevertheless takes the study of American music and "western songs" very seriously indeed.[35] A similar interest is apparent in the short 1914 piece on "The Little Old Sod Shanty on My Claim." But the privileging of such material in the *Folk-Song of Nebraska and the Central West* is something new, a striking departure in emphasis if not in placement from "Traditional Ballads in Nebraska." As it turns out, however, this innovation was accomplished not at Pound's initiative (she opposed and resented it) but at the insistence of Addison E. Sheldon, the editor of the Nebraska Ethnology and Folk Lore series.

Sheldon was an important figure in the Lincoln of his day. A proud Nebraskan passionately interested in the history of his home state (he had grown up on a farm in Seward County, just west of Lincoln), he was an active presence in early efforts to organize and promote the study of everything Nebraskan. He wrote one of the first comprehensive histories of the state (in two volumes) and prepared a shorter version (*History and Stories of Nebraska*) for use in schools. He began publishing (in 1918) *Nebraska History and Record of Pioneer Days*, the journal that continues today as *Nebraska History*, published by the Nebraska State Historical Society (of which he was a stalwart member and officer). Sheldon and his wife were also enthusiastic members of the Nebraska Ornithologists' Union. One highlight of the minutes of the 1922 annual meeting is a report on the "Home Life of the Brown Thrasher"—a nesting pair who set up shop in the Sheldon yard "were kept under constant observation by Mr. and Mrs. Sheldon" from the beginning of nest building until the last fledgling had flown. Constant observation, as understood by Sheldon and his wife, was no easy task: "every movement of the birds was noted and recorded during this entire period, from sunup till nightfall."[36] Sheldon somehow found time, amidst these scholarly, editorial, and ornithological labors, to produce in 1908 *Poems and Sketches of Nebraska*, dedicated to "The Pioneers of Nebraska."

He was also editor of the Nebraska Ethnology and Folk Lore series, and it was in this capacity that he not only insisted on the printing of full texts for the "Pioneer and Western Songs" in Pound's syllabus but added four captioned photographic illustrations (one as a frontispiece) to accompany them. From his perspective it was an obvious editorial decision, and it is only fair to note that most scholars today would agree with him.[37] Sheldon was charged with the publication of materials pertaining to Nebraska—songs with direct ties to the state were of far greater interest to him, and to his readers, than yet another version of some Old World ballad. The illustrations fleshed out the world of the songs, contributing an added ethnographic density.

Pound did not see things this way, and she was not pleased. More than twenty-five years later, sending a copy of her syllabus to her student and protégé Benjamin Botkin, Pound remained deprecating in her assessment and explicitly critical of Sheldon's contributions: "I am not at all proud of it though it came first among accessible lists of state folksong. The editor of our State Historical Society had a lot of money that he wished to use printing pamphlets and got hold of my syllabus, though I hardly wished to print it, and 'edited' the document himself, 'with illustrations.' I would have been glad to edit his editing if I had had a chance to do so but I never saw it. Since I cannot suppress the publication, I might as well send it around."[38] This is more than a little disingenuous, though the slightly exaggerated "first among accessible lists of state folksong" is an entirely characteristic touch, yet another competitive first for the holder of the Heidelberg record for "extras" on her dance card. (Pound clearly found the Shearin and Combs compilation from Kentucky accessible, since she accessed it—plus there is the Kittredge-edited Pettit collection, also from Kentucky, which appeared in the eminently accessible *Journal of American Folklore*.)

Still, it is easy to sympathize with Pound's dismay. Sheldon in her eyes would have been an unimpressive figure, as much booster as scholar. Attempting a collection ordered and presented according to prevailing academic standards, she bridled at what she saw as cavalier alterations made by a male editor with little expertise in the field. Lomax's *Cowboy Songs and Other Frontier Ballads* did not appear with pictures of cowboys or sod houses with cute captions ("A Bunch of Nebraska Cowboys," "The Little Old Sod Shanty on the Claim"); neither did Kittredge's *Journal of American Folklore* articles. From her perspective, a bumptious editor was throwing his weight around, using her material to advance an agenda she did not share. His roots were in the world of the western songs; hers were in Lincoln's professional and educational elite. Sheldon, in short, came from the mudflats outside, and credited them with forging the state's identity. Pound, by contrast, was rooted in the Boston within; she looked down from a great height upon *Poems and Sketches of Nebraska*. It is another instance of the insider/outsider oscillation so prominent in Pound's correspondence—in her dealings with Sheldon she is still, for all her attainments, and for all her obvious sense of her own more up-to-date scholarly approaches, something of a subordinate figure, compelled against her will and judgment to accede to decisions imposed from above. But when she writes to Botkin it is Pound who occupies the chair, and she writes as very much the superior insider, sharing with a (junior) colleague her frustration with the obtuseness of the help.

Some indirect evidence suggests that Pound did not keep her views entirely to herself. There is a hint of defensiveness in the "Editor's Preface," where Sheldon always refers to Pound as "Miss Pound" (never as Professor Pound or Dr. Pound, though by 1915 she was a full professor), devotes a paragraph to explaining the decision to print full texts of the western songs, and adds a final sentence addressed to the illustrations Pound found so offensive: "For the illustrations the editor is to be held solely responsible."[39] Surely, compiler and editor had words (or correspondence) over the matter; the editor insisted; the compiler insisted in turn that he make his authority explicit. And for her part there is more than a hint of distancing in Pound's little note at the head of the "Pioneer and Western Songs" section: "At the request of Mr. A. E. Sheldon, the editor, selected texts of the songs of this group are given in full."[40] The whole exchange made up the first visible home-turf scuffle of Pound's long career, but it would not be the last. Other figures in authority, most but not all of them male, would find her at times an acerbic, "difficult" colleague. But if she was mostly wrong in her disagreement with Sheldon, she would much more often be mostly right. What is more, her quarrels would usually be conducted not on her own behalf but in support of others, especially other women.

Folk-Song of Nebraska and the Central West is first and last a collection, and thus it exhibits only minimal commentary. And within that commentary one element might easily be missed altogether, confined as it is to a footnote. But it is a lengthy footnote, and in it, for the first time, Pound enters the ongoing scholarly controversies surrounding folk songs and their origins. Her concern, rooted in support of her inclusion of "popular lyrics of many classes" so long as they are found in oral tradition, opens with the question of the status of newer songs as "folk-poetry." This she affirms, despite obvious differences in "style." A basic error, Pound suggests, is that which takes fifteenth- and sixteenth-century ballads as "standard-giving," the better to rule out as "spurious" (and therefore "'art' poetry" instead of "folk-poetry") the productions of other times and places. Quick (too quick) to concede a "superiority for persistence in the popular mouth" to the older ballads, based on the fact that they were products of a time that "composed for the ear," Pound nevertheless insists that acknowledging "that the period of the English renaissance had the most memorable style in folk-song is not the same thing however as acknowledgment that only such folk-songs as conform to this style are genuine." She will agree, that is, with critics of the "popular lyrics of many classes" as to quality; they may often be "unsingable and unrememberable." But if people are singing them anyway they are folk songs.[41] That is, ballad making is not a "closed account," despite assertions to that effect by highly placed authorities (in this instance Kittredge). New ballads may not be as excellent as old ballads, especially if they are measured to a standard of excellence evolved to describe old ballads, but new ballads are still being made and still being sung.

Pound also, in the same footnote, makes her initial jab at the "communal" theory of ballad origins that would be her primary target in the future. The fifteenth- and sixteenth-century ballads featured in Child's collection are not only inappropriately held up as "standard-giving" but are also "assumed to have some romantic-mystic 'communal' origin." Pound will hammer this assumption again and again in her subsequent studies, but it is already suspect in 1915: "The making of popular ballads—that variety of folk-song having especial interest—is not a 'closed account,' though the making of ballads or songs in the older and more memorable style may be; nor is some hypothetical communal-mystic manner of origin, based on this older style, a valid test for determining what is folk-poetry and what is not."[42]

Meanwhile, as *Folk-Song of Nebraska and the Central West* was being assembled and edited for publication over a three-year period (1913–15), Pound produced an article-length study for *Modern Philology* where the focus fell entirely on just these issues. "The Southwestern Cowboy Songs and the English and Scottish Ballads" explicitly addresses Harvard professor Barrett Wendell's suggestion (made in his introduction to Lomax's *Cowboy Songs and Other Frontier Ballads*) that the American songs collected by Lomax might "go far to prove, or to disprove, many of the theories advanced concerning the laws of literature as evinced in the ballads of the old world."[43] The rationale behind the idea is one of analogy: the songs of unlettered cowpokes in the American West and the old ballads of England and Scotland exhibit similarities both in themselves and in the communities where they are or were sustained and within which they presumably originated. Lomax himself, in his prefatory "Collector's Note," waxes eloquent on the comparison: in a "wild" West of remote mining camps and cattle ranches "yet survives the Anglo-Saxon ballad spirit." These cowboys and miners, "cut off from newspapers and books," finding themselves "thrown back on primal resources" to express and entertain themselves, end up creating "somewhat the same character of songs as did their forefathers of perhaps a thousand years ago."[44]

Pound, then, proposes having a close look at the two bodies of song, with the explicitly stated intention of ascertaining which (if either) of "the two leading schools of thought concerning the genesis of the English and Scottish ballads" might find support by the comparison. The competing "schools" are briefly described: one, which Pound designates as "the Harvard school," espouses a "definition by origins for genuine popular ballads" and "emphasizes the idea of real communal composition"; the other, the "English school," defines instead "by destination and style." (By "destination" Pound means distribution. By "Harvard school" she means but does not name Kittredge and especially Haverford professor Francis B. Gummere. By "English school" she means and does name in a footnote four scholars, of whom the most important for her purposes are W. P. Ker and T. F. Henderson.)[45] Her purpose, for all the tone of objective inquiry, is polemical from the first (and was already clear in the footnote in *Folk-Song of Nebraska and the Central West*). In a steady stream of shorter and longer studies, beginning with this one, Pound will press her attack upon the communalists of the "Harvard school" (she will deploy the term repeatedly).

Examining Lomax's cowboy songs first, she groups them in two categories. One consists of songs that "are perhaps genuine cowboy pieces." These focus on the group and its activities—they "are related very closely to the life of the communities which originated and preserved them." Sample stanzas are provided, followed by an evaluation striking both for its novel application of aesthetic criteria and for its tone of disdain. These songs, while "often forceful" and "picturesque," are nevertheless "crude and nearly formless," lacking anything of "real poetical quality," and "unambitious" in the bargain. These are fatal flaws, Pound concludes, accounting at once for the limited distribution of these pieces and for their poor prospects for long-term survival. It is a class distinction at bottom: "To reiterate, they deal as a mass with the life and interests of the same class of people that originate them and sing them. And among this class, it is tempting to add, the pieces so composed are likely to die!"[46] (Exclamation points are rare in Pound's writing; a good-humored understatement will soon emerge as her more characteristic stance, even in the rigors of scholarly controversy. It is difficult to avoid concluding that an implied "and good riddance" lies just beneath the surface here. These "crude" songs—this is the recurrent term, used twice, like "class," in the same paragraph—appear here as interlopers, uninvited guests at the dignified scholarly investigation of traditional ballads, as unwelcome to Pound's interests and sensibilities as the "insolent street children" whose presence disturbed the Heidelberg tennis courts.)

The second group of songs from Lomax's collection consists of "those which have found widest diffusion and greatest promise of permanence." These, in contrast to the former group, were most often imported from other regions, were sometimes written by professional songwriters, and focus attention not upon the local lives of cowboys and miners but upon "widely known and interesting events and persons." They also exhibit more impressive formal qualities, "more sustained and 'artistic' execution," and are "too regular of rhyme and too symmetrical of structure" to have originated in the western communities in which they are now sung.[47] Sample interesting persons (Jesse James, Cole Younger) are listed, along with one widely known event (the death of President Garfield). "Young Charlotte" is offered as an instance of artistic execution, while "After the Ball" and "Juanita" (among others) serve as examples of songs written by known composers.

It is not at all clear, of course, how "promise of permanence" is to be measured, other than by widespread distribution. As it turns out, the difference between the two groups rests upon aesthetic criteria, upon what are at last matters of taste. Even cowboys and miners are understood as appreciating the distinction: their own compositions may be crude and lacking in poetical quality; they cannot originate songs with symmetrical structure, regular rhyme, or artistic execution, but even they pay homage to these qualities by singing songs that do possess them much more widely than their own humble creations, and by persisting in singing such songs "long after their local improvisations have perished."[48] Both groups of cowboy songs, as is made clear in the footnote in *Folk-Song of Nebraska and the Central West*, are made up of folk songs; one is no more "genuine" than the other; all have been collected form oral tradition. People are singing them. But the second group, by reasons of broader subject range, wider distribution, inherent "poetic quality," and the "promise of permanence" that somehow results from these traits, is judged superior.

Pound then turns from Lomax to Child, from cowboy songs to English and Scottish ballads. Surely, she begins, "the 'humble people' of mediaeval communal conditions" created songs. The admission comes across as grudging, even patronizing—"A liking for or the gift of song may surely not be denied them"—but it is made explicit. And what sort of songs would such folks make? Here Pound speculates, citing no actual songs; would not they most likely be, given analogous social backgrounds, "the mediaeval counterparts of the crude pieces for which modern communal origin may be affirmed?" These would deal, like the western songs, with "matters belonging to daily life"; their protagonists would be humble people; they would be "the 'homely traditional songs of simple people.'" The point, of course, is a negative one: such songs are precisely what the English and Scottish ballads are not: "In direct contrast with our western pieces, the kind of people who are supposed to have preserved them are the very people who do not appear in them." The world of the ballads is not humble but "aristocratic"; they are not "crude songs" but "well-wrought poetical tales"; they feature not humble "spinsters and knitters in the sun" but "kings, princesses, knights" and other elites. (Pound on several occasions employs phrases from literary works to indicate humble folk—"spinsters and knitters in the sun" comes from *Twelfth Night*; she identifies an earlier mention of "poor folk in cots" as from *Piers Plowman*.) The comparative examination, then, results in conclusions supportive of the "English school": if either "school" finds support for its position "regarding the origin of the English and Scottish ballads" in songs collected in the American West, "it is not that school which defines by origin in folk composition, but that which presupposes a higher descent, and defines by style and by destination."[49]

Thus Louise Pound entered, with this article and the notes to her Nebraska collection, the scholarly battle she would still be fighting in the 1950s, long after many of her auditors had come to think themselves witnesses to the flogging not merely of dead horses but also of their bleaching bones. Even in 1913 the so-called ballad wars were far from new—Pound's reference to an "English school" makes clear her awareness of an ongoing controversy—but 1913 was for her just the beginning, the opening salvo of the most protracted battle of her career. Between 1917 and 1920 she would produce three lengthy studies devoted to the issue of ballad origins. Then, in 1921, she would collect them, with additional material, in *Poetic Origins and the Ballad*, and the scholarly equivalent of all hell would break loose.

But long before that, back in the years when only the 1902 note on the Colorado version of "Lord Randal" had appeared to suggest her interest in traditional music, with "Traditional Ballads in Nebraska" and *Folk-Song of Nebraska and the Central West* still nearly a decade away, Pound had also been busy with other studies of a very different feature of Nebraska's culture. Her first study of colloquial speech, a 1903 article on negative verb contractions ("ain't" and "hain't" as well as the older "an't" and "han't") in the University of Nebraska journal *University Studies*, is a general survey of English and American usage, but "Dialect Speech in Nebraska," from 1905, inaugurates Pound's long and illustrious career as a student and collector of American speech. In this article and in its two successors—a second Nebraska word list appeared in 1911 and a third in 1916—she does for Nebraska folk speech what she did for Nebraska folk song in her Sheldon-edited syllabus. The first is the most extensive, opening with a series of general observations and closing with an alphabetized listing of more than 220 entries beginning with "against" meaning "in preparation for" ("Sweep the porch against some one comes!"), and closing with "wuzzy," "yap," and "yolk," the first meaning "confused" or "bewildered," the second (along with the better-known "yep" and "yeah") a variant of "yes," and the third presented not for nonstandard meaning (it is part of an egg) but for variant pronunciations.[50] The two others are supplements, introduced as such, with much briefer commentary attached to the second as "Miscellaneous Notes" and confined in the third entirely to the entries themselves. By 1916, with the publication of "Word-List From Nebraska (III)," Pound had gathered more than 600 Nebraska speech forms to go with the 330 songs collected in *Folk-Song of Nebraska and the Central West*. Especially helpful contributors (with women again in the majority) are acknowledged by name, as in the music collection.

The study of American speech, like the study of American folklore, would occupy Pound for the rest of her career. In both fields she would write her name in capitals, publishing her work in the profession's best journals and producing discipline-shaping studies. She was less active in the study of literature, but in this area too she concentrated most of her work on American topics. In time her contributions would be recognized by her peers—Pound would eventually serve as president of the American Folklore Society (1925–27), the American Dialect Society (1938–41), and the Modern Language Association (1955–56). In the study of American speech she also contributed sustained editorial and organizational service—in no field, not even folklore, was her leadership so influential. As Pound credited H. M. Belden with initiating her work in traditional music, she singled out George Hempl for encouraging her interest in dialect study. In 1951 she looked back over a half century's activity in the American Dialect Society:

> I joined the Dialect Society in 1901, and my name is on the printed list of members for 1902. My impetus to enlist came from Profes-

sor George Hempl of the University of Michigan, who gave a summer session course at the University of Chicago at the end of the century, when I was a graduate student there. I believe that the course was in Chaucer. Professor Hempl was an enthusiastic pioneer collector and investigator of dialect. I do not recall that Chaucer's poetry loomed large in the course save as regards his pronunciation. The Professor sandwiched in somehow a brief preliminary treatment of phonetics and drafted us for the discussion of dialect words and phrases. He made the subject so engaging that . . . I joined the Society as soon as I could and my interest has maintained itself down the decades.[51]

"Down the decades" is no overstatement. More than fifty years separate the first (1903) piece on negative verb contractions from Pound's final (1956) *American Speech* article, "More Plural Singulars." In between were scores of other studies—in 1916 alone some sixteen separate pieces, some very short but others much more substantial, appeared in the fourth volume of *Dialect Notes*.

The major study of these years was her 1914 collection, *Blends: Their Relation to English Word Formation*, which appeared in the same series that had published her dissertation thirteen years earlier. Though unusually thorough even by Pound's standards, it seems in many ways typical of her collecting method and presentational style. Opening remarks offer a rationale for the study itself and make a case for its worthiness as a matter of scholarly investigation. The tone walks a tightrope between apology and insistence, with the former offered first. Blends, defined as amalgamations or fusions of two or more recognized terms, like other "abnormal forms," often "impress many students of language as negligible, if not actually repellent." Nevertheless, they should be investigated for at least two reasons. The more obvious is "contemporary popularity"—and Pound's "Prefatory Note" calls attention specifically to "the section dealing with the present-day vogue of blend formations." A less apparent motive is historical. Blends are not new, and many terms now regarded as standard "have worked their way slowly upward from vulgar speech or provincial usage; what is objectionable in one century may be beyond reproach in the next." Here Pound's old-school philological training backs up her growing interest in contemporary slang and dialect usages. She may call special attention to her section on present-day blends, but she is able, in prior sections, to offer examples not only from literature (Rostand and Kipling) but also from Old French and John Wiclif. In the end, insistence obliterates apology: "More is often to be learned, as regards words and their ways, from dialect than from literary speech."[52]

In general, despite such instances of special pleading, the bulk of Pound's scholarship in dialect is markedly less polemical than her work in traditional music. If she at times felt a need to make explicit a claim for the academic worthiness of her topics, she nevertheless did not see herself as confronted on all sides by a reigning scholarly paradigm held by her to be ill founded. The skills of meticulous and painstakingly ordered assembly and classification that had served her so well in her dissertation project were also of great use in her work with dialect and language. The blends study, for its part, first explains at some length various terms not regarded as blends for present purposes, then discusses the contemporary popularity of blend formations (this is the section especially recommended in the "Prefatory Note"), next organizes words that are admitted as blends into nine classes, pauses for a brief defense of the "value of such a word-list," and only then presents the words themselves, organized according to parts of speech with nouns (by far the largest category) first and verbs last. The material is remarkably varied, with items drawn from sources as canonical as Jonson, Nashe, Swift, and of course Lewis Carroll, appearing side by side with others taken from yesterday's newspapers. "Comrogue," for example, is attributed to Elizabethan dramatists' conscious combination of "comrade" and "rogue," with its use by both Jonson and Swift noted. "Donkophant," on the same page, is listed as "an animal representing a cross between the *donkey* (democratic party) and the *elephant* (republican party)," and explained as the 1911 creation of a cartoonist at the *Minneapolis Tribune*, while "alcoholiday," defined as a "holiday spent in absorbing intoxicating drinks," is credited to the *Boston Transcript* for July 9, 1913.[53]

Pound also notes that for many such terms "consciousness of the mode of origin becomes quite lost"; these she calls *"obscured compounds,"* and her knowledge of Old English again proves useful in supplying examples ("barn" from "bere-ærn" or "barley house"; "daisy" from "dæges-ēage" or "day's eye"). For contemporary readers, additional terms have surely fallen into this category even since Pound's time—how many contemporary speakers would consciously think of "electrocution" as a compound of "electric" and "execution"? Pound not only lists it as such but cites a source deploring it as a "barbarously constructed word." "Cantankerous" is probably another instance—most people using the word today would not think of it as a fusion of "cankerous + contentious," as Pound lists it.[54]

The 1914 article on blends is also notable, among other things, for the suppression of a speculative note much more prominent in a shorter study of the previous year. "Indefinite Composites and Word-Coinage," appearing in *Modern Language Review*, focuses attention on a particular type of blend, called by Pound *"indefinite blending or reminiscent amalgamation."* Of interest in this piece is the relatively freewheeling speculation as to the origin of such terms. They arise, she suggests, italicizing the phrase to emphasize the point, by *"unconscious symbolism of sounds."* Interesting examples are provided. Addressing "sqush," for example, she first suggests that the initial "sq" in "squeeze," "squirt," and "squirm," among other terms, "may unconsciously convey the idea of impetus or motion, rather violent motion, perhaps." The final "sh," on the other hand, known from "crush," "splash," and "dash," among other terms, "also suggests motion, in this case motion which is continuous, as symbolized by the final spirant." "Sqush," then, may have originated as an "indefinite or eclectic" mixing, and the antecedent terms, "vaguely recollected, may well have entered into its composition."

A similar analysis is offered for "snuzzle"—a now-lost term more or less synonymous with "nuzzle," described by Pound as "recent" and "now admitted to dictionaries." The initial "sn," she suggests, is often found in words "associated with the nose, or the sense of smell," and so the "s" in "snuzzle" may have added itself by unconscious association with words like "sniff," "snout," "snuff," or "sneeze."[55]

Such extended speculations are striking departures for the scholar whose first publication trumpeted its dedication to "tests," "figures," and "calculations" in contrast to the "vague theorizing or speculations" scolded in Rev. Skeat's work. This comes across, in 1913, as a new note, perhaps even a strikingly up-to-date note in its explicit reference to unconscious processes. It seems a daring foray away from the tables and calculations of Pound's apprentice work, the Chaucer study and the Heidelberg dissertation. And perhaps it was too daring—it is almost wholly expunged from the later and longer 1914 blends study, where both unconscious processes and symbolism go unmentioned, and readers interested in "indefinite composites" are referred in a footnote to the earlier piece. It even seems possible that the speculative note was judged acceptable for the American *Modern Language Review* but insufficiently grounded in data for a German Anglistische Forschungen series presumed to be starchier and more traditional in its approach to academic writing.

Pound's early studies in American speech and dialect also differ from those in folk music and ballad origins by the more than occasional presence of a humorous note, both in the material itself and in her commentary. Her seventh class of blend formations ("Coined Place-Names; also Coined Personal-Names") offers an especially rich field for such breaks from scholarly seriousness—among the "arbitrary amalgam formations" used as honorific baptismal names, Pound lists "*Eldarema*" as bestowed upon a child "whose four grandparents were named respectively Elkanah, Daniel, Rebecca, and Mary." In another instance, "relatives and friends of twins named Fritz and Max" resolved all perplexities of address by giving to both, "in cases of uncertainty, the name 'Frax,' as in 'Here comes Frax.'"[56] For neither Eldarema nor Frax is a citation provided, though it is specified that they inhabit the same town—the clear suggestion would be that the town was Lincoln and that Pound drew both examples from her own experience.

There is in this note, new in Pound's published work as the twentieth century entered its second decade, something of a finding of her own most characteristic mature voice. For the rest of her long career as a prolific writer and frequent speaker she would have at her disposal a marvelously nuanced style that served her well before enormously varied audiences. The accomplishment, at its core, was the achievement of a more wide-ranging rhetoric—to the rigorously impersonal academic style she had learned from her mentors she now added when occasion suited an informal, even gently self-deprecating tone to the presentation of even the weightiest subjects. In this she seems also to embody an almost perfect combination of her parental influences. The day would never come when she could not serve up a title like Rector Magnificus with an absolutely straight face—Pound would all her life be the daughter of the Laura Pound who helped organize the first Nebraska chapter of the DAR; she would be a great joiner of honorary societies, a sincere respecter of persons and their titles, a careful tender of her own *Who's Who* entries. She was herself a member of the DAR.

But at the same time, she had also mastered before she was forty the art of sending up just such sonorities. As early as 1908, according to a copy preserved in her papers, Pound was "expert of the first part" (and surely at least co-composer) in an elaborate, two-page, comic "Contract" obliging her to travel on roller skates by September 1 from her home to (presumably) the home of Marguerite McPhee, "inexpert of the second part." Detailed conditions are spelled out—she cannot ride, seated or standing, in "any sort of vehicle, carriage or automobile, whether run by gasolene [sic] or electricity, or by hand or foot (as with an Irish Mail)." Upon her successful arrival Pound is owed a "seven-layer cake," prepared by Ms. McPhee "without the aid of any person or persons." The cake is also described in detail. Ms. McPhee is accorded no titles (other than "inexpert") in this contract, but Pound has attached to each occurrence of her name (four times) a lengthy list: "Ph.D., A.M., B.L., P.B.K., K.K.G., English Club, Black Masque, Silver Serpent, Xi Delta, L.W.C., A.C.A., E.S.L., M.L.A., U.L.S., A.D.S." That most of these are genuine—perhaps all are (Black Masque and Silver Serpent were University of Nebraska student groups)—in no way alters the basic comedy, the deployment of a bogus legalese to describe a bet involving roller skating and cake baking. A 1959 note preserved with the contract notes that Pound won the bet by making the trip on horseback while wearing skates, and adds that the cake was duly baked by Ms. McPhee and eaten by the ten signatories and witnesses.[57]

This of course is Pound, though winning again, exhibiting at the same time her father's gift for the gentle mockery that succeeds at least in part by its clear inclusion of the mocker. The judge who poked such gentle fun at the many Nebraska hamlets calling themselves cities in 1897 no doubt heartily enjoyed the whole episode, and especially the legal spoof of the mock "Contract." His daughter, once in possession of this nuanced and supple voice, would deploy it again and again in a wide variety of situations as an element in her self-presentation. It would prove an especially invaluable resource in times of stress, when Pound found it necessary to protest an injustice done to others or to defend herself against criticisms that were at times surprisingly harsh. In her subsequent editorial labors with *American Speech* she would make the humorous "Miscellany" her special interest, continuing to edit it even after relinquishing the editorial reins in 1933.

In 1917, at the request of three undergraduate students, Pound demonstrated a similar enthusiasm for spoofs and send-ups by agreeing to sponsor on campus the Order of the Golden Fleece, a group of redheaded women organized in celebration of their hair. "The Golden Fleece," she wrote thirty years after the group's demise, "met for luncheon once a year at Ellen Smith Hall. A hard-boiled committee passed judgment on eligibles, fixing the exact tint of the applicant's hair and rejecting the many attempting to chisel in though not genuine reds." Some twenty-eight shades of red were "approved as enabling membership," and a bit of slightly edited Goldsmith served as a sort of motto: "Sweet Auburn, loveliest plumage of the plain." The Order of the Golden Fleece enjoyed a seven-year run as an unofficial campus group, gaining membership with each passing year and awarding a wide variety of prizes at the annual luncheons. "At first only two prizes were awarded," but in later years up to "ten prizes were awarded as admiring outsiders from Lincoln and elsewhere offered them." One year's luncheon featured a "panorama piece" from H. L. Mencken, "which was printed later in the *Smart Set* of which he was then editor."[58] Mencken's tribute, a one-page lyric effusion on "red-haired girls," appeared as "Dianthus Caryophyllus" (the Latin name for the flower popularly called carnation) in the May 1921 issue of *Smart Set*. Mencken wrote it as "Major Owen Hatteras," one of his several pseudonyms. It consists entirely of sentence fragments, most of them opening with "red-haired girls," though near the close the "girls" become "brides," "widows," and "grass-widows," before ending as "women": "Red-haired women marrying their fifth husbands. Red-haired women in battalions, regiments, brigades, divisions and army corps. Red haired women. . . . Red haired women!"[59]

The party ended in 1924, at least partly due to the notice of the faculty committee charged with the regulation of student groups. The Order of the Golden Fleece was suspect on several grounds, having "no constitution, no officers, no regular meetings and no worthy purpose." Apparently, the Dean of Men also took an interest, as Pound's retrospective account describes him (in a nicely phrased gentle dig) as "an active arbiter of girls' events."[60]

This same reminiscence mentions two other comic "honorary" societies. One, the Dumbbells, "a small organization emerging from the physical education department," was permitted to exist for only "a few days," though Pound reports that she was "proud of being asked to be an honorary member." Even more short-lived was the Beta chapter of Nu Upsilon Tau Tau, an organization founded at the University of Texas and "popular with the faculty there and given an annual garden party by the Chancellor." Pound was at the center of this latter organization—a guest on the university campus in Austin the previous year, she had been introduced to some Texas "Nutts" by the Dean of Women. Enthusiastic over the opportunity to expand, the Texas Alpha chapter contributed yellow ribbon and "goobers" for the induction of their Nebraska sisters.

The Dean of Men at Nebraska, however, apparently still rattled by the Golden Fleece episode (if in fact it was earlier), was decidedly not pleased to find a group of Nebraska coeds wearing yellow ribbon peanut necklaces in attendance for the announcement of new inductees on Phi Beta Kappa Day. "The new Nutts were queens of the campus in the morning, but by afternoon the Deans had banished the institution ignominiously from the campus," Pound wrote. "One Dean termed it 'an insult to Phi Beta Kappa,' the other Dean took the goober from about the neck of a member and reduced her to tears."[61] Pound, as faculty sponsor of the anathematized sisterhood, wrote a chiding letter of protest to the *Daily Nebraskan*, explaining the group's Texas origins and describing the "new 'onery' feminine society" as "a harmless travesty of our numerous Greek-letter organizations." Insisting on the good scholarly standing of the Nutts—their grades would compare favorably with those of the Innocents, she adds, naming a long-standing organization of male students (initiated by her brother)—she closes by "mildly" suggesting that the Dean of Men "give fuller rein to his sense of humor when he is presiding over the destinies of girls' organizations."[62]

Another, much later example of Pound's gift for a gentle humor directed at herself and her own honors occurred in February 1940, when Pound was in Washington DC for a meeting of the executive board of the American Association of University Women (AAUW). Speaking for the *Washington Post*, she first scoffed at the reporter's notions of wintry weather, then referred to herself as the "Mrs. Throttlebottom of American education."[63] The reference is now recondite, but in 1940 many readers would have recognized the reference to Alexander Throttlebottom, the powerless vice-president of Gershwin's *Of Thee I Sing*, a hit in 1931. Pound, who was vice-president of the AAUW at the time, thus managed in one stroke to insist upon the superior rigors of Nebraska winters, allude to her own impressive list of offices, and still come across as winningly self-deprecating. She had been active in the AAUW from her earliest days, too, addressing the Nebraska branch of its precursor organization, the Association of Collegiate Alumnae (ACA), on June 11, 1901, on "Graduate Work in Heidelberg, Germany." By 1913 she was a member of the ACA's national council (the ACA merged with the Southern Association of College Women to form the AAUW in 1921).[64]

After a decade and a half of full-time teaching in Lincoln, then, Louise Pound had every reason to feel that she had made very good use of her time. Starting as an adjunct professor in 1900, she had rocketed through the academic ranks to full professor by 1912 (and half of that time was spent getting the first step accomplished, to assistant professor in 1906). She had also made a name for herself as a scholar, publishing one review (an approving notice of George Philip Krappe's 1906 edition of the Anglo-Saxon narrative poems *Andreas* and *The Fates of the Apostles*), some sixteen articles in respected scholarly journals on language, literature, and folk music, and three collection-based monographs (including her dissertation). On top of all this, she had from the beginnings of her career also edited school texts, beginning with *Tennyson's Lancelot and Elaine* in 1905, an edition of Goldsmith's *Deserted Village* in 1906 (this latter volume a job she did three times, adding Gray's *Elegy in a Country Churchyard* for one printing), and Shakespeare's *I Henry VI* in 1912.[65] Pound never did a great deal of this kind of work, but even in the 1940s she was involved in the production of a *College Book of American Literature* in one- and two-volume editions. She did it for the money—Robert Knoll remembered her telling a class how she "earned the money for her first car by writing an introduction to *The Iliad*"—but it also put her name (and the University of Nebraska's) on widely distributed books.[66] (The cars were a story in themselves. Professor Pound apparently gave them names—The Whippet, Rosinante, Henry—and piloted them around town with little regard for either safety or traffic regulations. The recollections of several colleagues and students testify to her spectacular incompetence as a driver.)

Pound's teaching load throughout the period was standard for the time, though astonishingly heavy by today's standards. In the first semester of the 1901–2 school year, for example, she was teaching the introductory Old English class, the history of Anglo-Saxon literature, and the advanced Old English seminar. In addition, she is listed as teaching the Shakespeare II course (reading *Hamlet* and *Othello*), a survey of nineteenth-century English literature, and "Phonetic and Philologic Studies in English"—a six-course load. Just over a decade later, in the first semester of the 1912–13 term, the list had shortened to a mere five, and Pound's folk-music studies had evidently brought about the addition of a course in English ballads. The Anglo-Saxon courses were by this time labeled "Old English" and "Advanced Old English," but Pound still taught both that fall. The survey of nineteenth-century English literature had narrowed its focus to English poets of that period, but an even more general survey of English literature had been added.

Even with all this collecting and publishing and teaching, Pound retained her strong interest in competitive athletics. Her tennis career would feature no more matches against the likes of Juliette Atkinson, but she continued to play in tournaments when opportunities arose. In 1901, the *Arrowhead*, a short-lived, turn-of-the-century student publication, carried a second poetic tribute to her triumphs as part of a series titled "The Arrow-Head's Gallery of Good-Looking Profs." The poem, accompanied by a cartoon figure of a racquet-wielding "Dr. Louise Pound" drawn by Herbert Johnson (a student who went on to make a career as a political cartoonist), stresses both athletic and intellectual achievements:

She's at home in Gothic lore.
She knows how the Vandals swore.
And the Iceland roots of Sagas
Are as tasty to her tongue
As the yellow rutabagas
That she ate when she was young.
She's an athlete; she's a scholar.
She is brighter than a dollar.
She won honors from the Germans
In their woman-hating schools.
She's a mighty clever maiden
Judged by any sort of rules.[67]

With Carrie Neely, a former "not liked" opponent in the Chicago tournaments from the 1890s, Pound enjoyed great success in doubles competitions, winning the Women's Western Championship in 1915. (Neely and Pound became friends off the court as well—a Lincoln newspaper report of a 1927 trip by Pound to Chicago noted that she "attended the Chicago Symphony concert with Miss Carrie Neely, who was her former partner for the women's western tennis championship in doubles." The whole trip was a glossy affair—it also included an evening at the opera with Vice-President Charles G. Dawes and his wife as well as a private screening of *The Big Parade* at the same couple's home.)[68]

Pound's career as a basketball player ended with the 1898–99 season, but she continued for a decade afterward as manager/coach of a powerhouse University of Nebraska varsity squad that lost only one game in its first decade (1896–1906) of competition. The *Sombrero* for 1904 lists her as manager of both the 1901–2 and 1902–3 teams and provides a record of their undefeated seasons. If she had starred as a player in the 1898 contest with the Iowa squad from Council Bluffs that broke new ground as the first "formal match between girls' teams at basketball" in the West, it was as manager/coach of the 1901–2 team that she raised the bar another notch.[69]

A match between the Nebraska varsity and a team from the University of Missouri, played in Lincoln on November 9, 1901, was celebrated as "the first intercollegiate match for girls played in the west."[70] The Lincoln papers provided a detailed account, billing the contest as "the most notable event in the history of intercollegiate athletics for women in the west" and stressing the good sportsmanship of the large crowd: "The armory was crowded until standing room was at a premium, by an enthusiastic and representative body of spectators, the best the city could turn out. Applause was frequent and impartial." The social dimensions of the event also received extensive coverage, just as they had in the earlier contest against the Iowans, and this time "Mrs. S. B. Pound" was listed as one of ten "patronesses" (up from seven in 1898). The Missouri athletes and their chaperones were guests at a reception held in their honor (the committee of hostesses is also named in the newspaper account) and also "taken in carriages about the city." The contributions of Mrs. Pound's daughter were also recognized: "The manager and amateur trainer of the Nebraska team is Miss Louise Pound, a former captain of the team."[71]

Three years later, in a home-and-home series with the University of Minnesota, the Nebraska team suffered the only defeat of its first decade of competition. The setback came in Minneapolis on March 26, with Coach Pound's charges on the short end of a 30–22 score. Two days before the game, the local papers carried a short story on the squad's departure for Minnesota the previous day; it named Olivia Pound as one of several "basketball enthusiasts" accompanying the official party.[72] The return match took place a month later in Lincoln, with the *Nebraska State Journal* for April 9 carrying a brief announcement of the delicate negotiations surrounding the event: "A telegram received by Miss Louise Pound, manager of the girls' basketball team, at the university yesterday morning finally assures a game with the young ladies of the University of Minnesota." The story goes on to emphasize that this agreement constitutes something of a breakthrough, as "Minnesota authorities have been very conservative in allowing the girls' team to play away from Minneapolis" and have never before endorsed a trip outside the state.

The notice concludes with an excerpt from a letter written by the University of Minnesota's president explaining both his position and his reasons for modifying it in the current instance: "While I am on general principles opposed to having our girls roam around the country in pursuit of athletic contests, nevertheless the impression made upon me by your team was so favorable, and your whole intercourse with our girls seems to have been so delightful, that I shall be disposed, in case our girls desire to accept an invitation from you[,] to be less strenuous in opposing their wishes than I should be under ordinary conditions."[73]

The game was played two weeks later, on April 22, with the Nebraska women evening the series with a 30–18 win. Once again newspaper coverage devoted as much space to the social aspects of the event as it did to the athletic contest itself. Patronesses were listed by name (Laura Pound sat this one out, but Mrs. W. J. Bryan stepped up in her place), as were Mr. and Mrs. A. E. Hargreaves, who entertained the visitors at a postgame gathering. Before the game, Mrs. Clapp treated them to a "trolley party . . . in a special car." The spectators' enthusiasm and good sportsmanship was again stressed: "While the rooters favored the home team both the Minnesota and the Nebraska yell were given with vim during the progress of the game."[74]

All this makes clear that Pound, as a player and as a coach and organizer, in the company of Anne Barr (later Mrs. Clapp), played a central role in the turn-of-the-century years that were a glorious time for women's athletics at the University of Nebraska. By their persistence and by their successes both on and off the court, Nebraska's women's teams gradually overcame a variety of long-standing conventions standing in the way of their goals. A summary report by Anne Barr, the "Director of the Women's Gymnasium," made clear the importance of the team's accomplishments:

> The first event of the of the year, in point of importance, was the interstate game in November. Here, when Missouri and Nebraska played against each other, was established in the Mid-West the precedent for intercollegiate games between women's teams which it is hoped marks the beginning of a new period in basket ball history. . . .
>
> Perhaps it is not modest, but it may be a pardonable vanity which leads one in concluding this summary . . . to speak of the team's record since its organization in 1896—a record unbroken by a single defeat. This would not be so just a cause for pride if it meant victory and nothing more; but the winning of a game implies training of body and mind, and self-control, and capacity for self-sacrifice; so it is not so small a thing to win, after all.[75]

Pound would have agreed wholeheartedly with such sentiments and the pride that went with them. Her pleasure in those glory days of pioneering intercollegiate athletic competition for women was still evident in a 1945 newspaper interview:

> Where else do you imagine should I have had the fun of playing amateur basket ball coach as I did under Mrs. R. G. Clapp? Why, our teams won matches with Missouri and Minnesota University teams, with the Omaha YWCA, Peru Normal, and the Haskell Indian girls from Kansas.
>
> Those events were great fun. We had to stop them, finally, because the Dean of Women thought such activity inadvisable for the girls' health. The last game we played was with Minnesota in 1910. In the audience of five thousand people was the governor of Minnesota and the University band. Yes, we won![76]

When her days as a long-distance bicyclist and basketball star were far behind her, and when tennis too had to be abandoned when the need for bifocals "completely wrecked my game," Pound was nevertheless not prepared to give up the pleasure of athletic competition.

In fact, she had long since found a new sport in which to excel. The same 1945 interview provides details of her career as a golfer: "Although she never had 'more than a half-dozen lessons,' Miss Pound was ranking Lincoln woman golfer from 1901 to 1927. 'Most of that time,' she says, 'I held the championship. But—I didn't always enter. I never cared so much for golf.' (That notwithstanding her state championship in 1916, [and] her position as vice-president of the Nebraska Woman's Golf Association 1916–17.)"[77]

Golf, as this summary makes clear, provided Pound with yet another opportunity to win athletic glory. Her exploits on the fairways and putting greens never gained her the national notice of her 1890s tennis victories, but in 1916, a month after her forty-fourth birthday, she made a final triumphant splash in Nebraska sports pages with her triumph in the initial match play tournament of the Nebraska Women's Golf Association. (There would be one later, explicitly retrospective blaze of glory, in 1955, when she was admitted to the Nebraska Sports Hall of Fame as its first woman member.) The tournament was held in Omaha, and Pound enjoyed a sensational week; playing the tournament course at the Field Club for the first time on Sunday, July 23, she recorded an eighteen-hole score of 94, "one of the best scores ever turned in there by a feminine player."[78] In Monday's qualifying round the "dark horse" did even better, running away from the field with a 90, at that time the best score ever recorded by a woman. Her closest competitor was five strokes back. In match play Pound saved her best for the final round, on Friday, July 28, defeating Mrs. J. T. Stewart of Omaha and posting yet another course record with a score of 88. In between, at a Wednesday luncheon meeting, she was chosen second vice-president of the newly formed Nebraska Women's Golf Association.

The Omaha papers covered her march to the championship in considerable detail, printing stories on the tournament in each day's edition. Friday's preview of the final match praised both Pound and Stewart for playing "consistently and brilliantly," calling the upcoming match a "toss-up now as to the outcome," but held out hope for the hometown favorite: "Shot for shot, it must be said that Mrs. Stewart has the edge on her opponent, inasmuch as her game appears to have more polish—more form, or finish—than Miss Pound's."[79] Pound's spectacular final round, however, elicited nothing but admiration in the next day's summary: "Lincoln Woman Wins a State Golf Title," read the headline, followed by a subhead calling the contest a "Splendid Match" and a story praising both players and noting that "a gallery of nearly 100 men and women watched the entire match."[80]

By 1916, then, as she headed, quite deliberately, into the biggest battle of her academic career, Louise Pound had assembled all the weapons she needed. Even with all the time devoted to playing and coaching basketball, and later to golf, she had moved to the top rung of the professorial ladder and made a significant name for herself in two fields (and kept her hand in as a literary scholar as well). Her work had appeared in the profession's most prestigious journals, and it had not been ignored. She had developed a more personal and even disarming presentational voice without sacrificing one iota of the authority of her more formal and impersonal earlier style. There had been one major loss in the years since her return from Germany—Stephen Pound had died in 1911 at the age of seventy-eight. "My father died suddenly," she wrote in a 1935 letter expressing condolences to her friend Klara Collitz for the loss of her husband, "just *after* mowing the lawn. He was 78 and had hardly known a day's illness in his life."[81] But Pound was more deeply at home in Lincoln than ever, happy in her teaching and secure in her position at the university that had educated her. Even in her mid-forties she was still a star athlete—the state's first female golf champion. By 1916 Roscoe had been gone for several years—1915–16 was his first year as dean of the Harvard Law School—but she was buoyed by the familiar company of her mother and sister in the family home at 1632 L Street. The days of preparation and apprentice work were over, and she was ready to take a stand.

FIVE

" Incapable of orderly thought "

Pound's initial forays into the "ballad war" had been the relatively low-profile notes in *Folk-Song of Nebraska and the Central West* and the markedly more polemical comparison of Lomax's cowboy songs with English and Scottish ballads. Nothing in these would have encouraged the expectation of anything like the sweep and bite of what followed in an astonishing five-year period running from 1916 to 1921. In five lengthy articles (there were also two shorter pieces devoted to specific songs) subsequently gathered and expanded into *Poetic Origins and the Ballad* in 1921, she launched an all-out assault on the entrenched "communalist" position. According to D. K. Wilgus's history of the controversy, Pound chose the role of "the dragon-slayer" and established herself as "the nemesis of the communalists": "She challenged the theory, its evidence, and its interpretation. Her view of the matter was not particularly new, nor is most of her evidence. But her attack was loud and long." Her book was "the first book-length refutation of the communal position which met the popular school on its own ground."[1]

The opening salvo was a 1916 piece in the *Mid-West Quarterly*, "New World Analogues of the English and Scottish Popular Ballads," which announces itself as a piece of controversy in the opening sentence: "I wish to question in this paper, for the second time, two currently accepted affirmations concerning the processes and the development of English popular ballads in the Old and New World."[2] These affirmations are "the theory of 'communal' origin" and the view that "real ballads and ballad-making are extinct." A second paragraph, a bit surprisingly, launches into a procedural comparison of scholarly investigation as conducted "in our day" with those of less-enlightened times. Progress these days is "from the concrete to the theoretical," not the other way around: "the methods of the transcendentalist yield to those of the scientist." Furthermore, "a good thing to do before reaching conclusions concerning the processes of the past, is to make sure what is true of the present."[3] A look at present-day "New World analogues" may therefore guide conclusions concerning the "processes of the past" responsible for the generation of the ballads under discussion.

What follows is for the most part a reprise of Pound's 1913 piece on cowboy songs and ballads—in fact, two pages are given over to a numbered summary of that article's major points. Its conclusions are also repeated: New World songs originating among cowboys, miners, and "plantation negroes" are strikingly unlike the famous English and Scottish ballads of earlier times; they are "too crude, too structureless, too unoriginal, too lacking in coherence and in striking or memorable qualities, to have much chance at survival." Two songs from Lomax's collection, "The Old Chisholm Trail" and "The Boll Weevil Song," are offered as samples of these failings, after which it is concluded that they "have nothing in common with 'good' ballads."[4] The real "analogues," again, are not such "communal" compositions but rather popular pieces of outside origin persisting in the singing of such communities. Lomax got something of a pass in the 1913 article, though a careful reading would not miss Pound's disagreement with his enthusiastic evocation of the "Anglo-Saxon ballad spirit." But by 1916 Pound is ready for direct confrontation with all comers: she is "unable to accept the conclusions" of Lomax; the general "Harvard school" of the earlier article is now identified by name, with Gummere and Kittredge at its head and Lomax listed with two others as "disciples"; and even "ex-President Roosevelt" is scolded for a Lomax-solicited blurb letter affiliating the prestige of his office with their positions.[5]

The matter of the extinction or persistence of ballad making receives much briefer attention. Listing many examples and citing H. M. Belden's 1912 article urging their nationwide collection, Pound affirms that "there are in America many short narrative pieces, current over the countryside, lyric-epic in character, the authorship and their mode of origin of which are lost." These are not as "good" as the Child ballads, and they will not last as long—"The older style is the more memorable; it was of higher quality and it persisted longer than will its successors"—but they are ballads nevertheless, and folk songs too, for the good and sufficient reason that people are singing them.

The article then closes on a strange note: such intense and sustained interest in ballads, even "good" ballads, seems to Pound rooted in a leftover "romantic attitude" now "out of key in a distinctly anti-romantic period like our own."[6] This passage, more than any other, drove Professor Gerould around the bend when he saw it reprinted as the closing paragraph of *Poetic Origins and the Ballad* in 1921. It was the most sweeping criticism Pound ever mounted—and even in its first articulation it is only a suggestion, offered almost as an afterthought. But in her most "anti-romantic" frame of mind she can almost question the worth of ballads themselves as focal centers of academic attention. A 1924 article, "The Term 'Communal,'" would be the most sustained expression of this cranky though persistent strain in her thinking (it is on prominent display as early as her 1892 graduation oration deploring the "apotheosis of the common"), but this passage comes close to the same note. Perhaps that very worry helped drive her move to a more general examination of poetic origins.

A much wider view linked to a even stronger polemic followed in Pound's first PMLA article, "The Beginnings of Poetry," published in 1917 (it was read as a paper on December 27, 1916, at a regional Modern Language Association meeting in Chicago). Here the procedure is exactly the reverse of the previous article: instead of examining contemporary ballad making to illuminate medieval practice, the attempt is to throw light forward to balladry from an investigation of truly ancient and/or "primitive" practice (the two are at times assumed to be one). The opening paragraph makes its new breadth clear—the lengthy quotation at its head comes not from studies of ballads or cowboy songs but from a recent ethnographic investigation of American Indian music. Much is made of such music in the pages that follow, as of the music of other communities understood as "primitive"—the discussion ranges across the inhabited continents, standing Chippewas next to Andamanese, South American Botocudos alongside South African Akkas. Many authorities are cited—a thirty-one-page article features fifty-six references, several to multiple sources. The perspective is resolutely anthropological, and Pound's impressive acquaintance with the scholarly literature (in both English and German) may be the piece's most striking new note.

All these data, their appropriateness for the purpose having been insisted upon, are promptly turned to polemical ends. One after another, the central tenets of the "Harvard school" position, represented most conspicuously once again by Gummere, are brought under scrutiny. First is the "communal" authorship of primitive songs in general and of ballads in particular. The idea is easily caricatured, as its proponents claimed it often was, but in essence it held that poetry originated in dance, that "festal throngs" of primitives, possessed somehow by a spirit of "choral composition" by their shared rhythmic movement, created the earliest songs by collective utterance of collective emotion. A flurry of five citations from Gummere's *The Beginnings of Poetry* illustrates this view, described as the "accepted or orthodox view" among "literary" scholars: "'Poetry begins with the impersonal, with communal emotion.' 'The ballad is a song made in the dance, and so by the dance.... The communal dance is the real source of the song.' 'The earliest "muse" was the rhythm of the throng.' 'Festal throngs, not a poet's solitude, are the birthplace of poetry.' 'Overwhelming evidence shows all primitive poetical expression of emotion to have been collective.'"[7]

Pound thinks all this is nonsense, and proceeds to say so in blunt terms: "That it is an absurd chronology which assumes that individuals have choral utterance before they are lyrically articulate as individuals seems—extraordinarily enough—to have troubled very few." Instance after instance is cited, taken from a broad range of ethnographic reportage from peoples regarded as "primitive," of songs authored by individuals (and of songs regarded as owned by individual composers). The mention of Chippewa "dream songs" even elicits another exclamation point, this one overtly sarcastic and encased in a parenthetical phrase: the dream, Pound affirms, is "surely not a 'communal' form of experience!" The point is reiterated with similar asperity near the article's close: "The assumption that group power to sing, to compose songs, and to dance, precedes individual power to do these things, is fatuously speculative." The supposed originary connection with dance is dispatched by similar means. A host of ethnographic citations, including one reference to a group of "recumbent Kaffirs" who sing from seated positions, are offered to demonstrate that there is no "indissoluble connection between singing and dancing."[8]

Next, having disposed of the "dancing throng," both adjective and noun, as the primitive ground of song making, Pound turns to the idea that "ballads" are well understood when described as developing from such origins. Again her verdict is sharply negative. After first deploring the wide variance in usage of the term itself, Pound points out that "primitive" songs (lullabies, the healing songs of medicine men, love songs, and hunting songs, among others) are more often lyrics than narratives. Additional references from the anthropological journals, as wide ranging as those from earlier sections, are offered in support. The article's final section recapitulates many of the points first put forward in the earlier study of ballads and cowboys songs, arguing again that ballads of the sort appearing in Child's collection exhibit none of the qualities apparent in so-called primitive song. Affirmation is not at the heart of this essay—it is first, last, and always an attack upon the entrenched communalist position, a fierce urging of how and in what communities ballads do not originate. But there is in this section, almost as an afterthought, a suggestion as to how and where ballads might actually be produced: "It is far less likely that primitive man established the lyrical species we now call ballad than that this species derived from the aristocratic song, or dance, or minstrel modes, of the mediæval bower and the hall."[9]

Pound might logically have been guided to this strikingly enlarged interest in the origins of poetry by the similar interests of her "ballad war" opponents—Gummere's ideas about ballad origins, after all, were embedded in the more overarching theories articulated in *The Beginnings of Poetry*, the very volume cited so extensively by Pound as embodying the orthodoxy she wished to attack. But apparently there was another stimulus closer to home. As she had done earlier with H. M. Belden for the study of folk music, and with George Hempl for her interest in dialect, so for her interest in poetic origins Pound gave explicit credit to "Professor H. B. Alexander of the University of Nebraska, to whom she owes her interest in poetic origins and in much more besides."[10]

Hartley Burr Alexander is mostly forgotten now, but in his day he was both a respected philosopher and a well-known creator of the hugely popular spectacles of civic congratulation and celebration known as "pageants."[11] Pound considered him a friend as well as a colleague. A fellow Nebraskan who grew up in a small town, he entered the University of Nebraska in 1892, the year she graduated. She admired him enormously. In a tribute published in 1948 (Alexander died in 1939) she honored both his accomplishments and his aid to herself: Alexander, she wrote, is remembered by many as "the University's most distinguished professor in the humanities" and for his contribution of the inscriptions and "art symbolism" for the state capitol building; his "elaborately presented pageants" for Lincoln and Omaha were "given before thousands of people"; and "in my own instance I owe more to him for his unflagging interest and encouragement than to any other scholar, with the possible exception of my Heidelberg professor for two semesters, Dr. Johannes Hoops."[12] Alexander's interest in "poetic origins" is most apparent in his 1906 book, *Poetry and the Individual*, which at several points anticipates Pound's concerns with folk music and balladry. There is even a reference to Gummere's *The Beginnings of Poetry*, with Alexander approving the notion that in "earliest times" poetry's "occasionings and applications were mainly social," but explicitly noting that "I cannot agree with what seems to be the author's thesis, that poetry is essentially a phenomenon of 'social psychology.'"[13]

In 1933, Alexander had published his own tribute to Pound. Written very carefully—it appeared in the university's alumni magazine, where he knew Pound herself would see it—Alexander's essay is nevertheless a uniquely sustained public analysis of Pound's personality. It is first asserted that from her earliest years at the lectern, Pound has been regarded with "a feeling akin to awe" by students, who find her an "enigmatical" and "almost cryptic" personality. Students know her first for her athletic accomplishments, Alexander guesses, many students being "alive to athletics . . . before scholarship seriously excites them." The union in Professor Pound of athletic and intellectual attainment would thus seem to some students "an incongruity," but even this "by no means sufficed to explain the hold upon imagination which she exercised." This personal magnetism or charisma, as Alexander describes it, is located finally in "her quite striking appearance"—she projects "the impression of alert and vivid seeing," a sense of "innerly contained and controlled expression." Her face "carries a dignity, and sometimes for others a discomfiture," and it is the adding together of all these qualities of mind and spirit made visibly manifest that "attached to her description the adjective 'hypnotic.'" Alexander's essay closes with a wonderful anecdote—it is written in his stilted, vaguely archaic (even in 1933) prose, but it is perfectly aimed to please Pound herself, who was surely its primary audience: "And I remember, too, my own dear lady [Alexander's wife] once remarking anent our mutual friend [Pound] (it was in a day when 'tatting' had vogue), 'I just cannot imagine Louise tatting.' The nearest holiday brought her a beautifully tatted handkerchief with Professor Pound's compliments. Even in those first days, with which I started out, folk used to inquire, 'Is there anything Louise Pound cannot do?'"[14]

Nineteen eighteen saw the publication of yet another lengthy article by Pound, "Ballads and the Illiterate," again in *Mid-West Quarterly*. Many points are repeated, but the primary targets this time are the exaggerated stresses laid by orthodox opinion on "the part played by oral tradition" in the preservation of ballads, the "unlettered character of the audience to whom they were addressed," and the "total lack of literary quality" in the songs themselves.[15] The usual suspects—Gummere, of course (mentioned in no fewer than seven epigraphs!), but also Kittredge—are quoted in support of these mistaken views. In contrast, Pound points out that many of Child's texts did not come from oral sources or from unlettered informants. Many collectors, including Child, "drew also upon Elizabethan and later song-books, or 'Garlands.'"

Outstanding informants, too, are often literate and even highly educated—"The celebrated Mrs. Brown of Falkland, that source *par excellence* of superior ballads, was no spokesman of a humble and homogeneous society but the daughter of an Aberdeen professor and the wife of Dr. Brown, minister of Falkland." The subject matter of the ballads suggests that "they were composed primarily for the delectation of the upper classes," and the texts themselves often exhibit qualities of "cohesion, cumulative effect, economy of words, use of suspense, and climax—all of which belong to art."[16] Once more the tone is sharply polemical, rising at times to open sarcasm. Noting that a rigorous application of orthodox definitions of ballad (artless compositions by unlettered dancing groups) to the songs themselves would drastically reduce the number of qualifying texts, Pound observes that "those who so define ballads never apply their definition in practice," for if they did "they would have left nearly no ballads to which to apply them."[17]

"The Ballad and the Dance," published the following year in *PMLA*, goes over similar ground and trains its argumentative fire upon the same targets. Copious annotation is once again supplied, though here the evidence cited is more literary and folkloristic than anthropological—there is even an excerpt from Chaucer's *Romaunt of the Rose*. "Ballad" is an old word used with many meanings over the centuries, but its primary use by "specialists" to describe narrative songs is a recent development: "In the nineteenth century, ballad continues in loose popular reference as synonymous with song. In the use of specialists it is increasingly applied to narrative songs; by the twentieth century, this has become the primary meaning."[18] It is pointed out at greater length than before that songs recognized as dance songs are most often not ballads, that "primitive" peoples not only "do not dance to narrative songs" but often "hardly know" them, and that "dancing plays hardly any role" in English and Scottish balladry.[19] Pound closes again with sweeping indictment of the "theory currently accepted in America": "The beliefs that from the dance emerged music and rhythmical utterance, or song, that dance songs are the earliest lyrics, that narrative songs are the earliest dance songs, and that the English ballad type had its genesis in the dance, are neither borne out by the evidence, nor intrinsically probable."[20]

"The English Ballads and the Church," coming at the end of the series in 1920, again in *PMLA*, shows Pound moving at last from critique to setting forth her own ideas about ballad origins. The title makes her point clear: a focusing of analysis on the oldest surviving ballad manuscripts reveals that "the oldest ballad texts existing have to do rather strikingly with the church." Here the evidence offered is neither anthropological nor literary, but centered upon the earliest manuscripts themselves. Viewed in this context, Pound suggests, with regard to "lyrical quality and style the closest affinities of the ballads of the pre-Elizabethan period seem to be with carols and with religious songs."[21] As such, they might be best understood as "a part of that great mediæval movement to popularize for edifying reasons biblical characters and tales." More or less in passing, the authorship of such pieces is attributed to what Pound calls "clericals"—that is, the monks and priests who then made up a sizable portion of the literate population. "The ecclesiastics and the minstrels," she writes, "were responsible for all or nearly all the new types of mediæval poetry, and (possibly enough) for the ballads too."[22] What is markedly different in this piece is the tone. So aggressive in her attacks upon the "communalist" position, Pound is much more diffident in affirming her own views. She concedes at the outset that her "new angle of approach" is "far removed from the theory of genesis enjoying the greatest acceptance at the present time." Then, still before laying out her view, she further concedes that it "may not take us very far."[23] She then follows the presentation of her case by calling attention to the small number of surviving religious ballads, "too slender for a very solid structure to be based upon them," before closing with the relatively mild insistence that the "possibility that ballad literature began with clericals deserves to be taken into account."[24]

The vigorous polemics of these pieces (all but the last), and the subsequent book that collected them into a single volume, was nothing new to the world of ballad scholarship. Joseph Ritson's eighteenth-century attacks upon both the sources and the editorial practices of Percy's *Reliques of Ancient English Poetry* were more vitriolic than anything Pound would later endure from the pen of Gordon Hall Gerould, and Christian Molbech's critiques of the great nineteenth-century Danish collector and editor Svend Grundtvig were characterized, according to one prominent "ballad wars" historian, by "needless malevolence."[25] So much heat seems surprising in a merely antiquarian issue, a teapot tempest, until it is remembered that the collection and analysis of ballads was entangled with notions of nationalist pride from a very early date. The "ballad war" skirmishes of the new century's first quarter took place at a time when the world was very much occupied with a real war; interest in matters of national identity and character ran at a high pitch.

Ballads as expressions of a nearly autochthonous folk ethos also fit nicely into major eighteenth- and nineteenth-century intellectual currents, from the German romanticism of Herder and the Grimm brothers to the cultural nationalism of Motherwell and Scott. Grundtvig's labors as a pioneering collector of Danish ballads were driven by a conviction of their worth as founding landmarks of a national literature, a mother lode of national identity. A thumping nationalism is no less evident in Lomax's celebrations of the "Anglo-American ballad spirit" displayed by singing cowboys and lumbermen. Much more than music was at stake in these scholarly disputes, and humble folk on both sides of the Atlantic were descended upon in their isolated settlements not solely or even primarily for love of their musical entertainments. Their gentrified betters sought them out most of all as embodiments of authenticity, and were often fascinated by them most of all as a cohort of surviving ancestors.

This note of cultural patriotism is almost wholly absent from Pound's writing. Her ancestors were distinguished Quakers, not peasants, and even the earliest expressions of her own cultural politics make clear her antipathy to any glorification of rabbles. The touchstone here is of course "The Apotheosis of the Common," her "oration" from the 1892 commencement celebrations. But her views on such topics, class based at their heart, never changed. In the Nebraska of her youth the loudest celebrators of the common man were Populists—William Jennings Bryan, known as "The Great Commoner," was a fellow Lincolnite. The staunchly Republican Pounds, it is an understatement to observe, were not of his party. Louise, however, except in her devotion to feminist causes both athletic and academic, was (unlike her brother Roscoe) neither political firebrand nor devoted party partisan. In one of her student letters from Germany, she went so far as to put in a good word for the dreaded "pops"—they were "as good friends of the institution [the University of Nebraska], really, as any are."[26]

When the Great War came, in the very years she devoted to the ballad controversies, Pound made her patriotic contributions in different ways, serving on various wartime committees. She was a member of the Women's Committee of the State Council of Defense and was chair of the National League for Women's Service, which provided overseas relief. Judging by the names alone this seems like wholly praiseworthy service, but the Council of Defense was a generally unsavory group that devoted its best energies to harassing German American citizens and others who for various reasons questioned the necessity and wisdom of American involvement. Olson and Naugle, in their history of Nebraska, refer repeatedly to "excesses of the home front of which few would later be proud," adding that "the atmosphere was favorable for the settlement of personal grudges." "It was often easy," they conclude, "to charge an annoying neighbor with being a slacker, and self-appointed patriots found a new use for yellow paint, liberally applying it to the houses and property of those they so labeled."[27]

Pound, however, given her study in Germany, her admiration for her German mentor Hoops, and her ongoing friendship with Ani Königsberger, along with her long-standing admiration of a spirit of individualism she understood as somehow "Teutonic," is an unlikely candidate for mindless anti-German xenophobia. Overseas relief, in fact, was the major focus of her efforts. Her old friend Dorothy Canfield, now Dorothy Canfield Fisher, was in France at the time, working full-time to aid the victims of the war's ravages. She worked most especially with blinded soldiers, but also established a home for orphaned and displaced children. Back in Nebraska, Pound worked directly with Fisher to obtain supplies (a particular focus of their efforts seems to have been soap) and also served on a Food for France Committee.[28]

Pound topped off her five years of concentrated labor in the field of ballad studies with the publication in 1921 of *Poetic Origins and the Ballad*. It would be her most important single book, recognized by friend and foe alike as the flinging down of a gauntlet, as raising the stakes of the battle beyond the pages of the scholarly journals to the larger world of more general readers. At least one approving reviewer saw right away that she had in a single stroke (or what looked like a single stroke to readers who had not followed Pound's five-year approach to it) altered the basic landscape of the field: "All the king's horses and all the king's men cannot put the question of ballad-origins back where it was before the appearance of Miss Pound's book. Her sharp challenge of widely accepted views is supported by a wealth of definite evidence and able reasoning that cannot be ignored. She is to be warmly congratulated."[29]

A more measured but also generally positive response came from the *Modern Language Review*. Noting the "avowedly destructive" tenor of the work as a whole, the reviewer called it "an important contribution" and praised it as "stimulating and provocative" even as he was unimpressed by its "highly tentative" suggestion that "the clerics had a large hand" in the creation of ballads. The "destructive" sections, however, are judged more positively: "In a series of incisive, pointed and well informed chapters she endeavors to demolish one by one the main positions of the romantic critics."[30]

Far stronger than either of these, however, was a staggeringly negative review—a tantrum in print—delivered by Princeton English professor Gordon Hall Gerould. Discussion of Pound's work is subordinated throughout to attack upon her person—the first sentence says she is "incapable of orderly thought," and the last concludes that "she should not be writing about ballads at all." In between, she is said to lack "sobriety and good judgment" as well as "tact" and scholarly integrity—"she has never learned, it is clear, how to deal fairly with evidence." Aligning himself openly with the communalist position held by "most of us," Gerould appeals most of all to the sheer authority of his distinguished predecessors: "Some very good minds have gone over the same material before, and have come to very different conclusions from Miss Pound's. Professor Child of Harvard and Professor Gummere of Haverford were great scholars—and had exquisite literary tact withal, which Miss Pound seems not to possess. Of the living, Mr. Kittredge, to name no other, is rightly credited with a mind of singular acuteness. Such men have understood the difficult problem that Miss Pound undertakes to solve for us and have tried in various ways to deal with it."[31]

Where to begin, with such twaddle? Perhaps with Child, who is sheer ballast here. Pound never criticized him, however fiercely she went after those who claimed his mantle. Furthermore, as Wilgus's survey points out, Child himself was by no means a committed communalist: "Child explicitly denied three fundamental tenets of the communalists: that ballads were dance songs, that they were of group authorship, and that they originated among the peasantry or in a classless society."[32] As for "exquisite literary tact"—surely Gerould's review disqualifies him from even raising the issue of tact. The "withal" requires no comment beyond noting it as thoroughly, even charmingly archaic in 1921. The residue, then, seems to be this: Gummere was a very smart man and Kittredge is a smart man; both have turned their impressive intellects upon the matter of ballad origins; both have in turn favored the academic community with their conclusions; Miss Pound now arrives, a woman from Nebraska, not a man from Harvard or Haverford; she exhibits no deference and presumes to conduct her own investigations and arrive at her own conclusions; shame on Miss Pound.

Gerould's review is an astonishing performance by any measure. Pound's own articles were themselves aggressive pieces. Words like "absurd" and "fatuous" push the envelope of polite argument; sarcastic exclamation points do the same. But there is a line she does not cross—it is always the "chronology" that is absurd, the "speculation" that is "fatuous," never the chronologer, never the speculator. Certainly, *Poetic Origins and the Ballad* received other critical reviews—after all, Wilgus's survey describes the book's reception as "mixed." H. S. V. Jones's assessment in the *Journal of English and Germanic Philology* is at times sharply negative, but his review took issue with Pound's arguments, offering no estimation of her capacities.[33] For Gerould, on the other hand, the target is Pound herself, again and again. Even Norm Cohen, an admirer of Gerould introducing a recent reissue of his folktale study, *The Grateful Dead*, characterizes his review as possessing "an acerbity that fairly pounded on the gates of incivility."[34]

Pound was nearly fifty in 1921. She had been a full professor for nearly ten years and a holder of a PhD for more than twenty. But her situation must have seemed strikingly familiar. Once again, despite all her achievements, she found herself cast as the provincial outsider, subjected to what was at bottom a snobbish dismissal based not primarily upon her work but on an intangible mix of class, gender, and regional affiliations. It was the now familiar drama. Gerould (who held no PhD) was another avatar of Skeat, of Juliette Atkinson, of the students at Heidelberg who had been there longer or had studied at Oxford. Well, Pound had defeated Atkinson and won her doctorate in an unprecedented two semesters. Gerould's attack was different—it was an open and public assault upon not only her work but upon her capabilities—and it took her longer than a tennis match or the completion of a dissertation and oral examinations to consolidate her victory. But she neither forgot nor forgave, and least of all did Laura Pound's daughter surrender her position. And her moment of triumph did come—many moments, in fact, the most spectacular in 1932 when Gerould produced his own ballad book and Pound took her turn as reviewer.

Poles apart from Gerould's attack, however, were the responses of Pound's friends. Hartley Alexander, writing a little more than a decade later in the *Nebraska Alumnus,* cast the episode into heroic terms: "Some years ago the English-literaturists of the country were under the spell of a biological romance as to the origin of balladry, English and other. The whole fictitious scenario was solemnly accepted dogma, with ponderous books supporting. Turning aside from her real concern for linguistic development, Louise Pound brought forth a book, *Poetic Origins and the Ballad,* and the whole house of cards collapsed, before a woman's single-handed challenge."[35]

H. L. Mencken penned an even more aggressively phrased encomium for his *Smart Set* review. Pound's book "completely disposes" of the "idiotic" views "cherished as something almost sacred by whole droves of professors and rammed annually into the skulls of innumerable candidates for the Ph.D." Mencken's close is unreserved in its praise: Pound's book is "extraordinarily learned, and yet the writing is clear and charming. It is a capital example of what scholarship might be in America if there were more of her acute intelligence among our scholars and less of the ponderous mummery of sorcerers and corn-doctors."[36] Mencken's review appeared in June; on May 11 he had written to "Dr. Pound" in person, praising her new book and noting in particular that the "form of it seems to me to be excellent." "But I can't help thinking of poor Gummere," he added. "To spend a whole life-time cultivating a theory, to come to fame on the strength of it, and then to have it wiped out at one stroke. You leave nothing of it save a faint, delicate perfume."[37]

Of course, ballad scholars who read Pound's articles and book did not rush into print with conversion narratives or confessions of prior error. Evangelists do that, but scholars do not. In the academic world, positions no longer tenable or fashionable are conceded tacitly, not explicitly. Least of all do academics customarily express gratitude in print to those who have enlightened them or pointed out the error of their ways. Decampings occur almost surreptitiously, in intervals between meetings and publications; a mocking irony is the default tone for expressions of thanks for criticism. What did follow upon Pound's work, according to Wilgus's survey, was a decade-long "gradual shift of position" best interpreted as "an attempt to get off the hook as gracefully as possible." Gerould himself, writing in 1923, just two years after his cantankerous review, offers in "The Making of Ballads" a nearly perfect illustration of these practices. As Wilgus notes, this piece "pointedly relinquishes any immediate concern with ultimate origins" and also "jettisons" any insistence upon dance origins, association with primitive poetry, and the claim that the era of ballad making is over. It goes without saying that Gerould and his fellow "communalists-in-retreat" do not credit Pound (or anyone else) for the disappearance of these no longer cherished tenets of the communalist faith. Wilgus chides "The Making of Ballads" for a general "failure to give credit to any predecessor except [Cecil] Sharp," and notes in particular that "the lack of even a bow to Phillips Barry is almost insulting."[38]

Pound's own comments were similar; if her tone is one notch more polite (she does not use any term as strong as "insulting"), she makes up for it by developing her critique at much greater length. A 1929 PMLA piece devoted entirely to Gerould's article both opens and closes with apparent praise. Gerould's article is "an attractive essay," possessing both "charm of style" and refined "appreciation of the poetical quality" of ballads. It has "real value for the student." On the other hand, there is "little that has novelty for the special scholar." This point, as it turns out, stressing the difference between a summary piece useful as an introduction for "students" and a contribution to scholarship of interest to specialists, will be the article's dismissive leitmotif.[39] One subsequent paragraph notes that while Gerould's "underlying thought" "may seem new to the author of the article," it has been old news to "practical collectors of folk-song for many years." Another reiterates the point: "Professor Gerould has gone a long way around to arrive at something that most scholars who are not arm-chair theorists but practical collectors would have conceded without discussion."

In yet another passage, Gerould is inconveniently called to account for the positions he has just abandoned: "It is not very long ago that Professor Gerould, terming himself a communalist . . . felt that the question of origins did matter."[40] Her close repeats the tepid compliment of the opening—Gerould's "excellent essay . . . deserves to be read attentively by ballad students"—before closing with her strongest critique. Anticipating Wilgus's scolding of Gerould's failure to credit his predecessors (and citing several of Phillips Barry's studies), Pound finds it "regrettable that he did not take into account the fact that most of the ideas he advances were held by his predecessors. Few, I think, among the leading ballad scholars of the present day would have failed to concede his leading positions before his article was written."[41]

Readers alert to the traditional gender resonances of this piece's prose might take particular delight in Pound's subtle feminization of her Ivy League antagonist. Gerould's "essay" is "attractive," written with "charm of style"; he is an indoor figure, a cloistered eastern academic, an "arm-chair" appreciator of the "poetical quality" of old English and Scottish ballads. He cuts a pretty effete figure, especially in contrast to the down-to-earth Pound, a hardheaded "practical" collector, a "field worker" in that rugged trans-Mississippi West where cowboy songs are actually being sung today. Reading this lambasting, one might almost sympathize with Gerould, despite his egregious offenses. Like his fellow easterner Juliette Atkinson thirty-two years before, he had run into a Nebraska cyclone. Surely by this time the Princeton don was regretting ever messing with Pound. And his punishments were just beginning.

Three years after absorbing this first drubbing, Gerould resurfaced in 1932 with *The Ballad of Tradition*, his major contribution to folksong scholarship. Pound's review appeared promptly. Again there was the opening bow to "felicity of style," followed this time not by repeated reminders of the lack of novelty in Gerould's arguments but by a statement of her personal pleasure in his reorientation. "Naturally," Pound says in the opening of her second paragraph, "I find the views expressed in this new book very gratifying."[42] The rest of the paragraph does not discuss Gerould at all but recapitulates positions Pound herself has taken in print since "about 1915." Then, in the third paragraph, the knife really comes out, though it is wielded by a writer deploying that tone of wry self-deprecation evident later in her "Mrs. Throttlebottom" reference. Noting first that her views, especially as expressed in *Poetic Origins and the Ballad*, had elicited "a shower of brickbats" from her opponents, and second that the criticisms "thrown with the most vehemence came from Mr. Gerould," Pound proceeds to quote his offending 1921 review at great length. All the most overblown phrasings are repeated, beginning with the "incapable of orderly thought" canard. Given this abuse, Pound concludes, her "gratification" is understandably heightened by Gerould's reorientations: "Now, in 1932, I find it pleasant to read that the positions advocated by me in 1921 and earlier have been tacitly conceded." Another lengthy listing follows, a collection of "stray citations showing the present beliefs of my critic," which of course exhibit a remarkable similarity to the just recapitulated positions advocated by Pound since 1915.[43]

The coup de grâce then follows: "Since Mr. Gerould's well-made and very readable book comes from a scholar once a strong advocate of peasant emergence of ballads, surely controversy concerning the origin of the ballad type in prehistoric times, or its development from the dance, or its composition by the illiterate, may now be termed at an end, and the matter dropped." The review goes on for two more pages, devoted entirely to Pound's astonishingly detailed replies to "scattered references" to herself in Gerould's book. Even she recognizes them as "less personal than his earlier tributes, those announcing to his readers that my ballad ideas were the maunderings of a disordered mind," but they nevertheless leave her "restive," and only a point-by-point rebuttal will bring relief.[44] No Gerould remark, however insignificant, is passed over. "Tributes," however, is a perfect touch, as is "maunderings"—Pound in sure control of both the serious and the jocular poles of the rhetorical spectrum.

But all this is mere mopping up—the real close came with Pound's announcement, as if from the bench, of a wholly satisfactory ending of the controversy. Pound is victorious, the east goes down before the west, more than corn and hogs are raised in Nebraska. In the wake of her review, Pound received a congratulatory letter from Indiana University English professor John Robert Moore. Her essay, he said, "arouses much enjoyment. . . . You must have had a great deal of fun in writing it." Moore goes on to scold Gerould for appropriating his own work without credit, noting that "Professor Belden has written a review for *JEGP* in which he has rebuked Gerould."[45]

Actually, the victory of Pound's positions was already a done deal in 1921, even before the brouhaha with Gerould began. Pound's essay on "Oral Literature," her contribution to *The Cambridge History of*

American Literature, appeared that year, and she would not have been asked to write it were the positions she espoused so vigorously not already ascendant. For "Oral Literature" has nothing whatever to do with folktales or with the great epic narratives of oral poetry. It is devoted entirely to songs, and consists primarily of a wide-ranging historical and generic survey. Ballads are discussed at some length, but the controversies carried on a such length since 1916 are here mentioned only in passing. Folk songs are songs people sing and preserve within their own communities; debates over "origin, quality, technique, or style, are secondary"; songs of recent American composition ("Jesse James," "The Death of Garfield," and "Casey Jones" are named, among others) are "genuine ballads." Criteria that would exclude them—"some communal-mystic origin" or "the preservation of a mediæval song style"—may not be logically insisted upon.[46] And this is all. Louise Pound, standing tall in the profession's ranks, surveys the field as a recognized authority. Battle over.

Pound would continue to write about music for the rest of her career. Most importantly, in 1922, just one year after *Poetic Origins and the Ballad,* she assembled and edited *American Ballads and Songs,* dedicating the anthology to Belden and crediting Carl Van Doren for the original suggestion. Kenneth Goldstein, introducing a fiftieth-anniversary reprint edition, is detailed in his praise:

> *American Ballads and Songs* was a "first" on at least two counts: (1) it set a model for organization, presenting its song texts in sections beginning with "English and Scottish Ballads in America" (the Child ballads), followed by "Other Imported Ballads and Songs" and "Native Ballads and Songs," and closing with several smaller miscellaneous sections; and (2) true to its title, it was the first *American* anthology, containing selections not only from Pound's Nebraska collection but including songs and ballads from other sections of the United States and even a few texts from Canada.[47]

Goldstein also credits Pound with not imposing her own "esthetic criteria" in choosing her material, deferring instead "to the singers' tastes." With the advantages of half a century's hindsight, he is especially impressed by her appreciation of the role of "broadsides, popular songsters, sheet music, newspapers, and phonographs" in disseminating and preserving songs: "Her statement on the importance of professional entertainers and of mass communication media in the circulation of songs is a clearer statement than that of any who came before her and of most who follow after."[48]

In 1932 Pound published a final *PMLA* article, "On the Dating of the English and Scottish Ballads." Much later, in 1953, at eighty-one, she published a summary article on "American Folksong" based on a paper read for an academic meeting in 1951. Finally, in 1957, at the age of eighty-five, she published her third (and most thorough) piece devoted to "Joe Bowers," the widely popular comic song chronicling the adventures and eventual jilting of a Missouri swain who joins the California gold rush in an attempt to "raise a stake" for his beloved Sally Black, only to learn via a letter from his brother Ike back home that Sally has married a red-haired butcher and borne to his red-haired child.[49] In between, Pound was for many years a steady reviewer of folk-music and other folklore publications (including in 1940 a highly favorable *Journal of American Folklore* notice of *Folk-Songs from the Southern Highlands*, the work of the same Mellinger E. Henry who had written her at epic length about his adventures in Italian jails in 1900) and the author of several encyclopedia entries and other pieces.

Pound was a teacher throughout her entire scholarly career, and as such she was always aware of the lag between up-to-date research and its incorporation into school texts. She found especially galling the persistence of communalist assumptions in the introductory material for sections devoted to ballads—as late as 1942 she took the time to produce "Literary Anthologies and the Ballad," a study calling for a final salting of the communalist earth. Poor Gerould gets blasted one last time. His "incapable of orderly thought" sneer was more than twenty years old, but it was warmed up and thrown back in his face again, along with his other choice phrasings, characterized as "pretty personal." His 1932 book, then headed into its second decade, is described, accurately enough, as an about-face, a claiming for his own of "most of the views he had condemned. This time his references to me were few, mostly unimportant though mostly derogatory, and in some instances wrong; but naturally I liked the book's positions."[50]

All this reflogging of the hapless Gerould is mere sideshow, however. The real focus falls on recent school texts, three of which are examined in the second section and generally praised, except for their treatment of ballads: "All are fine well planned books," Pound concludes, "abreast of the times unless for their ballad sections." These errors are then lamented in some detail, though Pound finds hope for the future in other anthologies, cited in the article's fourth section, which display more up-to-date attitudes. A second concern, discussed in the final section, has to do with misleading chronological placement of ballads in literary anthologies. They are always, Pound notes, placed too early. Seventeenth- and eighteenth-century texts are offered as instances of fourteenth- and fifteenth-century practice, and sometimes placed even earlier, alongside selections from Chaucer. Of "Sir Patrick Spens," to pick one example, Pound notes that "we know nothing before Percy's *Reliques* of 1765" and so have little right "to associate Percy's text with mediaeval composition."[51]

Pound had also produced, back in 1924, a strange article only half focused upon music. Her most thorough assault upon the communalists, "The Term 'Communal'," was a broad PMLA piece, on its face the most wide-ranging, philosophically ambitious study of her career. Its opening section is a general discussion of "The Doctrine of Communal Origins," understood as rooted in the wholly lamentable enthusiasms of the French Revolution, German romanticism, and "our own demagogic admiration of the undifferentiated demos."[52] Brief summaries of developments in theories of law, language, economics, and literature follow, with communalists in each field (Savigny, Grimm and Sapir, Maine, Herder and Wolf) corrected in turn (by Ihering, Jesperson, Lewinski and Lowie, Jacobs and Newell). But then there is a new paragraph, and suddenly all thought of communal origins is abandoned. "But in this connection," she opens, "it ought to be in place to point out that there is another and classical concept in criticism which might well have its value restored." A stirring defense of the *"consensus gentium"* follows, defined as "the critical agreement of instructed opinion" and understood as "poles remote from the romantic *Volksgeist* figment." The former, to be admired and restored to a deserved eminence, "calls for a deliberate and trained conscious effort," where the latter, the "'mob soul,' . . . seeks formlessly to express feeling."

Both the paragraph and the digression end with dismissal of a whole century's intellectual movements: "Obviously, conscious effort, cool judgment, and creative intelligence are gifts of men, not of mobs; and it was perhaps too much to expect from a romantic century interest in these qualities."[53] The whole section bristles with lengthy footnotes, featuring substantial citations in French and shorter ones in Greek, Latin, German, and Old English. Aristotle is cited, along with Longinus, Cicero and Bacon; there is an extended attempt to rescue Rousseau from the "mire of sociological mysticism." For help with this astonishing range of topics Pound expresses gratitude in a footnote to her brother, "Dean Roscoe Pound of the Harvard Law School," and also "to J. E. Le Rossignol, Professor of Economics at the University of Nebraska, and especially to H. B. Alexander, Professor of Philosophy at the University of Nebraska."[54] The article's lengthier second section, "The Term 'Communal' and Folk-Song," reviews yet again the discredited communalist orthodoxies. Gerould's 1923 article is mentioned in a footnote as an expression of communalism not yet wholly surrendered.

Read in sequence with her prior studies, "The Term 'Communal'" seems unusually wordy and repetitive, though Wilgus's reminder of its context is a salutary corrective for impatience—"if her voice was strident, we must remember that urbane scholars were prone to dismiss any deviation from the communalist line as fatuous. Polite criticism met with stony silence. . . . Her almost endless repetition of identical points was made necessary by an audience who did not want to hear them."⁵⁵ Taken as a whole, however, even with Wilgus's injunctions in mind, "The Term 'Communal'" comes across in the first section as slapdash, perhaps the only instance in Pound's career where she is guilty of overreaching, in over her head, striving for an overarching synthesis she cannot manage. And the second part, more than half, missing the leavening of the "Mrs. Throttlebottom" voice, reads as a cranky, even peevish performance, a portrait of the author as a sore winner. The whole *consensus gentium* passage seems a throwback, "The Apotheosis of the Common" with footnotes, or a reappearance of the outraged tennis player in Heidelberg dismayed by the laxity of local access rules.

Tonally, such strident passages are relatively infrequent, but Pound's fundamental cultural attitudes are wholly consistent. Songs and tales are composed by individuals, Pound insists, not groups or the "undifferentiated demos," and the best, most memorable ones, moreover, are composed by the "deliberate and trained conscious effort" of the best individuals. The famous English and Scottish ballads are not the rude effusions of peasants but derive from upper-class sources ("the medieval bower and the hall"),⁵⁶ just as more enduring American songs do not originate with cowboys, miners, or "plantation negroes"⁵⁷ but are often once-popular parlor tunes or stage numbers preserved in the traditional singing of such groups. Pound's predilection for creation by literate ("instructed" and "trained") individuals is deeply held and cuts across genres.

Investigating African American spirituals, for example, Pound on two occasions belittles the notion that they reflect "an African source for the striking rhythmical character of Negro religious song." Reviewing George Pullen Jackson's 1943 study, *White and Negro Spirituals: Their Life Span and Kinship*, she cites with approval his concluding chapter, "Farewell to Africa," where he "disposes summarily of African origins."⁵⁸ Twenty-six years earlier, in "The Ancestry of a 'Negro Spiritual,'" for *Modern Language Notes*, she had taken the same line, noting that a song titled "Weeping Mary," identified as a "negro spiritual" in H. E. Krehbiel's 1914 collection, *Afro-American Folksongs*, was known to her maternal grandmother by 1830, "a period long antecedent to its recovery from the negroes."[59]

(Even here, however, where Pound is clearly out of her depth—she had virtually no direct experience with African American song, religious or secular—she manages in spite of everything and against the grain of her own class biases to get her conclusions close to the mark. The conclusion of the second, later piece opens with praise for the spiritual's excellence—it is "the best product, the finest distinctive contribution of our American folksong"—and closes with recognition of its hybrid character: "If not fundamentally African, the spirituals are not of distinctive white character either. They are Negro-American and that is probably the best characterization of them."[60] Clean up the conflation of geography and ethnicity, substitute "African American" for "Negro-American," and Pound's sixty-year-old characterization of the genre holds up remarkably well today.)

But despite all these continuing efforts and ongoing settling of scores with Gerould, it is fair to say that communalism, ballad origins, and folk song in general were increasingly peripheral interests for Pound after the intense focus of the 1916–21 articles. She had joined an ongoing scholarly controversy and given it her best energies; she had fought long and hard, in the company of like-minded figures such as Belden and Phillips Barry, and their views had won the day. Her primary attention, beginning in the mid-1920s, would turn again to language studies. Here she would again produce an impressive body of scholarly work and in addition contribute the most significant editorial efforts of her career. She would establish herself as an authority on a wide variety of slang usages, entertaining and impressing students and a broad range of other audiences with her gift for translating literary and oratorical touchstones into contemporary argots.

An especially vivid instance of this talent in action comes from the memory of University of Nebraska historian Robert Knoll, himself Pound's student in the early 1940s:

Once when she talked about Spenser, she said she guessed she would describe the *Faerie Queene* in contemporary slang, and she did. Her knowledge of contemporary terms was so astonishing that we all laughed very loud. She was right up to the minute, and combined the current expression ("that dragon was no ball of fire, and the knight was a pretty green type") so accurately that I have never forgotten. Years later I heard her address the local chapter of PBK talking of current professional jargon, and she translated her morning activities into educationist language with hilarious results.[61]

Like her earlier (and later) dialect pieces, Pound's wider studies in American speech would be less controversial in content and less aggressive in tone than her folk music articles. Here too there would be occasional critics and conflicts, but no angry Princeton professors hurled "brickbats" at her studies of American speech. In yet another emergent field of study, Pound would establish herself as a major player on a national and international stage. And this field had an appeal that reached beyond the academy: Pound's explorations of various neologisms and slang usages appeared regularly in newspaper and magazine features. Even more than her folklore contributions, her studies of contemporary American speech made her something of a public figure. H. L. Mencken, much more widely known and surely at the time a contender for the title of the nation's fiercest polemicist, addressing her from the beginning as "Dr." and "Professor," would be firmly in her corner, praising her fulsomely and publishing her in the *American Mercury*. If the 1915–25 decade was Pound's great time of scholarly conflict and controversy, the next two decades, from 1925 through her retirement in 1945, would consolidate her greatest triumphs.

SIX

" There is always zest "

Even when she was busiest with her folk-music controversies, Pound continued to produce language studies. Following the outpouring of *Dialect Notes* pieces in 1916, she reappeared with "Popular Affixes in Present-Day Word Coinage" in the same journal in 1918 and with "The Pluralization of Latin Loan-Words in Present-Day American Speech" in the *Classical Journal* at the end of 1919. The last piece is especially interesting (and almost unique) for Pound's open expression of pleasure in her work. Pound often includes an assertion of her subject's worth as a part of her opening paragraphs, but her most common phrasings employ terms like "interest" or "value." Here she uses both, but in we encounter a much stronger and more personal statement: "It is of interest to watch the process of regularization in the living speech and to record the new words to which it is extended. There is always zest in observing linguistic phenomena, especially in following the transformations which are taking place under our eyes, as it were. To both the linguistic student and the lexicographer it is of value to survey the creation of new forms and to try to help fix the chronology of their acceptance."[1]

"Zest" catches perfectly her engagement with American language, especially when Pound goes on to indicate the specific sources of her pleasure in what might be called the fieldwork aspects of the subject, in "observing linguistic phenomena" and undertaking to "survey the creation of new forms." It was a perfect fit—an emergent field of study meeting the ideal scholarly temperament of a leading proponent. Pound always turns her solid philological training to good account, as she does, for example, in her examination of Latin loan words. Introducing a list of Latin plurals sometimes employed as singular in American English (curricula, data, insignia, etc.), she is careful to provide a precise grammatical description: "The following plurals of Latin neuter nouns in -*um* are treated as singulars of the first declension feminine." But her real interest lies with the other end of the story, not the "Latin loan-words" but the "present-day American speech."[2] Again and again, beginning with her earliest studies for *Dialect Notes* and continuing in the articles from 1918 and 1919, she is most interested not in Old English or fifteenth-century usages but in the language she hears on the streets of Lincoln, sees on the examination papers of her students, and reads on billboards or in magazines and newspapers.

Six years after "The Pluralization of Latin Loan-Words in Present-Day American Speech," Pound helped establish the scholarly journal that would most fully establish the academic legitimacy of such work. *American Speech* was apparently born in the brain of H. L. Mencken, whose groundbreaking study, *The American Language*, had gone through three editions between 1919 and 1923. But it was Louise Pound who acted on his suggestions, writing in 1924 to the Baltimore printers suggested by Mencken of her vision of a new journal addressed to a wider readership than the existing academic publications. "I'd like to help it START," she wrote, "to make sure that it gets away from the professorial formalism of the existing journals.

... There are enough of the formal kind of philological journals, dealing mainly with the past, already."³

The inaugural issue of *American Speech* appeared in October 1925 and listed Pound, Kemp Malone, and Arthur Kennedy as editors. Malone had just been appointed at Johns Hopkins (in 1924), where he would become a well-known Chaucerian and editor/translator of medieval literature. Kennedy was at Stanford, but he was a native Nebraskan, born in Weeping Water in 1880, and twenty years earlier he had been Pound's student at the University of Nebraska (he earned a master's degree in 1905 and completed his thesis, "The Substantivation of Adjectives in Chaucer," under her direction). In 1949 he would provide a foreword to a collection of her essays which includes both a general assessment of her impact on the field and her work with *American Speech* in particular. Kennedy is a stodgy writer—he was wise to choose bibliography as his specialty—and only an extended quotation can elicit his meaning. But his sense of indebtedness is clear; he clearly means to praise his old mentor:

> It was just forty-five years ago today that a little group of us, all graduate students, enrolled in her classes for Old English, for Middle English, and other philological subjects. Her courses moved along with a clarity and finish that gave to the earnest seeker after philological learning a real satisfaction. . . .
> At the time I have referred to, nearly a half-century ago, English philological scholarship was concerned for the most part with the study of Anglo-Saxon and Middle English, and earnest consideration of contemporary or recent American speech was eschewed by many English philologists as wasted on superficial and perhaps somewhat questionable linguistic material. It has required most of that fifty years to bring such study of the language of the present . . . to a generally recognized status of respectability and sound scholarship. Much of the credit for such a development in the field of English philology belongs, I should say, to the leadership of Louise Pound.

Kennedy goes on to describe Pound's work on *American Speech* as providing "leadership, courageous and of a very high scholarly order."[4]

That both leadership and courage were necessary in this search for scholarly respectability is made clear by even a cursory examination of the struggle for "American English" to be recognized at all, let alone understood as worthy of scholarly attention. Even in the seventeenth century, English writers were including novel words in reports from the colonies, and before 1750 complaints concerning "barbarous" neologisms originating in the New World had surfaced in print. For at least the next century and a half, Americanisms of all sorts were routinely derided and attacked. The very idea of a dictionary of American English (Webster's earliest appeared in 1806, with a much fuller edition in 1828) was greeted with scorn, and not only from across the Atlantic. Americans themselves, most especially those who aspired to recognition for scholarly or literary achievements, were often at least as hostile to American locutions or pronunciations as the sternest English critics.

As late as 1905, Henry James subjected a graduating class at Bryn Mawr to a "harangue" on the shortcomings of American speech. Mencken worked him over for it, too, describing the remarks as "ill-natured" and noting that James had little direct experience of American speech but "imitated very effectively the lofty air of an Oxford don."[5] Pound described the situation in a retrospective 1940 piece titled "American English Today": American English, she wrote, had "little interest to outsiders for a long period, unless to serve as an object of transatlantic disparagement." Even through the close of the nineteenth century, "everything distinctively American in language was thought bad and modifications of British usage held to be corruptions."[6]

Kennedy's high estimate of Pound's work is echoed, with more direct phrasing, by Allen Walker Read's remembrance. Recalling the founding of *American Speech* in 1925, Read stresses both Pound's encouragement of his own work and her early editorial struggles with the journal:

> The prime mover of this enterprise was Louise Pound. She published several studies of mine, especially my delving into the Iowa roots of the word *blizzard*, as applied to "a severe snow storm." I first met her on a trip she made to the University of Missouri on behalf of Phi Beta Kappa, and she was always a strong inspiration to me. She was not afraid to take a firm position in controversies that arose, especially in the field of folklore. . . .
>
> At first, *American Speech* was a monthly, and she had trouble filling it. She had to accept some articles that she was ashamed of. Especially I remember a vapid piece called "A Ramble in the Garden of Words." . . .
>
> Pound was a giantess in the field, and I owe much to her.[7]

Most telling of all, however, is the opinion of Mencken himself, irascible godfather and tireless promoter of the study of American speech ways. As author of *The American Language*, the field's most famous single book, Mencken was generous in praising those who encouraged and assisted his work, but he singles out Pound's contribution for special mention. First noting that *Dialect Notes*, where Pound got her start as a student of American speech, had for many years "offered the only outlet for the work of the few American scholars who took the national language seriously and gave it scientific study," Mencken goes on to emphasize the wider range of Pound's contribution: "Of these few, the work of Louise Pound, of Nebraska, was especially productive, for whereas most of the other members of the Society confined their investigations to regional dialects, she and her pupils studied the general speechways of the country."

Mencken goes on to stress that Pound's students produced a solid body of published work in the same years that their mentor was establishing herself at the forefront of the field: "Her first contribution to *Dialect Notes* was in 1905 [the first Nebraska word list]; thereafter, for twenty years, she or her pupils were represented in almost every issue." He then turns specifically to *American Speech*: "In 1925, in association with Kemp Malone, of Johns Hopkins, and Arthur G.

Kennedy, of Stanford, she founded *American Speech*, becoming its first editor, and serving in this capacity until 1933."[8] Mencken is characteristically generous here, quietly eliminating his own initiating role (and elevating Pound just slightly to the position of sole editor, a job she shared with Malone).

A somewhat fuller treatment of the journal's founding appeared in a retrospective article published in *American Speech* in 1945, "'American Speech,' 1925–1945: The Founders Look Back." This piece consists entirely of reminiscences by (in order) Mencken, Pound, Malone, and Kennedy, but Mencken, though he admits his role as the "pa of *American Speech*" (claiming surprise, since "I am not normally given to good works"), once again shifts the lion's share of credit to Pound. He also provides precise dates, citing correspondence on his idea with Pound (on October 5, 1924) and Malone (November 20) and remembering a dinner in Baltimore at the very beginning of 1925 (January 2) where Pound agreed "to undertake the editorship, but shrank from doing it alone." Mencken lined up Malone "as her associate," and Kennedy "was added at Dr. Pound's suggestion."

When the first issue came out the following October, Mencken "was so charmed by it that I gave it a florid welcome in the *American Mercury* for December, 1925." (Mencken had celebrated Pound's research in both language and literature even before this "welcome," publishing her four-part "Notes on the Vernacular" in 1924 and two Whitman pieces in 1925.)[9] On top of all the dates and data, this reminiscence stands out as the place Mencken chose, three years before his disabling stroke, to look back over the quarter century since the first publication of his own epochal work and award Pound the most sweeping of all his accolades: "It was her work, more than that of any other philologian, that had set the investigation of American English on its legs, and all my own writings on the subject since 1910 have leaned heavily upon it."[10]

This wonderfully magnanimous assessment is altogether typical of Mencken's treatment of Pound. Pound was then seventy-three, twelve years retired from her editorship and just that year stepping down from her teaching duties in Lincoln, and such a tribute, from such a figure, must have seemed a nearly unassailable validation of her labors in the field. Here was no dyspeptic Princeton don harrumphing about her intellectual capacities and lack of exquisite literary tact, but an infinitely more significant figure paying her the highest of compliments. The pleasure of that long ago day, in 1897, when she had won her way into the finals of the Women's Western Championships ("I've made a name for myself now and won a prize and am content") — surely it was repeated in maturer form nearly a half century later when she saw Mencken's words.[11] Pound had done most of her work by 1945, and that work had been judged successful, again and again, by the highest authorities. She had long since "made a name" for herself, and her scholarly and athletic accomplishments had been fulsomely praised in print ever since the "Nebraska cyclone" stories of the 1890s. But Mencken's glowing assessment stands out even in this chorus of applause. Here, in the study of American speech, she had not only accomplished her own important work but had made it possible for a host of others to contribute theirs as well.

Malone, for his part, contributed to the retrospective a fuller description of the "division of labor" between the two editors, calling Pound the "senior editor" and himself the "managing editor." Both "read all the articles submitted for publication," and both also, when submissions proved insufficient to needs, "kept the hopper full with writings of our own." In addition, Pound was charged with "the special task of soliciting contributions," while Malone "undertook to see each number through the press."[12]

Pound's contribution to the same retrospective focuses on the attempt of the founding editors to create a journal appealing to a wider readership, stresses the "hand-to-mouth" situation in its first years, and thanks a lengthy list of contributors (including her Nebraska colleagues Mamie Meredith, Lowry C. Wimberly, and Melvin Van den Bark). Recognizing that in a field addressing itself to contemporary language practices "valuable contributions may come from outside colleges and universities," *American Speech* was designed to be "not so academic as to attract only the austerest scholars as contributors and subscribers." The new publication started out as a monthly, making it "a pretty precarious matter to obtain enough articles for it." Sometimes pieces like the "Ramble in the Garden of Words" lamented by Read got published (it appeared in the very first issue), but just "when the situation seemed desperate, the next mail usually brought something good." The change after two years to a bimonthly schedule was "welcome," according to the self-described "pioneer" editor working in "remote Nebraska" who combined her editing responsibilities with "teaching five university courses, sometimes to between three hundred and fifty and four hundred students" with a staff consisting of one "undergraduate student at thirty cents an hour as my typist."[13]

A survey of the fledgling journal's early years makes clear that the two editors lived up to Malone's description of their job—they "kept the hopper full" with their own writings when necessary. The first volume—twelve issues running from October 1925 through September 1926—includes seven articles by Pound and three by Malone (both contributed articles to each of the first two issues, and Pound contributed a signed review to the fourth). Pound even reached out to her sister, Olivia, for a contribution, publishing a short piece on "Educational Lingo" in the sixth issue. *American Speech* cut back to a bimonthly schedule for volume three, but Pound and Malone were still going strong, contributing two pieces each to that volume's issues.

Pound would continue as a regular contributor long after her duties as editor officially ended in 1933. All in all, between 1925 and 1933, the year she turned over the editorship to William Cabell Greet, Pound published twenty-two signed articles in the first seven volumes. She also wrote several reviews, and composed brief notices and announcements for every issue. The articles themselves were a remarkably diverse group. Some are brief, often single-page treatments of single terms, like the discussion of "chorine" (a chorus girl) in 1928 or the comparison of the modern use of "park" as a verb with the medieval "Among wives and widows I am wont to sit, Y-parked in pews" from

Piers Plowman in 1927.[14] Other pieces are lighter in tone. "Curious Club Names," another of the first year's contributions, is a whimsical listing of bizarre group names. Some of these are well known—Altrusa, for example, the women's organization allied to the Rotary Club, named itself to suggest "altruism in the U.S.A."—but others still more unusual are "mostly local in character." The naming of the Homac bird club, for example, is explained by a member: "*Ho* stands for Mr. Hoskinson who encouraged us to organize, *m* for me because I was elected president, *a* of Audubon, the great ornithologist, and *c* for Charley who was elected secretary and treasurer."[15]

Other articles were more substantial, and ranged widely in their subject matter. Pound's second article, appearing in the second issue, was "The Value of English Linguistics to the Teacher," a wholly serious and even hortatory urging of the need for "a *scientific attitude toward language*" among teachers. "Scientific" translates here as first of all historical, rooted in an understanding of changes in vocabulary, grammar, spelling, and pronunciation "from the period before the Norman Conquest onward," and second as promoting an "*evolutionary point of view*" in a sense explicitly analogous with "sciences like zoology and botany."[16]

The spring of 1926 saw the publication, in the eighth issue, of a very different piece, "Walt Whitman and the French Language," combining Pound's interests in dialect and literature. Pound is almost always a straightforward writer, and this piece is no exception. The essay's purposes are announced and their "interest" explicitly asserted—an "exhibit" of Whitman's "Gallic importations has interest both for the student of his poetical dialect and for the linguistic student." The "exhibit" that follows strings numerous citations and lengthy extracts on the thinnest of narrative threads (close to half the words in the piece must be Whitman's). This structure, however, is no accident, but very much a matter of design: "The aim has been to display in inventory fashion the French element on which he relied."[17]

The following year, "The Dialect of Cooper's Leather-Stocking" brought an almost identical procedure to another American author. Once again, Pound opens with her topic and a statement of its worthiness: "the speech of James Fenimore Cooper's frontiersman" possesses "no little interest for present-day students of speech, an interest that is partly historic and partly intrinsic." This article is more wide-ranging than the Whitman piece—it opens with the suggestion that twenty-first-century scholars interested in "linguistic retrospection" might focus the same attention she is bringing to Natty Bumppo's speech upon the utterances of George F. Babbitt (Lewis's novel had been published just five years earlier), and closes, after concluding that "Cooper's forte was not dialogue," with a return to "slang usages" in contemporary novels, cartoons, and newspapers.[18]

From the very beginning, too, *American Speech* included a "Miscellaneous Notes" section which was soon recognized, over and above her myriad other contributions, as Pound's special province. Here the "zest" she found in the study of contemporary speech found its fullest expression—so much so that even when she handed over the editor's job in 1933 she retained her "care of the Miscellany." From the beginning, each issue contained at least a page or two of brief items, invariably humorous. Malapropisms from student papers, unintended double meanings from newspapers, inflated pomposities from academic articles—everything was grist for Pound's mill, and the "Miscellany" quickly became a favorite of readers. It was here, more than in any other section, that the editors lived up to their announced intention of producing a journal of a more-than-academic appeal, one that got "away from the professorial formalism of the existing journals." Many correspondents assisted Pound's work by sending in amusing items, but it is clear that Pound was remarkably well placed to gather material. Any teacher who encountered the spoken and written work of three or four hundred students each term would inevitably collect a trove of hilarious mistakes. Any academic who read regularly in academic journals would no less surely encounter a steady supply of professorial pomposities. Any close reader of newspapers was rewarded on an almost daily basis with the humorous typographical mistakes of hurried compositors.

Pound was all of these, and was in addition a widely traveled speaker active in the meetings of many academic and professional organizations who maintained an enormous personal and professional correspondence. She was, in short, perfectly placed for an editorial labor she clearly loved. Even on the golf course she was on the lookout for material. A glance at "The Contributors' Column" for the first issue (a "Miscellaneous Notes" section would be added for the second issue) shows every sign of her work. Several student papers are cited: one praises Antony's love in extravagant terms: "The charms of Cleopatra, Queen of the Egyptians, vaccinated all those about her." On the same page, a learned paper is lampooned as a "Specimen of a Professor's Simple Diction." In an address titled "Shades of Longfellow," the savant laments the present-day influence of Whitmanesque verse and yearns for a return to less-barbaric yawping: "His imagistic manner has fostered a multifarious poetic effort, lively but thin, that eventuates in satire. His free but inchoate vision, to be fruitful in our national poetry, needs to be freed from the cult of intensity, and integrated with the steady Longfellowan zest for poetic tradition and design." On the following page, a country club solicits golf tournament entries from area cowpokes: "Any man wishing to play will be furnished with a pardner. If you have no regular golf pardner, come any way, and pardners will be found for you."[19]

In issue after issue, year after year, Pound enlivened the pages of *American Speech* with hundred upon hundreds of these hilarious linguistic pratfalls. Readers told her it was their favorite section of the journal, and surely the collection and presentation of such snippets was at the very heart of the "zest" Pound found in her studies of American speech. In her obvious pleasure in such work Pound appears in her most engaging guise, her striking paradoxes prominently on view. The fierce, doggedly insistent polemicist of the "ballad wars" is nowhere to be seen; in her place is the smiling (though equally tireless) collector of puns and bloopers, the scholarly dictionary consultant and delegate to international language councils who nevertheless delights in the unending vitality of "substandard" American speech. Here, to offer just one additional instance, are the "Excerpts" from a single "Miscellany" page, complete with Pound's introductory headings, taken from the February issue of the fourth volume (1929):

HEADLINE IN AN IOWA PAPER.—"Bomb Much Damaged When It Exploded."

NEWS ITEM.—"The plaintiff lives at 1830 North 31st Street, in a small gray house with a paralyzed son."

HELP WANTED.—"Fancy lady pressers. Must be experienced. No other kind need apply."

LOST.—"Between the Rialto Theater and the Capitol, Black lady's fountain pen with loose clip."

FILM ITEM.—"While still in the high school Betty Compson's father became ill and died, and she began to help support the family."

PROMISING.—"The prisoner's statements have never once varied an iota during each and every time he was repeatedly questioned by the States Attorney."

AUTOCHTHONS.—Society note in an Ohio paper: "Mrs Adeline Tatman, Mrs. B. Y. Williams, and Mrs. Buchanan, are all natives of Brown County and were born and reared there."

THE END.—"Walter Conley of Beemer was married on April 17 to Miss Eva Hunter of Centerville. The marriage brings to a close a romance of several years' standing."

DUBIOUS PHYSICIANS.—"Robert M. Payne and his wife who were injured last week in an automobile accident on Farnam and High Streets are getting along as well as may be expected under the care of the doctors at St. Theresa's Hospital."

THIS IS SAYING IT.—The following paragraphs are from the society columns of Ohio newspapers. In this the coming of spring is announced—The green bridges over rivulets and winding streams that twist and turn among the dells, give hostages to golfers' fatigue and renew the youth of every one crossing their bright-tinted boards in search of new laurels of driver and putter.[20]

The 1920s, it is clear in retrospect, opening with *Poetic Origins and the Ballad* as the culmination of her sustained "ballad war" efforts, and devoted from the middle of the decade onward to the establishment and nurturance of *American Speech*, marked the high point of Pound's career. She was before its close a well-established academic star with a national reputation and a deep résumé of published work in two fields. In the summer of 1923 she had been invited to Berkeley as a visiting professor at the University of California, and before the decade was over she had served in a similar capacity at both Yale (in 1928) and the University of Chicago (in 1929). Her teaching in these sessions included courses from both of her special fields. At Berkeley she taught a ballad course, while the Yale visit was devoted to language study—Pound taught one of thirty-eight courses offered (hers was titled "American English") in a Linguistic Institute sponsored by the Linguistic Society of America. In between these summer school duties, in 1927, she made another trip across the Atlantic, serving as one of nine American delegates (her fellow *American Speech* editor Malone was another) at the initial meeting in London of a group called the International Council for English. That same summer, Pound picked up an honorary doctorate from Smith College and was appointed to the advisory council of the Guggenheim Foundation, initiating a four-year term.

In the spring of 1928, just before the trip to Yale, Pound had a brief scare when she found herself blacklisted for "radical, socialistic or communistic sympathies" by the Massachusetts Daughters of the American Revolution. "D.A.R. Names Dr. Pound on Black List," said the *Daily Nebraskan*'s front-page headline. Evidently she had had nice things to say about a very questionable book (Norman Hapgood's *Professional Patriots*), though by her own account she had found just one chapter "laudable." The whole charge was laughable, of course, an earlier (though hardly the first) outbreak of the militant yahooism that had McCarthyism and Freedom Fries in its future. Pound was of course herself a member of the DAR, and the Bay State chuckleheads even included her brother on their list, at a time when the Harvard dean, as fierce an anti-Communist as ever lived, was headed toward a position on the political spectrum somewhere to the right of Tamerlane the Scourge of God. Pound pulled out her best "Mrs. Throttlebottom" humor for her response, noting after reading other names on the list, "Well, it seems to be an honor." Mrs. C. S. Paine, vice-president of the Nebraska DAR, was also quoted, suggesting that there must be some mistake. "'That family is loyal, I know,' she said. 'Why their mother organized the D.A.R. in this state and was the first state regent.'"[21]

The meetings of the International Council for English stand out among these professional activities. Pound was in distinguished company—in addition to Malone, the American delegation included (among others) John Livingston Lowes, chair of Harvard's English department; George Philip Krapp of Columbia (the same scholar whose edition of two Anglo-Saxon narrative poems she had reviewed with approval back in 1907); and W. A. Craigie of Chicago, editor of the *Dictionary of American English*. The English contingent was even more glittering, headed by the Earl of Balfour, a former prime minister, and George Bernard Shaw. Pound also enjoyed her by now familiar role as the only female at the table, and was still (as she turned fifty-five) sufficiently devoted to tennis to arrange for a visit to Wimbledon as well. A letter she sent back to Olivia, enclosing clippings and instructions to save them, not only provides a succinct account but shows her in top form, not in the slightest abashed by the occasion, the company, or the setting, and proud as ever of her physical gifts:

> The meetings are over. The *Times* clippings tell the news. We sat (about 24 of us) about a table in the rooms of the Royal Society. I talked too, having more concrete material in mind than the oth-

ers and thinking of many new subjects. The Britons were not expecting a woman delegate and seemed a little embarrassed at first. Lord Balfour would begin "Miss Pound and gentlemen." Bernard Shaw took it all in. . . .

I plan to read a few days in the Brit. Museum, to go for a day or two to Wimbledon, and to shop. Liberty's, Peter Robinson's, Selfridge's and all the good theatres are within walking distance, for *me*.[22]

Nineteen twenty-five, the very year she helped *American Speech* get started, was also a year of extraordinary service as an officer of professional organizations—Pound served as president of the American Folklore Society (beginning a 1925–27 term), vice-president of the Modern Language Association, and western vice-president of the American Dialect Society (closing a 1921–25 stint). She had been doing both sorts of work for a long time—even before going to Germany for her PhD, she served as secretary of the Nebraska chapter of Phi Beta Kappa, and by 1906 she was the state director for the Association of Collegiate Alumnae (the predecessor of the American Association of University Women). On the editorial front she initiated more than twenty years as senior editor of the University of Nebraska's *Studies in Language, Literature, and Criticism* in 1917. But by 1925 these local and regional appointments, both professional and editorial, had ascended to the national level. Wherever the nation's linguists, literary scholars, and folklorists gathered, Louise Pound had earned a seat at the head table.

This steady rise from state-level to national offices is chronicled in Pound's half-century run of *Who's Who in America* entries. Her first appearance in the famous biennial chronicle occurred in the 1908–9 edition; her last hurrah, an entry of much greater length, came in the 1956–57 volume. The story they tell is first of all a narrative of national eminence nourished by deep and remarkably stable local roots. Every entry opens with Pound's chosen occupational identity badge, "educator," and closes with her home address, the same from first to last, 1632 L Street in Lincoln. The entry from 1930–31 makes clear the density of her editorial activities—in addition to her continuing labors with *American Speech* and her even more extended service at the head of the University of Nebraska publication series, Pound was also serving on the editorial boards of the *New England Quarterly*, *American Literature*, and *Folk-Say*. (The 1931 entry does not mention it, but she had by then also joined the board of *College English*, and she would add the *Southern Folklore Quarterly* to the list in 1939.) In her 1956–57 entry she also listed membership in an astonishingly wide range of social and professional organizations, including the University of Nebraska chapter of Phi Beta Kappa, where she served over a forty-year period as corresponding secretary (1898–1905), vice-president (1911–12, 1926–27), and president (1915–17, 1936–37).

The list of "Professional Societies, Activities and Honors" at the back of Pound's 1949 *Selected Writings* provides the fullest listing available, including no fewer than nine Greek letter organizations with parenthetical indicators of each one's focal interest provided for the uninitiated. Of these, only Kappa Kappa Gamma is described as purely "social." Two others (Chi Delta Phi and Sigma Tau Delta) are listed as "literary" (Pound was also, in 1925, a founding member of the Nebraska Writers Guild). Pi Gamma Mu is described as "sociological," Delta Omicron is "musical," and Theta Sigma Phi is "journalistic" (Pound was also an honorary member of the Omaha Press Club). More directly tied to Pound's interests as an educator were Alpha Lamda Delta, labeled as "scholastic," like Phi Beta Kappa, and Delta Kappa Gamma ("educational"). Appearing before all these groups is Laura Pound's great favorite, the Daughters of the American Revolution, summarized as "patriotic." On the local scene Pound was no less active, belonging to the Copper Kettle Club (labeled "social-literary"), Wooden Spoon ("social professional"), the Lincoln University Club, and the Lincoln Country Club. Louise Pound, in short, was a joiner, and since it was not in her nature to follow, she also came in time to one or another leadership role in most of the organizations she joined.

Somewhat obscured by the sheer volume of such listings is Pound's lifelong special commitment, across a wide range of activities, to the expansion of opportunities for women. If she was especially well known from her student days onward for her groundbreaking achievements as a cyclist and tennis player and for her contributions as a player and coach to a golden age of varsity women's basketball at the University of Nebraska, she was no less active in her efforts to encourage increased opportunities for women in academic life. Thirty years after her service as state director for the Association of Collegiate Alumni, she would serve a lengthy term (1937–44) as the national vice-president of the same group, by then renamed the American Association of University Women (AAUW). In the busy 1920s, in the midst of her continuing teaching duties, Herculean editorial labors, dizzying rounds of professional meetings, and ongoing scholarly writing, Pound also produced several essays specifically directed to advanced academic study for women.

The earliest of these was "The College Woman and Research," delivered at the 1920 meeting of the American Association of Collegiate Alumni and published later that year in the association's journal. This is a straightforward piece of preaching to the choir. Opening with a description of a pecking order in collegiate life, it is (at least) as applicable now as it was nearly a century ago: "Much is made of 'research,' in these days, in the academic world. Engaging in it is supposed to bring prestige to its prosecutors. . . . Those who do not engage in research are likely to defer tacitly to those who do. Most of us recall people who utter the term in collegiate life as though spelled with an initial capital, if not as written wholly in capital letters." Pound follows this gentle send-up with an admission that such deference to faculty "investigators" who pursue "original work" is to some degree deserved, once "divested of some of its factitious glamour." Universities exist not only to "preserve the learning of the world" but also to "add to that learning and to train and to encourage those who are to add to it in the next generation."[23]

She then turns to her central question—"Is research for college women as well as college men?"—and answers it by stressing two obstacles that prevent the "lady professor" (Pound repeatedly encloses the phrase in quotation marks) from taking "her recognized place as an investigator alongside her men colleagues." The first is external—"there are not many 'lady professors' in advanced positions, or indeed in positions which are favorable for the prosecution of original work." Women, that is, are too often assigned to heavy teaching loads restricted to introductory-level classes where they are expected to "preserve the learning of the world" but not add to it (or even teach those preparing to add to it). The second is internal—women are trained to diffidence, and as a result lack self-confidence: "The tradition is that women shall distrust their abilities, shall lean on others, shall assume that they cannot rather than that they can."[24]

These two points make up the heart of the essay, but it ends on two other notes that come almost as afterthoughts and reveal very different sides of Pound's approach. The first is strikingly pragmatic, though it appears on the surface to urge the most undiluted idealism. Since "things are as they are," she suggests, the "conscientious professor" (specifically of English, identified by Pound as "my own subject") should take care, before encouraging a promising woman student to pursue an advanced degree, to spell out the realities of the professional world. The woman who pursues advanced work, that is, should be urged to "do so out of pure love for the subject or for the research itself—not because she expects to attain a higher position or immediate reward."[25] By this brief addendum Pound throws a cold shower over all the prior analysis, relocating the main body of her address to a better future where women are no longer raised from the cradle to distrust their own abilities and, when they complete advanced degrees, are appointed in larger numbers to advanced positions where investigative work is expected and encouraged. For the present, they should simply be more responsibly advised by their prospective mentors.

Pound's second afterthought puts forward the notion that opportunities for women in "the more humanistic branches of collegiate learning" must of necessity increase, men in ever greater numbers having abandoned "the furtherance of cultural subjects" for the pursuit of "commercial and industrial interests." The present may be grim, with research-oriented positions for women so limited as to require conscientious professors to warn would-be doctoral students of their limited prospects, but a future feminization of virtually all "investigation in humanistic or cultural subjects" may eventually provide a remedy: "This possibility is remote, perhaps, and perhaps unlikely, but it remains a possibility."[26]

Pound followed this piece with "Graduate Work for Women," first delivered in February 1922 to a meeting of the National Association of Deans of Women in Chicago and published later that year in the educational journal *School and Society*. The themes of "The College Woman and Research" are prominent here as well, though if anything the tone has darkened. Pound opens in optimism, observing that "those who are not yet convinced of the ability of women to do graduate work of high quality are a negligible minority." In a later passage she observes that "opportunities of today probably go beyond the wildest dreams of an earlier generation."[27] But between these happy moments she provides an extended discussion of dismaying developments. Statistical evidence combines with anecdotal account to suggest that opportunities for women are in fact shrinking: "The National Bureau of Education reported sometime ago that the number of women holding positions in higher institutions of learning is actually decreasing." One informant, labeled "an extreme pessimist" by Pound, provided a bleak analysis: "Now that salaries are better, women are less and less likely to receive appointments to academic positions. That they broke in at all was because, when they were admitted, their positions offered much work and little pay, and men were not available."[28]

Given such a picture of things as they are, it is no surprise that Pound repeats her injunction to the conscientious professor of "The College Woman and Research": encouraging "able women" to undertake graduate study in preparation for a profession that systematically excludes them is "unwise." Also echoed from the earlier piece is the notion that women in entry-level positions are not encouraged to think of research and publication, as men routinely do, as a means to advancement: "Very often the best the woman instructor can do is attend with all her might to the pedagogical details that are set before her, and take for granted that outside effort would not pay. If she prints some good piece of work, it hardly makes enough difference in her status to make her efforts worth while. She must be willing to work purely for the work's sake, and not with the expectation that it will count to her advantage, as it might for a man."[29]

In general, Pound contemplates this mixed message of long-term progress slowed by setbacks assumed to be temporary with what she calls "philosophic calm." But, she adds, there are limits even to her composure. In particular, there is one among the "current comments concerning women and graduate study which I cannot hear with undisturbed equanimity." From administrators in charge of appointments on both coasts she reports hearing the same line: "We have the positions . . . and we are perfectly willing to employ women, but no strong ones are available." "I never hear it with patience," she adds. Pound also refuses to apologize for dwelling at length on the "commercial side" of the question of graduate work for women. She is cognizant that such stresses do "not sound very idealistic," but she insists upon their importance nonetheless: "What brings returns, what is in contemporary demand is what attracts the strongest minds. The able are ambitious, and they go where their ambitions find scope."[30]

"Graduate Work for Women" ends with an almost formulaic optimism (exactly the same phrasing occurs near the essay's beginning)—"I look forward to a time when it will be neither necessary nor profitable to speak separately of graduate work for men and for women"—but the tone of the essay is decidedly less rosy. Consider, for example, Pound's assessment of male support for increased opportunities for women: "And time and time again, men—the larger-minded ones—have shown that when they get around to it, when they understand, they are glad to stretch out a helping hand."[31] This is an extraordinary sentence. Pound is no vivid stylist, but her prose is almost invariably straightforward and clear. At her best she is a master of the plain style, with a sure sense of both controlled asperity ("I never hear it with patience") and an understated humor ("if not written wholly in capital letters"). But here the syntax is strikingly clotted by multiple qualifications—the men must first be subdivided, the "larger-minded" winnowed from their more obtuse and bigoted brethren, then even this enlightened subgroup must be not only be enlightened again ("when they understand") but also granted a lengthy period of dithering ("when they get around to it"). Sound conveys sense perfectly—even the "larger-minded" men are slow to understand, and even when they understand they are slow to act. Dean Power and Professor Privilege, born on third base, sit at ease in their offices and feel like sluggers. Their no less accomplished sisters, meanwhile, struggle to gain entry to the ballpark. Despite the brave close, the essay as a whole suggests that anyone looking forward to a time when men and women enjoy anything close to a level professional playing field will be looking through a very long lens.

It is in this cause, then, in her dogged lifelong resistance to gender-based restrictions and her commitment to the forces seeking their removal, that Louise Pound found a standard she could wave. If she was an educator first—the *Who's Who* entries make that explicit—she was a feminist second. Feminist educator, noun and adjective joined, would be both succinct and appropriate. Proud as she was of her athletic achievements and her work as a scholar, when push came to shove, when even a schedule as busy as hers couldn't accommodate everything, Pound put sports and scholarly research on the back burner to serve her students and the advancement of women. In her tireless services to the AAUW and her battles on behalf of varsity athletics for women at the her university, she united her professional and avocational interests perfectly.

On every front, then, from *Poetic Origins and the Ballad* to *American Speech*, from high professional offices to struggles for better opportunities for women, the 1920s were a glorious decade for Pound. Hard times came, too, of course—no whole decade is an unclouded day. Surely its darkest hours came on December 10, 1928, when Laura Pound, mother, first teacher, and model of quiet confidence for her children, died in her bed at 1632 L Street. She was eighty-seven. According to the newspaper's account, her final illness was mercifully brief—she attended a meeting of her beloved DAR on Friday, fell ill on Saturday, "weakened rapidly" from pneumonia on Monday afternoon, and died later that evening.

The subheads for Laura Pound's obituary stressed her longtime residence ("Was Pioneer Resident of Lincoln"), her active role in civic life ("Club Woman"), her botanical interests, and her role in educating her children ("Mother of Dean of Harvard Law School," "Recognized as an Educator"). Her services to the public library were remembered, as were her charter memberships in the Hayden Art Club, the Ingleside Club, the Lincoln Women's Club, and especially the "Deborah Avery chapter, D.A.R., in the organization of which she was instrumental." On at least one occasion Mrs. Pound had managed to join two of her great interests, persuading the local DAR post "to plant a botanical garden at Twenty-seventh and D streets in Antelope Park." The obituary closed, appropriately enough, on her efforts as an educator: "Throughout her entire life Mrs. Pound was interested in educational affairs. Her daughters, Misses Olivia and Louise, received the greater part of their elementary education from her while at home. Friends have credited much of the intellectual prominence of the family to the personal attention she gave to their early mental development in the home. She took great interest in many young people who were striving for an education and because of her attention was affectionately called 'Mother Pound' by many of her younger friends."[32]

A vivid instance of Laura Pound's "interest" in action surfaced nearly thirty-five years after her death, when fellow Nebraskan Frank O'Connell published *Farewell to the Farm*, his account of life on a Lancaster County farm at the end of the nineteenth century. O'Connell's mother, before her marriage, had worked in the Pound home and witnessed Mrs. Pound's teaching: "While I worked at dusting . . . I'd listen to Mrs. Pound teach. Her lessons opened up a new world for me. I thought then if I married and had any children I'd do the same for them." Later, when she was discouraged at her oldest child's choice of the California gold fields over the college campus in Lincoln she had dreamed for him, a timely letter from Mrs. Pound renewed her spirits; "Mrs. Pound is a wonderful woman," she tells her daughter Ona, "so understanding. She tells me not to be discouraged." She then quotes from the letter: "You have such a fine big family. I am sure the day will come when your children will bring you great happiness." Near the book's end, when Mrs. O'Connell journeys to Lincoln for the graduation of two of her children, she again encounters her old employer and maternal role model: "'What a wonderful day for you, Emma,' Mrs. Pound said, when they accidentally met. 'Especially since the *Cornhusker* this year is dedicated to the mothers of Nebraska. Why, I do believe they had you in mind, my dear girl.'"[33]

This accolade, more than any obituary's praise, seems a fitting epitaph for Laura Pound, capturing not only her innovative teaching but also her indomitable optimism and generous happiness in the accomplishments of others. Here, in a family at one remove from her own, Laura Pound is glimpsed as she pursues quietly, diligently, and thoughtfully the same teaching and encouragement that launched her own children lives of learning and energetic service.

Ever since the death of Stephen Pound in 1911, "Misses Olivia and Louise" and their mother had opened their home at 1632 L Street to generations of female university students, allowing them to earn their room and board by helping with household maintenance chores. The best account of this long service comes from a letter written by one such student to Mamie Meredith after Louise Pound's death. It is worth quoting at length:

There had been quite a succession of students before me (1927) and an even longer one following me. . . . Our welfare was the concern of the Pounds, as was our progress. Messages, news, and visits from any of *the girls* were eagerly awaited. *The girls* under the roof were especially fortunate, but no one will ever know how many other students were assisted and encouraged nor how many loads were eased by the quiet, efficient, unpublicized acts of the Pound family, singly and collectively.

"Mother" Pound enriched the years I was privileged to know her. Like her daughters, she never complained, always saw the best in people, befriended many, exercised a wonderful sense of humor, and constantly improved her mind. She, too, had a "Green Thumb," and we shared many happy moments in her rose garden.[34]

Now, seventeen years after their father's death, it was just Louise and Olivia. They would remain at 1632 L Street for almost thirty years, making their home together and continuing to share it with a long line of young women short on money but long on a desire for higher education. They would be for the rest of their lives the closest of companions, sharing everything from daily chores to summer vacations. And they were devoted travelers—in particular, they made a habit of going to Denver in the summers to attend the Western Folklore Conference and take in the opera.

At the time of her mother's death, Olivia Pound had been assistant principal at the Lincoln High School for a decade (she eventually served a quarter century, from 1918 until 1943). Unlike her illustrious siblings, Olivia had only a modest reputation as a scholar or writer, though she was every bit as active in service to feminist causes as her sister. Louise, after all, topped out as vice-president of the AAUW—she was in Washington DC in that capacity when she made her "Mrs. Throttlebottom" remark. But Olivia, two decades and more earlier, had twice served as president of the National Association of University Women (1913–14, 1919–20). She was deferential to her sister almost to a fault, at times making jocular reference to herself in conversation with new acquaintances as "the dumb Miss Pound," but she too possessed in good measure the family traits that drove Roscoe and Louise to prominence.[35] Like Roscoe, she was a teacher and administrator, and like Louise, she was an educator who wrote textbooks, published studies in professional journals, and worked to develop greater opportunities for female students.

In 1918, for example, the *School Review*, described in its subhead as a "Journal of Secondary Education," published Olivia's article "The Need of a Constructive Social Program for the High School," listing her as "Advisor of Girls" at the Lincoln High School. Two years later, appearing in the same publication with "The Social Life of High-School Girls: Its Problems and Its Opportunities," she had upgraded her position to "Assistant Principal." Olivia was also, even in a family of formidable Latinists, the star classicist. Earlier than either of the education studies was her 1913 study, *On the Application of the Principles of Greek Lyric Tragedy in the Classical Dramas of Swinburne*, published in the same University of Nebraska series.[36]

The death of her mother was clearly Louise Pound's greatest personal loss of the 1920s, but the decade also saw disappointments and conflicts on the professional front as well. If Gerould's 1921 review of her *Poetic Origins and the Ballad* initiated the longest-running settling of a score in her career, a feud much closer to home, a quarrel with a fellow University of Nebraska faculty member over the place of women's athletics on the college campus, occupied her from about 1925 until her retirement in the 1940s. Mabel Lee came to Lincoln in 1924, charged with reviving the university's women's physical education program. Lee brought with her strong credentials—a graduate of Coe College, she completed postgraduate studies at Wellesley and the Boston Normal School of Gymnastics and had directed women's physical education programs at Coe, the Oregon Agricultural College (now Oregon State), and Beloit College. She came to Nebraska as a full professor with strong support from the administration.

Pound was initially delighted, reportedly congratulating Chancellor Samuel Avery for "his determination to have the department reorganized and freed of male domination."[37] But it did not take her long to realize that Lee was no friend to her dreams of reviving the glory days of women's athletics in Lincoln. Lee, fourteen years younger than Pound, was every bit as strong-willed, but her commitment was to a physical education program aimed at promoting the health of female students by encouraging moderate physical activities and wholly intramural games. She was interested in the great majority of students, not in elite athletes, and she was an outspoken opponent of intercollegiate athletic competition for women, fearing it on many fronts. For the women themselves such contests were to be rejected as encouraging the undue emphasis on winning that characterized varsity sports for men and frequently resulted in special privileges and relaxed academic standards. For faculty members the threat was no less serious; as a pioneer in the professional organizations that sought legitimacy for women's physical education instruction, Lee worried that varsity programs for women would both undermine the women's physical education classes (by removing the best athletes) and roll back the hard-won gains by women in the profession by placing women's sports programs under the direction of male-dominated athletic departments. Pound, of course, found Lee's genteel notions appalling and thoroughly retrograde. She relished competition, thrived upon it, and resented the notion that women would be physically or psychologically harmed by the strenuous and competitive athletic competitions deemed healthy and beneficial for men.

The quarrel between Pound and Lee was long and often bitter, but Pound's voice is once again entirely absent from the surviving record. Just as scholars interested in her schoolgirl friendship with Willa Cather have only Cather's letters to fuel their speculations, researchers into her clashes with Lee have only Lee's side of the story. Lee, however, makes up for this one-sidedness by providing what can only be described as a remarkably full account. Lee lived a very long life—she died at ninety-nine, in 1985—and in 1978 she published the second part of a two-volume memoir, *Memories Beyond Bloomers*, which includes a vivid account of her struggles with an unnamed antagonist. (Lee published the first volume of her memoir as *Memories of a*

Bloomer Girl in 1977, and by one report completed a draft of a thus-far-unpublished third volume, *From Bloomers to Bikinis*.)

Pound appears many times in *Memories Beyond Bloomers*, always identified obliquely—as an "English teacher on the faculty," as a "faculty sportswoman from another department," most simply as "one woman" or "this woman."[38] These references are in every case complaining. Pound's initial welcome, before she is aware of Lee's fundamentally different agendas, is overacted: "She had been more than cordial at first, in fact embarrassingly so. . . . Apparently she had assumed that with my coming there was to be a revival of the intercollegiate program. To my dismay she immediately took possession of me, told me which faculty members I should cultivate and those I should not bother to cooperate with. . . . I was shocked beyond words but hid my feelings. As tactfully as possible I avoided discussion with her of my plans."[39] The honeymoon, despite Lee's attempts at dissimulation, was brief: "By spring she realized I had no intention to revive intercollegiate athletics and, worse than that, I was not going to let her dictate the management of my department." From this point on, writes Lee, Pound was "my severest critic, becoming a thorn in my flesh for all the rest of my long tenure at the university, even past her retirement to the time of her death."[40]

On at least two occasions in the 1920s the disagreements between the "faculty sportswoman" and the new director of women's physical education flared into open hostility. The first came in 1925, when the reorganized Women's Athletic Association (WAA) printed a booklet featuring its new constitution and the current year's program of activities, with a fulsome dedication to Lee. Lee's account, including a complete reprinting of the dedication, focuses upon Pound's response when the enthusiastic students, as yet unaware of Pound's hostility, rushed to her office to present the second copy:

> She took the booklet, read the dedication to me out loud with much sarcasm, and to the amazement of the girls, threw the booklet down on her desk in disgust exclaiming, "Sissy! Just a sissy!"

For a split second there was dead silence. Then she picked up the booklet again and turned to the next page on which the officers of WAA had recorded their beliefs about sports for women which ended with "We play for the fun of the game." Reading that entire statement too, out loud, with a second burst of disgust she threw the booklet down once more, exclaiming: "Sissies! All sissies! Bah!"[41]

Several factors, of course, urge caution with regard to this account. The accuracy of the narrative is itself suspect, given that Lee, hardly an impartial witness in any case, was in this instance not a witness at all, not being present for the presentation of the booklet. Also, she relates that when the dismayed students, "deeply hurt, . . . ran back to my office to report this incident," she was "secretly delighted to sense their unshaken loyalty to me." These caveats being made, however, it must be admitted that the basic tone of Lee's account rings true. Pound was in fact deeply contemptuous of such genteel and restricted notions of appropriate athletic activity for women, and it is also true that the word "sissy" tripped easily off her tongue. Robert Knoll's history of the University of Nebraska, citing this very passage, notes that Pound made such remarks in "conversation with various persons, including me."[42] There are also later profiles of Pound, from 1955, one actually titled "No Sissy, She" and the other reporting her dismay at the discontinuation of women's intercollegiate competition in similar terms: "They finally stopped girls' sports at the University. They felt it would hurt their health. We played men's rules; we couldn't stand those sissy rules."[43]

The second incident, a clash over plans for a new women's gymnasium, occurred in 1928. As Lee tells the story, her own designs were still incomplete when she was summoned to Chancellor E. A. Burnett's office to examine and approve a set of blueprints she had not previously seen. From Lee's perspective, these plans were inadequate—their major flaw being that spaces were allotted for spectators at both the swimming pool and the basketball court—and her inquiries as to their source brought her old nemesis Pound back into the story: "Sick at heart, I asked where he had procured these blueprints. To my amazement I learned that the faculty sportswoman from another department who on various occasions had taken an interest in our department had submitted these plans backed by a group of prominent women in the state. A letter accompanying the blueprints said the women 'wished to restore to the university the days at the turn of the century when its women's basketball teams triumphed over high schools of the state and the neighboring universities.'"[44]

Presented with these plans and a stark "take it or leave it" choice by Chancellor Burnett, Lee did not hesitate. "We will leave it," she reports herself as saying, "and keep our dreams." This in turn opened her to charges, as she reports, of "selling the university women down the river." Pound's voice, Lee reports, was especially prominent:

> In fact, this accusation was made even in St. Louis at a Saturday luncheon meeting of the American Association of University Women when the faculty woman who had presented the plans was the guest speaker. . . . Blissfully unaware that a close friend of mine was in the audience, the speaker mentioned that the new director of physical education for women at Nebraska was holding up progress. But she admonished her listeners not to worry because a committee of prominent women throughout the state was organized to get rid of me which they hoped soon to accomplish.[45]

The plans to have Lee removed came to naught, whatever their origin and whatever role Pound may have played. Lee's career prospered, even without the new gymnasium. In 1930 she was elected president of the American Physical Education Association, and in 1937 she published *Conduct of Physical Education*, a pioneering textbook in the field. As Lee tells the story, however, these accomplishments only exacerbated her relationship with Pound, whom she reports as especially resenting the textbook: "No sooner was it off the press (and given a most generous review and acclaim in the local city press) than I was hailed to the chancellor's office to answer to the charge made by an unnamed accuser that I had had my manuscript typed by my department secretary on university time and therefore at the state taxpayer's expense." Lee denied the charge and produced checks written to her typist; the chancellor was pleased to have this "concrete proof," as he too was, according to Lee, "under attack by the same person who was attacking me." Lee's narrative implies that the "unnamed accuser" has now been named, at least in her conversations with Chancellor Burnett. Lee continues: "My accuser had up to this time been the only woman on the faculty whose publications hailed her as a recognized author in her field (though none of her writing was used as textbooks); apparently she was jealous of that reputation as the only woman author on campus and my book was now a threat to it."[46]

In fact, Pound's first publication, *A List of Strong Verbs and Preterite Present Verbs in Anglo-Saxon*, was explicitly intended for use in classes. And Lee's troubles over her book did not end with the charge that her manuscript had been typed at the taxpayer's expense—she further reports that "a person whose name was never known to me (although guessed at) complained to various members of the board of regents and . . . it was agreed to make a ruling that no faculty member could use a textbook which he had authored or co-authored."[47] But all this is small change in a dispute that evidently plumbed new depths of pettiness. It got to the point where Lee took pleasure in her accomplishments and honors at least in part for the imagined discomfiture of Pound. As late as 1979, when she was inducted into the Iowa Women's Sports Hall of Fame, Lee was still paying off scores with her old adversary, then resting comfortably for twenty years in Wyuka Cemetery: "she'll turn over in her grave when she hears that I've been inducted."[48]

And things got uglier still, at least as Lee reports events. Her final four years at the University of Nebraska, from 1948 until 1952, were "a veritable nightmare to me and from the distance of 25 years later I look back upon this period as the low tide of my career." Lee felt herself to be "the unwitting victim" of an organized off-campus "hate group" encouraged by "the one faculty woman who had resented my presence on campus throughout my tenure there."[49] Things hit rock bottom with Lee's account of her "harassment by telephone" and a series of forged "strange letters" sent to her friends and acquaintances on department letterhead. At least one of these addressed a "former student telling her that I was doing research on the subject of homosexuality . . . and that I suspected a friend of hers of being homosexual and would she spy on her and report to me what she learned about her." Eventually, in her final year, Lee told her whole story to Chancellor Reuben Gustavson (he had summoned her to his office when "a citizen had informed him that I was in danger"). Gustavson responded by directing Lee to a psychiatrist and arranging for her to have "special secret protection on campus."[50] Handwriting experts, says Lee, were called in to analyze the letters.

The whole story makes a bizarre and tawdry saga. Like most feuds, this one brought credit to neither party. As with the Cather story, however, it is important to stress again the absence of Pound's voice. Unlike Lee, she left no account, and it seems fair to guess that she worried far less about Lee than Lee worried about her, just as she had never, in the 1890s, come close to matching Cather's passionate obsession. Cather may have loved her, and Lee may have hated her, but Pound was by nature much more reserved. She surely disliked Lee, and no doubt gave forceful expression to her opposition on more than one occasion, but it is difficult to imagine her bringing to the quarrel anything close to the energy manifested by Lee. Her primary interests and attentions, as with Cather and even with Ani Königsberger, were always elsewhere. Gordon Hall Gerould, who hit her exactly where those primary interests were engaged, stands out as the only antagonist to draw return fire (very sustained return fire). The quarrel's closest student summarizes her investigation with a cautionary note: "The University of Nebraska's archives contain nothing to corroborate Lee's autobiographical telling. . . . It is possible that Lee greatly exaggerated the threat to her person to elicit sympathy for herself."[51]

Although this assessment seems compelling, it is also clear that the clash between the two local titans was rooted in a real and deep-seated disagreement over the place of women's athletics on the university campus. Pound was passionately committed to opportunities for intercollegiate competitions between elite women athletes; Lee was equally committed to more moderate exercise programs aimed at all female students. Both were clearly alpha females, scholars at the top of their fields, and it apparently occurred to neither that their goals were not mutually exclusive. Lee won in the short term—Pound retired and died without seeing a return to the glory days of women's sports at the University of Nebraska. But Pound was victorious in the long term—Lee's remarkably long life made her a witness to unwelcome developments; she survived "long enough to see all her anti-intercollegiate work unraveled" by the 1972 passage of Title IX legislation, which relegated "Lee's beloved physical education once again to the fringes of academic institutions."[52]

It would be a mistake, in any event, to close an account of the quarrels between Pound and Lee without noting that neither woman really interfered with the triumphs of the other. Both made major contributions to their academic fields, and both were honored for making them. Pound was by a great margin the superior scholar, but Lee published a pioneering textbook and was a recognized leader in efforts to establish her field's professional respectability. Both served as presidents of their professional organizations (Pound at the head of three), and each earned admission to a state-level sports hall of fame, with Pound's 1955 admission to the Nebraska Sports Hall of Fame preceding Lee's 1979 enshrinement in the Iowa Women's Sports Hall of Fame. Both women, in short, were very bright lights, ornaments to the university fortunate enough to employ them. Buildings are named in honor of both on the campus today, and Robert Knoll's spirited history of the University of Nebraska, by placing their pictures on the same page, may be subtly telling the two distinguished antagonists to give their spats a rest at last.

13. Louise Pound the golf champion. Nebraska State Historical Society, RG0909 PH10 9.

14. Mamie J. Meredith. (*top*) Nebraska State Historical Society, RG2239 PH1 7.

15. Ruth Odell. (*right*) Biographical/Bibliographic Collection, RG52/01, Archives and Special Collections, University of Nebraska–Lincoln Libraries.

16. Louise Pound signing copies of her *Selected Writings*. Olivia Pound (in dark coat) is standing behind her right shoulder. Louise Pound Collection, Archives and Special Collections, University of Nebraska–Lincoln Libraries.

17. The Pound siblings (*right to left*): Olivia, Roscoe, and Louise. Nebraska State Historical Society, RG0909 PH6 8.

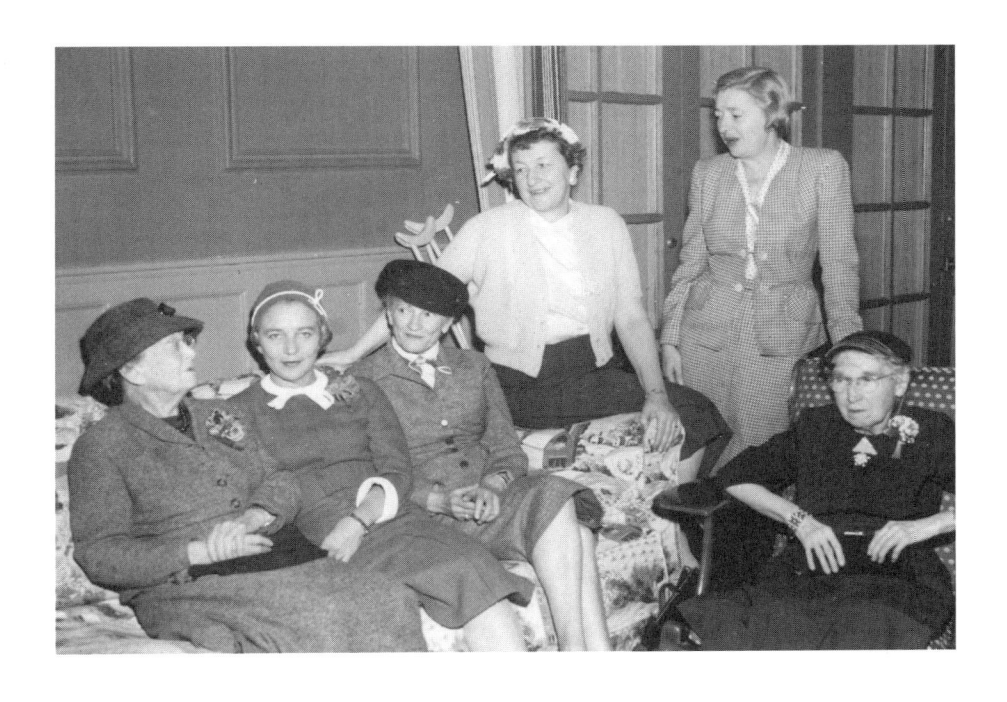

18. Louise Pound (*far left*) with Mari Sandoz (*third from left*). Olivia Pound is seated at right. Nebraska State Historical Society, RG0909 PH27 2.

19. Louise Pound. Louise Pound Collection, Archives and Special Collections, University of Nebraska–Lincoln Libraries.

SEVEN

"First woman again"

The 1930s dawned with Pound approaching her sixtieth birthday, the nation spiraling into the Great Depression, and the University of Nebraska already well into what its chancellor called a period of "retrenchment" and its historian described as a "long generation of economic and academic depression."[1] Laura Biddlecome Pound had died in 1928, and Stephen Pound had been dead since 1911. For ordinary people the approach of sixty is even now a point to start thinking of retirement; resting upon laurels begins to look like an appealing option. But Louise Pound was far from ordinary, as her many friends had known for a long time and as her few enemies were beginning to learn. She would spend the last third of her life almost as busily as the second, continuing to produce studies in the fields—folklore and American language—where she had earned her greatest reputation. Through the 1930s and 1940s she also sustained her editorial labors with *American Speech*, carrying on as editor through 1933 and continuing to produce the "Miscellaneous Notes" section through 1952, the year she turned eighty. "Twenty-seven years on it is enough!" she wrote to Benjamin Botkin in 1952.[2]

Pound was even more prolific as a reviewer in the 1930s and 1940s than she had been in the 1920s, and she also picked up the pace of her work in literary criticism. In the latter field her interests focused more closely than ever on American literature, where she interested herself most particularly in source studies. She produced two articles for *American Literature* (in 1934 and 1936) exploring Poe's use of classical and eighteenth-century narratives of sunken cities in his "The City in the Sea."[3] In 1940, in the same journal, she published "Lowell's 'Breton Legend,'" suggesting a Breton tale as a source for Lowell's patriotic Civil War poem, "The Washers of the Shroud."[4]

Pound's interest in Walt Whitman went deeper than sources, however; she returned to his work again and again, exploring neologisms and his love of Italian music in two 1925 pieces for *American Mercury* published just before the 1926 *American Speech* article on "Walt Whitman and the French Language." Another study from this period, "Walt Whitman and Bird Poetry," published in the *English Journal* in 1930, is notable for its extravagant praise of "Out of the Cradle Endlessly Rocking," which Pound celebrates as "one of the most devastating love elegies in poetry."[5] This is a note at far remove from her source studies or listings of French phrasings. Pound does not often produce a criticism rooted in her own aesthetic response or make reference in print to poems she finds "devastating"; that she does so here is surely a sign of her deep love for Whitman's poem. Five years later, editing an anthology of Whitman's prose, Pound produced a sweeping, forty-page introduction presenting Whitman's "deeply religious nature" with obvious sympathy. Citing Whitman's celebration of his own "powerful nonchalance," his stated desire to "confront night, storms, hunger, ridicule, accidents, rebuffs, as the trees and animals do," Pound stresses his escape from the old New England fear of death, "bound up with fear of future punishment and the judgment to come." Whitman, she says, "feels nothing of this terror.

To him the earth is not a battleground between the forces of light and darkness . . . but a place as divine as the next world."[6]

Pound took on many speaking engagements throughout her career; she traveled far and wide addressing audiences of all sorts. It is one thing to know this as a general truth, however, and quite another, in the absence of actual itineraries, to appreciate the sheer logistical labor involved. Fortunately, copies of Pound's own résumés for a four-year period (1937–40) have survived in her papers. These make clear, for example, that in 1937 alone she gave talks in seven Nebraska cities and towns in addition to five addresses in Lincoln. The same year saw her travel as a speaker to three towns in Kansas, two in Missouri, and four in Colorado. In some locales she gave more than one talk—in Colorado, for example, she lists two each in Greeley and Denver plus three in Gunnison. Laramie, Wyoming, was her busiest stop, with four talks listed. She also went to Austin, Texas, and Shenandoah, Iowa. A total of thirty-three addresses are listed for the year.

The listings for 1938 and 1939 are more precise as to audiences, making clear that Pound traveled most assiduously on behalf of the American Association of University Women—in 1939, for example, she addressed AAUW groups on twenty-nine occasions, ranging as far afield as Eugene, Oregon; Pocatello, Idaho; and Minneapolis, Minnesota. On nineteen other occasions she addressed various other groups, including an AAUP dinner in New Orleans on December 27. That adds up to a road-warrior total of forty-eight speeches for 1939 alone.[7] Pound also traveled in support of the "folk festival" movement that hit its high-water mark in the 1930s. These were direct descendants of the earlier "pageants" whose Lincoln productions engaged the talents of her friend Hartley Alexander. The prime mover of the festival idea was Sarah Gertrude Knott, dubbed "Go-Gettin' Gertie" by Pound, whose first National Folk Festival in St. Louis in 1934 set the standard for the genre.[8] Earlier festivals had focused on particular regions and had emphasized music and dance—well-known examples include Bascom Lamar Lunsford's Mountain Dance and Folk Festival (in Asheville, North Carolina), Jean "Traipsin' Woman" Thomas's American Folk Song Festival (near Ashland, Kentucky), and the less durable White Top Folk Festival in Virginia. But Knott cast a wider net from the beginning, opening the four-day St. Louis festival with Kiowa dancers from Oklahoma and including exhibits of traditional arts and crafts. Her second festival, in Chattanooga, featured Pennsylvania miners and the Fisk Jubilee Singers. Pound was involved in all these doings—she corresponded with Thomas, served on Knott's executive board, and gave a talk at the third annual festival in Dallas, in 1936.[9]

Even when Pound stayed home, her social and academic calendars were full. There were always meetings of her social and literary clubs, Copper Kettle and Wooden Spoon, and trips for Cokes or to movies with student groups. "After a 4 o'clock class in Old English," wrote one of her students, "she would sometimes fill 'Henry,' her little Ford car, with students and take them to the latest movie in town." At that time, she told them, she "felt it necessary to keep up with Rudolph Valentino and Clara Bow," but thirty years later, when that same student returned for a visit, "Miss Pound entertained us at 1632 L by playing her newest record album, *South Pacific*. She played her favorite record twice—it was 'There is Nothing Like a Dame.'"[10] The Pound sisters were also avid bridge players, and Robert Knoll's recollections make clear that Louise brought to these more sedentary games at least a portion of the competitive fire that she had carried to the tennis courts in her twenties and to golf courses in her forties. "She used to say, 'Breast your cards, Olivia,' suggesting that others at the table might not be above peeking. Oh yes, she was determined to win, no matter what."[11]

Frank Hallgren, who took Pound's Anglo-Saxon class as a first-year graduate student in 1941 and later served as her reader for a large composition class, remembered her as "a delight to work with" and told with relish the story of a star football player who registered but failed to attend class or turn in papers. "I reported the situation to Dr. Pound, asking if we should report him to the Dean of Students.

But she said no. 'I prefer to flunk him quietly at the end of the semester,' she said."[12] Hallgren, who later served as Dean of Men, also recalled wonderful dinner parties with the Pound sisters:

> At 9:00, without fail, Louise would announce, "We must be leaving, Olivia. Alexander will be missing us." Alexander was their house cat; a "supplementary" cat, Beelzebub, stayed in the barn. They were wonderful company, full of humor. Louise was very fond of driving, but she didn't trust the rear-view mirror. Olivia was posted to the backseat, to ride as a lookout. "Is it safe to go, Olivia?" she would ask as they backed out of their drive.
>
> They were both very devoted to their brother, though Olivia Pound once wrote a wonderful letter to him, filled with a spoof of the pompous legalese that lawyers use. I still have a copy. The opening lines went, "Comes now Olivia and prays her learned brother . . ."[13]

In 1938, amid all these addresses and dinner parties that ended in time for Alexander and Beelzebub to be cared for, Pound received what might be her finest tribute. Her old friend and ice-skating partner Dorothy Canfield returned to Lincoln in February as the university's Charter Day speaker. She was by this time, as Dorothy Canfield Fisher, a famous writer and Book-of-the-Month Club editor. Pound introduced her, and the two old friends and longtime correspondents had a fine visit. On her way home, from a Chicago train station between trains, Fisher was moved to "fish out writing-things from my bag and write you." What she wrote was effusive. Pound is, for starters, "by all odds the prize exhibit Lincoln had to show me after forty-three years." What is more, "it's not just that you're a first-rater . . . but that you've stayed in Lincoln to be a first-rater." Fisher goes on: "When I think what it has meant for the university, for the city, the state, and the west, to have you there, one of them authentically, and standing for the very best in taste, the sincerest, the truest *best*, with no compromises, —I shout hallelujah!"[14] This is an accolade to rank with Mencken's, a private letter from an old and cherished friend to treasure with the public tribute of her old co-worker in the study of American speech.

Amidst all this activity and honor, Pound continued with her scholarship. A steady stream of articles and reviews appeared, year after year. Then, in the decade leading up to and just following her retirement from active teaching in 1945, she shifted to a series of pioneering studies devoted to the traditional lifeways of Nebraska. In 1959 these were gathered together to make up her last book, *Nebraska Folklore*. A broader selection of her work, *Selected Writings of Louise Pound*, had appeared in 1949 while she was working on her Nebraska articles. Both volumes were published by the University of Nebraska Press.

The most striking new note in the 1930s, however, is her quiet pride in the accomplishments of her students. Pound told interviewers in the 1940s that nothing gave her more pleasure: "Today Miss Pound takes great pride in the accomplishments of her students, indeed, she dwells on them to the exclusion of her own. Many have been the master's and doctorate theses published by her students through Miss Pound's efforts."[15] A large cohort of grateful protégés, a group the folklorist Benjamin Botkin (himself a prominent member) referred to as the "Louise Pound alumni association," put its admiration on record, most often by dedications and printed acknowledgments in their own works.[16] Early among these are those appearing in the various articles published in *University of Nebraska Studies in Language, Literature, and Criticism*. When the first number appeared in 1917, Pound was already heading the three-person editorial committee; twenty-three years later, the eighteenth number was also supervised by a committee of three, but only the name at the top remained unchanged.

In between are perhaps a dozen pieces expressing thanks to Pound for everything from suggesting the whole enterprise to "practical editorial help," with the most usual template for such acknowledgment being a combination of both opening with the former and closing with the latter.[17] Maurice O. Johnson, for example, prefaces his

1938 *Walt Whitman as a Critic of Literature* with the following credit: "It was Dr. Pound who suggested that I might enjoy working with Walt Whitman's criticism of literature; who read the manuscript; and who accepted the finished essay as partial fulfillment of the requirements for the Master's degree." Johnson also notes his use of "the private library of Dr. Louise Pound."[18] *Modern Language Notes*, reviewing Johnson's work and another Pound-directed thesis in the same series, described them as "master's essays of unusual competence, directed by Professor Louise Pound."[19]

The sixth number, published in 1925, shows Pound again breaking new ground, this time overseeing the publication of a study she had directed: Lilian Linder Fitzpatrick's 1923 MA thesis, *Nebraska Place-Names*, the first thesis devoted to the study of American place-names. Fitzpatrick's acknowledgment sounds very much like Johnson's, crediting Pound with everything from initiating her work to helping see it through to completion: "I am indebted to Professor Louise Pound . . . for the suggestion that a study of Nebraska place-names might be both valuable and interesting, and also for her aid during the progress of the work."[20] Yet another thanks comes from Martin S. Peterson, whose MA study of Irish dramatist Robert Jephson appeared as number eleven in the series: "to Louise Pound, Professor of English at the University of Nebraska, who has given me valuable assistance in the revision of my study, I express my gratitude."[21] Twelve years later, in 1942, Pound updated her résumé to note additional services to Peterson, whose doctoral studies had developed in a different direction: "Martin S. Peterson made his book, *Joaquin Miller: Literary Frontiersman*, at my suggestion and I obtained the publisher for it, Stanford University Press. He had his doctorate under L. C. Wimberly."[22]

Two other issues in the series helped launch the distinguished career of yet another Pound protégé, the director in turn of Peterson's dissertation. Lowry Charles Wimberly's *Minstrelsy, Music, and the Dance in the English and Scottish Popular Ballads* came first, in 1921 (as number four), citing Pound's *Poetic Origins and the Ballad* and her 1919 PMLA article on balladry and dance, and was followed six years later by *Death and Burial Lore in the English and Scottish Popular Ballads* (as number eight). Wimberly is best remembered today for his role as the founding editor of Nebraska's distinguished literary quarterly *Prairie Schooner* (he served as its editor from 1927 to 1956), but he was also a distinguished English professor and folk-song scholar who was for a decade or two "the center of whatever literary life Lincoln had," hosting regular gatherings of young writers in his home on Sunday evenings.[23] When the University of Chicago Press published his *Folklore in the English and Scottish Ballads* in 1928, Wimberly dedicated the book to Pound and wrote a preface that echoes Fitzpatrick's acknowledgment and foreshadows Johnson's: "I owe my initial interest in the British ballads to Professor Louise Pound, whose contributions on the subject of ballad origins are well known." Wimberly goes on to thank Pound for continuing encouragement and for "reading the work in manuscript and proof."[24] Elizabeth Atkins did not publish her work in the University of Nebraska Studies series, but the phrasing of her thanks in the preface to her *The Poet's Poet* follows a similar pattern: "The value and interest of such an investigation was first pointed out to me by Professor Louise Pound. . . . It is with sincere appreciation that I here express my indebtedness to her, both for the initial suggestion, and for the invaluable advice which I have received from her."[25]

At least as distinguished as any of these was another female protégé and longtime friend, Viola Florence Barnes, who went from beginnings in Boone County, Nebraska, to a Yale PhD and a long teaching career at Mount Holyoke by way of the University of Nebraska. Barnes left behind a rich documentary record of her long life (she died in 1979 at ninety-three) that makes it possible to trace in some detail Pound's early influence and continuing support. Described by her biographer as "one of the major early American historians of the interwar years," Barnes first attended the University of Nebraska as a music student in 1902, was awarded her undergraduate degree (and admitted to Phi Beta Kappa) in 1909, and by the spring of 1910 had completed an MA thesis on "The Prometheus Myth in Literature" under Pound's direction.

During the same period, Barnes (with her younger sister Ruby) boarded at the Pound home, joined Pound's sorority (Kappa Kappa Gamma) and senior women's society (Black Masque), and served as vice-president of the University of Nebraska branch of the College Equal Suffrage League, a group organized in 1908 following a campus lecture by Maud Wood Park on "The Debt of College Women to the Suffrage Movement." Pound served on its board of directors.[26] By 1916 Barnes was at Yale (she completed her doctorate in 1919), but Pound's efforts on her behalf were far from over. In 1929 Pound wrote a letter supporting Barnes's successful application for a Guggenheim Fellowship (where Pound also sat on the advisory council). In March 1930, when the award was announced, she wrote in congratulation: "Lincoln is quite proud of you. You have gone pretty far since you lived at 1701 L Street and were drawn into the fraternity and family." In 1940 Pound urged Barnes's invitation to a "Women's Centennial Congress," and in the summer of 1941 she arranged for Barnes to receive an honorary doctorate from the University of Nebraska.[27]

Pound's mentoring of Barnes and their subsequent long friendship are unusually well documented, but there is enough evidence from other sources to suggest that Pound quite often made such sustained efforts on behalf of her charges. Leta Stetter, another Nebraskan, did undergraduate work in Lincoln at the same time as Barnes. As Leta Stetter Hollingworth (she married Harry L. Hollingworth, a classmate who outlived her and wrote her biography) she became a distinguished psychologist, producing several important studies addressed to the education of children (*The Psychology of the Adolescent*, published in 1928, became a standard textbook in the field). She is also recognized today for the searching critiques in large part responsible for discrediting the "variability hypothesis" and the notion of "functional periodicity," two linchpins of a widely accepted view of female inferiority. The first held that women were underrepresented at both the top and the bottom of the intellectual achievement spectrum because of a lesser biological variability; the second described monthly menstrual cycles as so incapacitating as to render women dysfunctional and thus unsuited for many occupations. Hollingworth, on the basis of many measurings, found both baseless. Pound, says Hollingworth's biography, was both "one of her favorite professors" and the "life-long friend" who told her in the spring of 1938 to keep her calendar for early June clear of engagements so she could come to Lincoln to receive an honorary doctorate.[28]

When Ruth Odell dedicated her pioneering 1939 biography of Indian rights activist and novelist Helen Hunt Jackson (whose *Century of Dishonor* [1881] and *Ramona* [1884] are in print today) to Pound, her by now standard expression of thanks included an added dimension. "Finally," Odell wrote in her acknowledgments, following the "To Louise Pound" on a separate dedication page, "I desire to express my long-felt affectionate obligation to Dr. Louise Pound, who suggested my subject and, by kindly assiduities too numerous to mention, helped bring the study to completion."[29] The "assiduities" in this instance included correspondence with members of Jackson's family hesitant to support Odell's project as well as intramural battles with (male) colleagues at the University of Nebraska hesitant to endorse the serious study by a (female) graduate student of a "popular" (female) novelist and historian. Knoll's history uses the example of Pound's support of Odell to point up a major shift of emphasis in higher education at the University of Nebraska:

> In the same generation, 1920–1950, subject-matter professors became increasingly oriented toward peer approval based on narrowly defined research.... Thomas M. Raysor, who came to the University as chairman of the Department of English in 1930, was typical. A distinguished editor of Coleridge, he would endorse research only when it dealt with original examination of high literary texts. Ruth Odell's study of Helen Hunt Jackson, author of the popular novel *Ramona* (1884), was impermissible, he thought, because her writing was "subliterary." Louise Pound protested this

view, arguing that Raysor and all those who were "homesick for Harvard Yard" drove prospective schoolteachers into the arms of Teachers College, where education courses, respected neither by the students nor by subject-matter specialists, replaced standard academic disciplines.[30]

Pound's protests eventually prevailed in this instance; Odell was granted a PhD in 1937. As it happened, the book she made from her dissertation was both a critical and biographical success, still cited in contemporary scholarship and credited with rekindling interest in Jackson and her work. Odell's experience in the academy, however, was all too typical for the time. Fifteen years after the publication of her *Helen Hunt Jackson ("H.H.")*, Odell was still at the University of Nebraska, still an assistant professor. She was never promoted, despite continuing to publish studies in professional journals, and (more egregiously) despite the fact that few colleagues had to their credit a work of similar impact.[31] When she retired in 1956 she had served in the same rank since 1937. Where Pound was often able to guide her top male students into good professional appointments—Kennedy at Stanford, Botkin at Oklahoma and the Library of Congress, Wimberly at Nebraska—she was much less successful in finding similar positions for her female protégés.

There were exceptions—Viola Barnes was a spectacular success, Elizabeth Atkins carved out a solid professorial career, and Lilian Linder Fitzpatrick was continuing her graduate studies at Cornell when health issues forced her withdrawal. Pound also "strongly encouraged and deeply influenced" fellow Nebraskan Mari Sandoz in long struggles to overcome her father's opposition and other formidable obstacles to make a significant name for herself as a fiction writer and historian. Sandoz studied Old English as Pound's student in 1926, but the teacher's real aid was given off campus, when Pound made sure Sandoz's work was given a local hearing: "at Sunday afternoon meetings of Chi Delta Phi, national honorary women's writing society, at the Pound home, or occasionally at tea in the home of someone interested in the arts, Mari was one of several asked to read their own work."[32]

Sandoz paid a warm tribute her mentor in *Love Song to the Plains*. Pound's advice—"Tell your stories in your own words, in the words and expressions that the people used, in the talk that is natural to the material"—is addressed there to a barely disguised Sandoz: "a student who had been struggling against the insistence of another professor that she write of her raw homestead childhood in Barrett Wendell English."[33] When east-coast editors sought assurance regarding the authenticity of Sandoz's *Old Jules*, now a recognized classic of Great Plains literature, they directed their inquiries to Pound. Pound apparently also promoted Dorothy Thomas, another star of the local scene—she is reported as holding the view that Thomas "held promise to be a better writer than Willa Cather" by the editor of *The Getaway and Other Stories*, a collection of Thomas's work. The same editor also refers to Pound as a "matriarch of the literary scene in Lincoln."[34]

Despite these triumphs, even a cursory examination of the record makes clear that the unhappy conclusions put forward in Pound's addresses and papers regarding limited opportunities for women in the academic world were generated by many concrete examples from her own experience. And that experience, disappointment piled upon disappointment, sometimes exhausted her goodwill. "I never hear it with patience," she wrote, and it seems she was telling the truth.[35] "Chancellors, deans, and chairmen all found Miss Pound difficult," writes Knoll. "One of them said her endless agitation took ten years off his life, and the women whom she sponsored were not advanced because deans were afraid they would become as difficult as Louise Pound."[36]

It is surely true that Pound was on occasion "difficult," and her "endless agitation" no doubt disturbed the equanimity of comfortably situated administrators. But she had her compelling reasons, rooted in her loyalties to promising students—female students in particular, who faced severely straitened career opportunities thanks to the attitudes of those in power. There was every likelihood, Pound knew, that Ruth Odell, given comparable encouragement and opportunity, would prove every bit as capable as Chairman Raysor and his like. Botkin, himself a spectacular beneficiary of Pound's mentoring and continuing assistance, makes clear his understanding of her situation in his prefatory remarks to his selections from her letters: "A pioneer and crusader in the fields of poetic and ballad origins and American English, she knew what it was to be lonely and under attack. What was more natural than for her to surround her disciples with the mutual aid and encouragement that give the scholar the feeling of security and the confidence that comes from knowing that one is not alone?"[37]

It is a brief note, as brief in Botkin's commentary as it is in Pound's own letters, but for all that it is unmistakable; Pound, born to privilege and long since risen to national prominence, was also, and most especially in her attempts to ameliorate the second-class status of women in the academy, often by reason of her gender alone a peripheral figure, obliged to do decorous battle with male administrators at best semi-oblivious and at worst openly hostile. This was the cohort—the suits and ties changing over the decades but the attitudes within mostly unvarying—that confirmed in Pound's experience the generalizations of her "Graduate Work for Women" article. By no means were all men in power "larger-minded," and even the best were slow to understand (and slower still to redress) inequities not disadvantageous to themselves. Yet again, Pound was a figure placed uneasily in two worlds, at once a to-the-manor-born insider and a stranger at the clubhouse gate. It was the old situation from the Kenwood Country Club, where she was the upstart Nebraska cyclone up against the champion from the East, or from University of Heidelberg, where she was the newly arrived American woman up against folks out of Oxford who had been there for years. Here, at home in Lincoln, she was a full professor with a major book under her belt and a growing national reputation. But Pound was no chancellor and no dean, not even a chair. Looking to advance her best students, she was at last, even (and perhaps especially) on her home ground, playing on uneven fields with odds tilted against her.

Eventually, as age sapped even her enormous energies, those same entrenched forces, resentful both of her stature and her long critique, moved from limiting opportunities for her students to circumscribing her own. A letter to Botkin from 1945, the year of her retirement, offers her wry assessment of the opposition: her department has "passed a rule, 'Miss Pound may have no more theses, M.A. or Ph.D.' (Isn't that *silly*) . . . I think it would have been a good idea to encourage me, just once, . . . and keep me at graduate theses so long as I was willing."[38] The "just once," coming as it does at the end of a distinguished senior teacher's career of conspicuous service, exhibits a momentary vulnerability, a glimpse of the toll taken by her long and often lonely struggles. Confronted with the stark choices offered by stature's claims—grow yourself or cut stature down—the comfortable middle, neither conspicuously gifted nor conspicuously inept, can be counted upon, in Lincoln as in Athens, to cut stature down. The tone of Pound's letter, only momentarily aggrieved and mostly accepting, suggests that her department's petty ruling was nothing new, and came as no surprise.

A more egregious instance even than Odell's might be the treatment of Mamie Meredith, a woman who combined a genuinely innovative intelligence with sustained diligence to a degree that must have suggested Pound herself to her colleagues. Meredith came to Lincoln as a student, earning her undergraduate degree in 1913, and returned for an instructorship and graduate studies in 1922, after nearly a decade teaching in Nebraska high schools. With the completion of an MA in 1929 she was advanced to assistant professor. Twenty-seven years later, in the same year as her colleague Odell, she retired at the same rank, again like Odell, unpromoted even to associate professor despite producing a steady stream of scholarly articles. Between 1927 and 1940 Meredith published forty-four signed pieces for *American Speech* alone. Her most impressive single work might be her detailed study of pioneer fencing, published in the *Southern Folklore Quarterly* in 1951. This is a brave and prescient piece, forty pages on a topic for which there was no established scholarship or prior literature—today it would be immediately recognized (and has been recognized by later students in the field) as a significant contribution to the then-emergent field of cultural geography.[39]

But it cut no ice in Nebraska's English department. Given Chairman Raysor's negative assessment of Odell's work on the "subliterary" figure of Jackson, it is easy to imagine a nearly apoplectic response to Meredith's careful attention to "The Nomenclature of American Pioneer Fences" (or to Odell's "Mid-Western Saliva Lore," published in the same journal). Writing to Melvin Van den Bark, Pound made clear her sense of Meredith's mistreatment: "Mamie Meredith has acquired for herself a national, almost international reputation. She goes happily and unperturbed on her way. The University ought to do something nice for her by this time, but the department seems rarely to miss a chance to do the opposite."[40]

All this is not to suggest, however, that conditions at the University of Nebraska were conspicuously inimical to women. Its chairs and deans were not ogres; the barriers impeding the advancement of women were hardly regional, and for that matter hardly confined to the academy. It could even be argued that the Lincoln campus offered a relatively welcoming environment for women—from the pioneer days when administrators were sometimes more interested in chemistry professor Rachel Lloyd's church attendance than in her work with sugar beets, women had found doors often closed and locked elsewhere at least slightly ajar in Nebraska. The University of Nebraska Press was created "out of thin air" by a woman, Emily Schossberger, hired in 1941 while Pound was still teaching. Schossberger in turn was followed (not as director but as editor in chief) by Virginia Faulkner, whose "editorial acumen brought international attention to the press and to the University."[41]

The English department, a decade after Pound's retirement, featured another formidable woman, Bernice Slote, author of a prize-winning book on Keats and later the third editor of the *Prairie Schoo-*

ner. Slote had been Wimberly's student, as Wimberly had been Pound's, as Pound had been Sherman's; gender barriers, formidable and as frustrating to Pound and her charges as they were, played a large but not determinative role at Nebraska. According to Knoll's account, English chair Jim Miller, wanting to promote Slote, hatched a plan for her to complete a doctorate, with Pound to "unretire" in order to serve as director. "She was willing, too, but Slote wasn't interested. 'Nothing doing,' she said. 'If I'd wanted a Ph.D., I'd have got one.' She wrote her book on Keats instead."[42]

It is difficult, then, to accept the notion that in the absence of the "difficult" Pound, women like Ruth Odell and Mamie Meredith would have been more speedily advanced, but it is also fair to say that on many other campuses there would have been no powerful woman present to champion them, that Odell might have been denied the PhD and Meredith might well have retired as an instructor or lecturer instead of an assistant professor. Meredith's summary of the situation, in a 1938 letter that reveals her as less wholly "unperturbed" at her own situation than Pound later thought, may be the most apt. From an opening where she says "it doesn't seem possible for so erudite a person to be so human," Meredith proceeds to a sweeping accolade:

> There are others besides myself who probably wouldn't have found it bearable to remain here if Louise Pound hadn't stayed here to champion just causes, whether popular or unpopular. She, more than almost anyone else I know, is free from envy and jealousy. She has time to help young scholars, young writers, young teachers, has the prestige to secure them a hearing, and the wisdom to aid them in the right way at the right time.
>
> ... [I]n the midst of teaching big classes at the University, writing articles and books on many subjects, editing magazines and books, helping direct many learned societies ... she yet has time to join University girls for hamburgers or ice cream at college lunch counters or on picnics.

You may find her at home in the afternoon painting the back fence a nice bright green, and in the evening presiding at a PBK meeting where the noted speaker has come because of a personal friendship for her.[43]

Pound's assistance to others did not stop, of course, at the doors to her classrooms. As one journal's editor and as a member of advisory boards for several others, she encouraged the initial efforts of several researchers who went on to prominent careers. Allen Walker Read, who gave tribute to Pound as a "giantess in the field," offers a conspicuous example, and James C. Olson's briefer acknowledgment makes clear his surprise at her initiative on his behalf: "For some reason or other, Louise Pound took a special interest. She engineered my first publication, a short article in the journal *American Literature*. She was a member of the Board of Editors."[44]

Vance Randolph, who went on to make his name as the great collector of Ozark folklore, got his start with dialect studies in *Dialect Notes* and *American Speech*: "I started in dialect studies, really. Louise Pound was at Nebraska then—I went to see her. . . . Pound encouraged my work. She even came down to Pineville [Missouri] once."[45] And Pound did more than publish Randolph's early articles. She offered in 1927 the prescient suggestion that his folk-song collection might find a publisher with "some state or local agency . . . as belonging to the history of the state," gave his first book, *The Ozarks: An American Survival of Primitive Society*, a glowing *American Speech* review in 1932, and praised the first and second volumes of his great *Ozark Folksongs* collection in 1947 and 1948 reviews in the *New York Herald Tribune Weekly Book Review*.[46] Randolph, for his part, repeatedly acknowledged his debt—Pound is thanked in both *Ozark Folksongs* (dedicated to Belden) and in his book-length study of folk speech, *Down in the Holler* (dedicated to Mencken). As an old man in a Fayetteville, Arkansas, nursing home he remained volubly grateful for Pound's help, remembering her vividly as "the callipygian folklorist."[47]

Viola Barnes, Leta Stetter Hollingworth, Maurice Johnson, Arthur

Kennedy, Mamie Meredith, Ruth Odell, Vance Randolph, Mari Sandoz, Lowry Wimberley—quite an impressive lineup takes the field for the "Louise Pound Alumni Association." But Benjamin Botkin, perhaps that cohort's most devoted member (his only challenger would be Mamie Meredith), may also have been her most successful protégé (though Mari Sandoz would also contend here). Botkin grew up in Boston and came to Nebraska in 1930, his Harvard (BA) and Columbia (MA) degrees balanced by nearly a decade in Oklahoma, where he taught at the University of Oklahoma in Norman, founded and edited *Folk-Say: A Regional Miscellany*, and wrote reviews for the *Daily Oklahoman* in Oklahoma City. His dissertation—completed, according to his preface, under Pound's "stimulating guidance"—was *The American Play-Party Song: With a Collection of Oklahoma Texts and Tunes*, published in 1937 in the University of Nebraska's University Studies series.[48] This is a remarkably thorough and meticulous study, a landmark in the field still useful to scholars today. Only his "classic study of slave folklore," *Lay My Burden Down*, rivals it as his most substantial scholarly work.[49] To have your dissertation be the acme of your achievement would be a disappointing outcome in a scholarly career, but Botkin soon left the academy to play important roles in the public sector—as editor of the folklore section of the Federal Writers' Project and head of the Archive of Folk Song in the Library of Congress, among other positions. He also edited a series of successful anthologies, beginning with *A Treasury of American Folklore* in 1942, following with several regional *Treasury* volumes (New England in 1947, the South in 1949, the West in 1951), and closing with two collections based on urban lore and a final *Treasury of American Anecdotes* in 1957.

Botkin also became a devoted friend to Louise Pound. The two corresponded regularly for almost thirty years, from 1929 through 1958. Her last letter, written five months before her death, invites him to visit on his way to California and promises a "good dinner and reunion" with Mamie Meredith.[50] Pound mentored and promoted his work; he in turn praised her generously, repeatedly, and in public.

He was founder, president, and chief publicist of the Louise Pound Alumni Association.

In this paying of appropriate homage, however, Botkin has conspicuously not been emulated by the scholars who have come in turn to celebrate his achievements. Botkin's various *Treasury* anthologies were as controversial with academics as they were popular with general readers (the controversy, of course, was not unrelated to their popularity), and he was at times attacked or dismissed in academic precincts as a "fakelorist" foisting material of dubious traditionality upon a gullible and unsuspecting populace. In the 1980s and 1990s, of course, the pendulum swung back, and Botkin has been happily rehabilitated. His mentor and champion, however, was in this revival almost wholly ignored.

Botkin's most thorough advocate, Jerrold Hirsch, in two otherwise persuasive *Journal of American Folklore* pieces and in a book devoted in large part to Botkin, mentions Pound once and in passing, not as Botkin's mentor and director of his dissertation (*The American Play-Party Song* is omitted from an otherwise impressive listing of Botkin's works) but as a member of the advisory board for *Folk-Say*. The order of authority is thus neatly reversed—Pound, almost thirty years Botkin's senior, and in 1930 a nationally prominent scholar, becomes the editor's adviser, not the student's dissertation director. A whole section of Hirsch's longer *Journal of American Folklore* piece is titled "The Oklahoma Years," but Nebraska is not mentioned. Discussing Botkin's "Lore of the Lizzie Label," Hirsch praises his cutting-edge definitions: "By referring to literate college students as a folk group and the printed material they created as lore, Botkin knew he was pushing far beyond his contemporaries' understanding of these terms."[51] Well, he might have been "far beyond" some of his contemporaries, but Louise Pound was waiting for his arrival—"Lore of the Lizzie Label" appeared in *American Speech* in 1930, with Pound as its editor, at a time when Botkin was, by his own report, sitting in her classes in "American English at the University of Nebraska."[52]

From the second article, as from Jerrold's 2003 book, *Portrait of*

America: A Cultural History of the Federal Writers' Project, Pound is wholly absent, despite index subheads for "Botkin, B. A." in the latter for "education" and "folklore interest."[53] Added up, these are striking, tendentious omissions, though Pound herself, could she rise from the grave to read them, would likely be unsurprised. A woman whose turn-of-the-century letter of inquiry regarding graduate study at Leipzig was returned with a one-word German negative scrawled across it, and whose 1920 book on ballads got her scolded as "incapable of orderly thought," would be well prepared for contemporary dismissals. Hirsch's article, after all, is explicitly concerned to "explore the role of Jewish intellectuals, such as Botkin, in developing the theory of cultural pluralism."[54] His book, similarly, notes "how similar key national FWP officials were in educational background . . . in many cases formal education at Harvard and Columbia or both."[55] This is, of course, the ghost of Gerould, with the difference that where in the first instance Pound is actively lambasted she is in the second simply airbrushed out of the picture. Professors Child, Gummere, Kittredge, and now Botkin have addressed these topics—Miss Pound therefore "should not be writing about ballads at all."[56] Or collegiate folk groups. Or printed lore. If your search is focused on Jewish (male, it almost goes without saying) intellectuals, you will fail to perceive the Quaker Professor Pound, even if she is directing your intellectual's dissertation; if your eye is reverently upon Harvard and Columbia, you will fail to notice Nebraska, even if your Ivy Leaguer is studying in Lincoln.[57] In short, renewed appreciation of Botkin is wholly to be applauded, and Botkin himself, most loyal and generous of students, sets an excellent standard for the appropriate recognition of mentors. His own champions would do well to emulate him.

In any event, all these dedications and expressions of thanks (and the listing here is by no means exhaustive) should not be taken as indicating that Pound in the 1930s and 1940s was resting on her laurels.[58] The two reviews of Randolph's folk-song collection, after all, were written in 1947 and 1948, when Pound was seventy-five and seventy-six, and in early 1954, at eighty-one, she was still promoting Botkin. Reviewing Paul Brewster's *American Nonsinging Games* for *American Speech*, she devotes almost the entire final paragraph not to Brewster but to Botkin:

> [Botkin] was the originator of the useful word *folk-say* now in dictionaries. His *Treasury of New England Folklore* is entered [in Brewster's bibliography], though not his earlier *Treasury of American Folklore* or his *Treasury of Southern Folklore* or his *Treasury of Western Folklore* of 1951; and his *Lay My Burden Down* made from the Slave Narrative Collection of the Federal Writers' Project when he was the folklore editor of the project is listed also. These books do not concern themselves with games, are indeed hardly germane at all to Dr. Brewster's field. Much more appropriate is Botkin's important *American Play-Party Song* (1937), which is not mentioned.[59]

And reviews, though beginning in 1929 she did more of them than she had before, were never her chief works. Most of her studies of Nebraska traditions appeared after 1945, as if the author had retired from a half century of teaching only to reinvent herself as a regional historian. Between 1946 and 1950 Pound published seven such studies; her usual practice was to develop a talk for the summer meeting of the Western Folklore Conference in Denver, then revise it for publication in the *Southern Folklore Quarterly*, *Western Folklore*, or *Nebraska History*. The first journal, especially, was a great favorite of Pound's in the 1930s and 1940s—in its first decade, from 1937 to 1947, she published at least fourteen articles and reviews in its pages.

The trip to the Western Folklore Conference became a regular expedition for the Pound sisters—Louise wrote to Botkin in 1947, enclosing "Old Nebraska Folk Customs," her talk from the previous year, and explaining that their motives were as much musical as scholarly: "I go on these annual Denver programs because the Uni. owns the Opera House at Central City and gives its guest speakers tickets. . . . Olivia loves to go. We enjoy it more than hearing the Met. in NYC. The conditions are so much more intimate."[60] Six years later, she wrote: "Olivia and I go to Central City, Colorado, day after tomorrow. Last time, my twelfth, was my last for folklore programs but we still plan on the opera programs of the NYC Metropolitan Company."[61] At the 1950 conference she compared herself to Old Faithful; like the famous geyser, she could be counted on to erupt every year.[62]

The gathering of these studies into Pound's third and final book-length volume in 1959 makes clearer a sort of standard compositional strategy that would be less apparent in scattered articles. Discussing "Nebraska Cave Lore," for example, Pound locates her subject on a world stage by opening with a quick survey of famous literary caves (the lair of Polyphemus and the "subterranean dwelling" of Grendel's mother are cited, among others) before closing down first to famous American caverns (Kentucky's Mammoth Cave and New Mexico's Carlsbad Caverns are among several listed, though Pound mislocates Carlsbad in Arizona) and finally to the legends associated with ten Nebraska caves.[63] When the topic is not caves but cliffs, in "Nebraska Legends of Lovers' Leaps," the approach is the same: the article opens with Ovid's story of Sappho's "fatal leap from the Leucadian promontory" and Virgil's account of Hero's despairing plunge to the Hellespont, before turning first to American authors, who tend to "specialize in fatal leaps of frustrated Indian lovers," and then, as with the caves before, to discussions of four Nebraska lover's leap stories.[64] Much the same method is followed in "Nebraska Strong Men," where Homer's Ajax and the biblical Samson join with the contemporary Tarzan and Superman to introduce a discussion of three Nebraska muscle men.[65]

Pound makes extensive use of personal and family reminiscence in her Nebraska studies. Judge Pound and (more often) his wife are both cited as sources, as is Roscoe. Pound's students and colleagues also come in for frequent mention—Mari Sandoz, by this time a noted regional historian, is a nearly ubiquitous presence, cited in at least six of *Nebraska Folklore*'s chapters, but Hartley Alexander, Benjamin Botkin, Lilian Fitzpatrick, Mamie Meredith, and Ruth Odell are also referenced. Even her old editor/antagonist from the days of *Folk-Song of Nebraska and the Central West*, Addison Sheldon, the pioneering historian and celebrator of all things Nebraskan, is accorded several citations. In "The John G. Maher Hoaxes" Pound makes use of her editorial correspondence at *American Speech* with "a philologically inclined convict" to explain a "watch-stuffing" scam long outlawed in Nebraska but no longer understood.[66]

The Maher piece is also notable for its inclusion of a sharp critique of government responses to the rise of messianic "ghost dance" religion among Plains Indians. Maher's role was that of publicist/provocateur—he "kept the New York papers full of stories of depredations and atrocities." None of these were true, of course, but in Pound's view they contributed to the atmosphere of alarm that got Sitting Bull killed and scores of innocent women and children massacred. The whole episode, she wrote, "is no credit to the white race. Far from it. It contributes another chapter in the story of our stupid and often brutal treatment of our Indian wards." The open paternalism of this is off-putting, but the disapproval is no less explicit—she goes on to label the Wounded Knee slaughter as the "inexcusable massacre by an uninhibited soldiery not only of Indian braves but of women and children."[67] For Pound, who generally keeps her political opinions (like her aesthetic ones) in the background, the whole passage constitutes an unusually forceful statement of her views.

Digressions of shorter or longer length intrude frequently, as might be expected in a series of articles including personal and family stories. At times these exhibit a dark humor (the exact tone is difficult to gauge). "Nebraska Legends of Lovers' Leaps," for example, ends far from Nebraska and does not limit its scope to unhappy lovers. Its final sentence is an astonishing flurry: "Mme. Kasenkina's leap to freedom from the Russian consulate, the leap of Masaryk in Czechoslovakia, and that of Lawrence Duggan in Washington, as well as James Forrestal's suicidal leap from a hospital, were all from windows, and all were in 1948–1949."[68]

Longer than these digressions are three essays separated into an appendix and published at the back of the volume, no doubt because none of them is specifically addressed to Nebraska traditions. They are instead general surveys, retrospective historical accounts of the development of folklore, dialect, and folk-song studies in the United States. Despite their subordination, these are among the volume's most interesting pieces; contemporary readers have singled them out for special praise. Reviewing the 2006 reissue, for example, Patricia Sutcliffe found "Folklore and Dialect" and "The Scholarly Study of Folklore" "the most important, because in them Pound explicates her pioneering view of folklore."[69] "My personal definition of folklore," Pound had written in "Folklore and Dialect," published in 1945, "would omit all delimitations of origin, characterizing it simply as lore traditional among homogeneous groups."[70]

Pound is of course once again digging up for additional drubbing the bones of the long-discredited "communal theory" (Gummere is mentioned in passing, but Gerould gets a pass on this occasion), but "Folklore and Dialect" is also interesting for its explicit consideration of the relationship between her two favorite fields. Its opening sentence makes her position clear: "Folklore and dialect have been less closely associated, in the past, than they should be. Surely dialect is a species of folklore, though the two subjects are usually treated independently." Pound goes on to define both folklore and dialect, describe the founding of learned societies devoted to each, indicate various types of dialect, and distinguish dialect from slang (slang "is characteristically ephemeral, dialect not"). Her close, having offered dialect as a "species" of folklore, steps back from the implicit suggestion of a unified field of study. The two learned societies should not be merged, she says: "Each has enough rich soil of its own to till, and it is ground that can be better tilled if they are kept separate."[71]

A decidedly skeptical tone is also a recurrent presence in the *Nebraska Folklore* pieces. The frequent association of lover's leap tales with American Indian traditions, stated as well established by no less an authority than Stith Thompson, for example, is examined and found wanting in "Nebraska Legends of Lovers' Leaps." Pound notes that despite Thompson's claim in *The Folktale* for "dozens of Indian tales of lover's leaps all over America," no such tales (or mention of them) appear in the same author's *Tales of the North American Indians*. Her further examination of the pioneering ethnographic works focused on Nebraska tribes (George A. Dorsey and George Bird Grinnell for the Pawnee, Alice Fletcher and Francis La Fleche for the Omaha) likewise turns up "no stories at all of suicidal leaps of despairing Indian lovers."[72]

Pound directs a similar skepticism to the stories of Nebraska strongman Febold Feboldson. Once again, printed assertions of Febold's popularity are cited (Carl Carmer's 1937 *Hurricane's Children* and a 1942 *Journal of American Folklore* article calling Feboldson "among the best known folk heroes"), only to be undermined by his complete absence from oral tradition: "Never, in more than a quarter of a century, has anything been contributed to me about Febold. Those persons I have questioned who have come from Gothenburg, Wahoo, North Platte, and Lincoln testified promptly that they had never heard of him."[73] Pound eventually traces the Feboldson stories to a series of 1920s newspaper columns written by a lumber dealer in Gothenburg. She assigns responsibility for their wider circulation to Paul R. Beath's 1932 *Prairie Schooner* article, "Paul Bunyan and Febold." By the 1940s Febold had been released to an even wider reading public in Botkin's best-selling *Treasury of American Folklore*. In 1949, six years after her "Nebraska Strong Men" article, Pound reviewed Beath's collection of Feboldson tales for *Nebraska History*. Here she reiterates the position that Feboldson, like the Paul Bunyan who directly inspired his elaboration, was "the synthetic creation of enterprising lumbermen," but she also concedes that while he "may have been created, not born," he had unquestionably "arrived." His tales "stand on their own, and it is with books and tall tales and gags . . . that they belong, not with the scholarly recordings of professional collectors."[74] (Such careful parsing was necessary if Pound wished to refrain from criticizing Beath, Carmer, or Botkin even as she insisted upon some presence in oral tradition for "folk" heroes.)

A working skepticism was nothing new for Pound, of course. It had served her well in her approaches to communalist theories of ballad origins, and she had recently deployed it again in a final piece on Whitman, casting doubt on fellow Lincoln resident Jennie Morgan's account of her great-grandfather's encounter with the poet near New Orleans in 1848 or 1849. Morgan's "Early Reminiscences of Walt Whitman," with annotations by noted Whitman scholar Emory Holloway, appeared in *American Literature* in 1941; Pound's cautionary "Doubtful Whitman Lore" followed in 1942, in company with Morgan's rejoinder "[Early Reminiscences of Walt Whitman]: A Reply."[75] Pound's tone is aggressive, sometimes bordering on sarcasm and in one spot portentously vague. Morgan had contacted Pound in Lincoln in the 1930s, "asking me whether I could suggest a periodical, preferably one paying for manuscripts," and had sent a manuscript of her article. Pound had her doubts even then—certain passages "sounded as though of contemporary composition and expression and as though influenced by stock characterizations of Whitman."

But these considerations were not decisive; it was an unspecified "something else that determined me to go no further in the matter." After the publication of Morgan's article, what most drives Pound's skepticism is a shift of locale—in the earlier manuscript, she is quite sure, the encounter with the poet took place in Kentucky; in the piece as published it occurs in Louisiana. Noting that Morgan had also recently published (in the *Prairie Schooner*, no less, with Wimberly as its editor) an account of a second Whitman sighting, this one involving her father, Pound rises (or sinks) in her penultimate paragraph to a rare level of derision: "One notes that it is her 'great-grandfather' who associates with Whitman . . . in the *American Literature* narrative, and her 'father' who knows him in Miss Morgan's *Prairie Schooner* sketch. How about her grandfather? How many generations of Miss Morgan's ancestors chanced to know Whitman as a contemporary?" Only by a short final paragraph noting that "details of remote facts . . . may easily become confused in the minds of their last inheritors" does Pound back off from the intimation of deliberate hoax.[76] In her reply, Morgan goes into great detail in giving plausible dates for the two encounters, noting that "generations came quickly when girls married and became mothers young," but she has little to say about the relocation of her great-grandfather's encounter, other than to describe the published version as "more complete," thanks to the recovery of additional "old letters" and other family materials when "the effects of my brother Daniel Kendley Morgan were sent me."[77] Professor Holloway, resting from his annotations of the original article, did not participate in the controversy.

The tiff with Morgan was minor compared to Pound's long feud with Mabel Lee or her spirited defense against Gerould's attack. But there were other squabbles as well, this time involving her activities as an officer of the American Dialect Society. If her work in American speech was never so polemical (or so strenuously resisted) as her folk-music studies, there were, nevertheless, moments when a figure as strong willed as Pound, placed in a wide range of leadership positions, inevitably attracted opposition and resentment. There is, for example, Allen Walker Read's vivid account of a conversation with dialect scholar Percy W. Long: When Pound's "name came up, he declared with great heat, 'That woman is a liar!' I have no idea of what she was supposed to have lied about, and was too stunned to ask; but he prevented her from being elected president of MLA, and she finally became president at an advanced age after he had left office."[78]

It is too bad that Read was so taken aback by the vehemence of Long's charge that he failed to draw a fuller narrative from the angry man (or even to date the conversation), but Pound's retrospective account of her tenure as president of the American Dialect Society (1938–41) may provide at least some hints at possible sources of Long's antipathy. In this general "historical sketch" of the society (written in 1952, a little more than a decade after her service as president), Pound's tone is at several points sharply defensive. She devoted several pages to a tediously detailed explanation of her role in arranging for the publication of Harold Wentworth's *American Dialect Dictionary*. Acknowledgment of the controversy her actions occasioned is sandwiched between that account and a following speculative guess at the consequences had she acted differently. "I have been criticized," she opens, "for not bringing up the matter of its publication for discussion before the Society. I merely announced it as under way and acceptable to a publisher of short practical dictionaries."[79]

The project apparently began in Lincoln, when Pound was "called upon once in my Nebraska office by Mr. Robert Crowell of a house that specializes more or less in turning out useful dictionaries of various types." At this meeting, Pound reports, she told Crowell "how very much I needed a dialect dictionary, however limited a number of pages he could allow it." Crowell, in turn, "promised to publish such a book if I found him an editor." Pound, noting the unavailability of two "experienced lexicographers" (Read and M. M. Mathews) and her unfamiliarity at the time with a third (Frederic G. Cassidy), reports that she gave Wentworth's "name to the Crowell Company as the likeliest possibility." It was, she insists, a good decision: Wentworth brought "extraordinary industry" to the job and "finished his work in a minimum of time" while teaching a full load of classes at the University of West Virginia "quite without assistance of any kind such as fellowships or grants in aid, probably with little or no cooperation." "Few could have done so," she concludes. In all of these dealings, Pound further insists, she acted "as a private person, not a president of the society."[80]

All of this has about it a distinct air of protesting too much, but Pound is as thorough and doggedly repetitive here as she was thirty years earlier in the multiple iterations of her "ballad war" arguments against Gummere and his communalist allies. Here even the detailed apologia is not sufficient; Pound follows up the blow-by-blow account of her negotiations with Crowell with a coolly pragmatic retrospective analysis of the end result: "Had I submitted the project, would we have had the dictionary? Straightaway it would have become a target. Think of the comments, divergencies, elaboration of plans, negative decisions, vetoes that would have arisen. A standstill of half a century seemed long enough. When an opportunity offered, why not seize it?"[81]

These two defenses, separated as they are by the acknowledgment of criticism, are tonally quite dissonant. I did not do anything out of the ordinary, says the first defense. And if I did, says the second, it was the only way to get the job done. It is easy enough to sympathize with Pound's impatience—her description is for all its overstated certitude ("would have become a target," not "might have become a target") a witheringly accurate picture of exactly how groups of academics tend to act (or not act). It should be noted, too, that Pound involved herself in other projects with Crowell and his company, and had been for some time involved in various dictionary projects—in 1949, a separate section for "Lexicographical" work appeared in the bibliography and vita included with her *Selected Writings*.[82] She provided the "Introduction," for example to *The American Thesaurus of Slang*, published by Crowell in 1941.[83] But the passage nevertheless conveys a bristling sense of affront. Pound has not in this instance been notified in public that she is "incapable of orderly thought," but the propriety of her behavior had been called in question, and her response makes clear that she was only marginally less displeased.

And there is more—an earlier section of Pound's brief history treats at considerable length the society's decades-long effort to prepare a dialect dictionary and includes a somewhat skeptical account of its archive of words and phrases collected with such a publication in view. The major mover in the dictionary project is none other than Percy W. Long. He was a longtime secretary of the society, serving from 1913 to 1928. As early as 1917, by Pound's report, Long "emphasized again the need of a dialect dictionary and suggested plans after twenty-seven years of discussion for indexing the 'many thousands of slips, representing perhaps as many usages as the 26,000 already printed.'" In a 1923 report, also cited by Pound, Long reiterated his point: "One chief aim in the Society has always been the preparation and publication of an American Dialect Dictionary. As materials to this end, it has, in addition to the 26,000 entries in the issues of *Dialect Notes*, some 15,000 other items." Long was, then, both a recognized authority on dialect and a longtime advocate of an American dialect dictionary—since 1906, as Pound's report also points out, he had been "editor of the dialect words in the Webster *New International Dictionary*."[84]

As for the society's collection of materials for the proposed dictionary, Pound first suggests that its size has been overestimated, then implies that it may have at times been carelessly handled. Where Long's secretarial reports repeatedly mention large word lists awaiting publication, Pound's account suggests that the existence of what she terms (in quotes, though the phrase is not used in the reports cited) a "vast collectanea" is "a myth." She then provides a personal anecdote: "At one time, I am not sure just when, I volunteered to alphabetize the contents of a volume [of *Dialect Notes*] when volunteers were called for. It was the fourth, I think. I made the alphabetized list and sent it to headquarters. When Dr. Harold Wentworth was searching for all available material for his projected dictionary, I tried to borrow for him the list I had prepared, this to save him time. But my slips had vanished."[85]

Next to nothing can be demonstrated from all this, of course, but there is ample suggestion of a prickly relationship between the dialect heavyweights. Surely Long, by virtue of his lengthy service, established reputation, and long involvement with the project, had every reason to expect a prominent role in the production of the long-awaited dialect dictionary. Perhaps he assumed he would edit it himself. In his 1926 *American Speech* article, "The American Dialect Dictionary," Long suggests that preliminary editorial work was already under way, with "Professor [W. A.] Craigie, at the University of Chicago," as "Director of Research." The assembly of a future board "of trained scholars" is also envisioned, for the purpose of "preliminary subediting . . . according to a concerted plan."[86] There is much to give pause in this prose, of course—the editing is forever "subediting," and "preliminary" at that, and a "concerted plan" is still to be developed by a yet unappointed body. But the fact remains that Long was for a very long time at the center of a large undertaking central to his academic interests. To have that project's summary assignment to a less prominent figure breezily presented as a fait accompli by Pound might well have been a galling, even infuriating experience.

There is also the matter of Pound's skepticism with regard to the size of the society's collections, which is in direct contradiction to Long's own reports as cited by Pound. Her story of the lost word list does not directly name Long as the careless party, but in the context of her sketch he is an obvious candidate. The 1923 call for volunteers, after all, was his, and his term as secretary continued through 1928.[87] This imputation, if it is there, would surely have affronted Long as much as criticisms of her actions displeased Pound. If the exact causes of offense are a bit vague after all this time, it is nevertheless clear that punching and counterpunching are going on just beneath the veneer of civility. It is probably fair to say that Pound at the very least played loose with decision-making protocols; her characterization of the dialect dictionary project as dead in the water (at a "standstill of more than half a century") also seems apt, however, and goes a good way toward explaining the impatience that led Pound to urge its undertaking upon the Crowell representative and to help find him an editor.[88]

In any event, it is obvious that Pound in the 1940s, like Pound in the 1920s, had her detractors, in Nebraska and elsewhere. It is also clear that they were both a minority and, in the long run, an ineffective minority. For every Gordon Hall Gerould or Mabel Lee or Percy Long there were ten like Lowry Charles Wimberly, Mamie Meredith, Benjamin Botkin, Ruth Odell, Vance Randolph, or Viola Barnes. As a mature scholar and editor, Pound retained the independence of spirit fostered by Laura Pound, who taught her as a child "the wonderful advantage one has who is able to decide and not change his mind."[89] She decided, then acted (tirelessly), and did not often change her mind. These traits appear most often in brief notes, but they are recurrent. Benjamin Botkin stresses her "unswerving devotion and loyalty"; Arthur Kennedy calls her leadership "courageous, and of a very high scholarly order"; Allen Walker Read notes her willingness "to take a firm position in controversies that arose."[90] And it was this large circle of friends who repaid Pound's encouragement and support not only with their thanks but also by celebrating her own accomplishments. Her *Selected Writings* was edited by Wimberly and reviewed by Botkin, and it appeared with a foreword by Kennedy and a thorough "Bibliography, Professional Activities and Vita" by Meredith and Odell. Botkin and Meredith were especially devoted and tireless in their support—both produced obituary notices (Meredith had a hand in three) after their mentor's death.[91]

Pound was probably right, given all these dedications, expressions of thanks, and posthumous testimonials, in taking her greatest pride in the work of her students. Certainly she produced impressive scholarship in an astonishingly wide range of studies. She was a superb collector, an able and efficient editor, and when the occasion called for it a formidable polemicist. But her deepest genius, it seems clear, was for mentoring, for teaching and encouraging others, for service in the most encompassing sense of the word. It was in service—not just in the classroom but in her lifelong engagement with the work of her students—that she found her truest calling and the fullest engagement of her faculties.

Three anecdotes reveal this gift with particular clarity and suggest something of its constituent elements. One day in the fall of 1940, near the end of the term, there was great rejoicing in Lincoln. The football team had enjoyed a triumphant season, losing only to national power Minnesota in their opening game, and had as a reward been invited to play in the Rose Bowl against Stanford. Edward Dosek, an undergraduate cheerleader and debate squad member, rushed about the campus on the day the invitation was announced, drumming up support for a parade down "O" Street. "I went from class to class," he recalled sixty-five years later:

> I broke into her classroom and proceeded to lead a few cheers. It was a fairly large class; I remember it had a sloped floor. Anyway,

she didn't take too kindly to that. She shooed me off the stage and reported me to the Dean's office. That was T. J. Thompson; his son was one of the quarterbacks. Anyway, I was called in and chastised very duly. He told me to apologize to her. I did, and she was very cordial. I think she understood my enthusiasm; she was eager to support the team herself.

But she was also very adamant about her classroom. That was the point, you see. The schoolwork came first.[92]

What shines out most brightly from this lovely story is Pound's attitude. Few people loved sports more, and no doubt she was a fervent cheerer when the Nebraska squad took the field in Pasadena. (Stanford won, however, 21–13; it was the first time, said Dosek, Nebraska had seen a T-formation attack.) But teaching was for Pound a true vocation, a calling. What she had believed in the 1890s, telling Alvin Johnson that scholarship was a "mission," she believed just as deeply in the 1940s. Her classroom was to her a nearly sacrosanct place, her own little piece of the ancient and ongoing academy.

A second anecdote, this one from the mid-1950s, is even more wonderful. Paige Fox was a girl of ten or eleven when she was taken with her younger brother to tea at the Pound home. For her parents, Ralph and Barbara Fox, it was a job—they were freelance photographers, and Louise and Olivia wanted pictures made while Roscoe was in town on a visit. Barbara Fox remembered that Louise was so impressed by the good behavior of the children that "she gave them her skates and golf clubs." The skates needed new straps, but Pound "told her she could get them at a harness shop across from the Rock Island train station. Of course that harness shop was long gone at the time, but my daughter still has the skates and the golf clubs."[93] This is a fine story in itself, but the mother's recollection is just the beginning. For Paige herself the encounter with Pound was a thrilling event, and her memories of it were vivid a half century later.

They open with Roscoe. He wore a tweed suit with a vest and "looked like Theodore Roosevelt." At one point he told a joke—"I thought I was supposed to follow it because he was looking at me. But the punch line was in Latin!" At this point, perhaps noticing that the young girl looked "desperate," Louise took her aside and saved the day:

> She told me that when she was a girl there was a neighbor boy who would come over after dinner sometimes and call through the screen door asking if Louise could come play ball. She was a wonderful storyteller, really vivid, down to the detail of how the boy's nose would press against the screen, and how pleased she was that she was a good player and this boy wanted her on his team.
>   I told her, I remember just what I said, "I love to feel the bat crack when it hits the ball." Then we talked about skating, and I told her there was some really smooth sidewalk on 16th Street by the Safeway store. She told me that Lake Street used to have five lakes. We commiserated about how unfortunate it is to misplace your skate key and have your knees scabbed over all the time.
>   It was the most wonderful thing you could imagine. She was eighty then, wasn't she? But she was so innocent! She just became a young girl again. Louise and I had sneaked out to play! We came back laughing—I don't think Olivia and Roscoe even noticed. Then Louise got excited and started running up and down stairs gathering up her sports equipment to give me—I went home loaded down with golf clubs, roller skates, and ice skates. She gave me her tennis racquet too. I still have it all. It thrilled me more than I can tell you, this great woman accepting me as a soul of equal worth. I think the skate key is beautiful; I cherish it as a kind of amulet or charm. Like she's still watching over me, still encouraging.[94]

If Ed Dosek's memory captures Pound's veneration for education itself and for the academy as education's institutional center, Paige Fox Namuth's wonderful story is no less perfect for its portrayal of Pound's astonishing ability to meet other people on their own ground, to identify (and identify with) their needs and goals, and to devote herself with prodigious energy to assisting in their realization. The image of the eighty-something Pound hustling up and down stairs gathering up sports equipment for yet another young protégé is unsurpassable for its vivid embodiment of this greatest and rarest of her many gifts.

A third anecdote, from roughly the same time period, demonstrates this same capacity directed to an older beneficiary, and exhibits at the same time a considerable dramatic flair. Michael Shugrue was a senior in 1956 when he was taken to meet the Pound sisters in their home by Dean of Men Frank Hallgren. "They were both very kindly," he recalled. "They served tea. . . . They were both remarkably acute; Louise in particular was full of questions about my own future plans." After that first meeting Shugrue "saw her pretty regularly—I would stop over, do some shopping for them. I enjoyed it very much—the tea and the company." It was on the first visit, however, that Pound showed her flair for the memorable moment:

> At some point, I think it was after we'd had tea, Louise took me on a tour of the house. Dean Hallgren may have stayed behind with Olivia, I'm not sure. But as we started along a hallway she told me she had something she wanted to read. She said it was from Willa Cather; I think it was *The Professor's House*, but I'm not certain. But as we walked and I listened to her it dawned on me that the passage she was reading was a description of that very house, that very hallway. It was quite an experience for an undergraduate literature student. I was very impressed.[95]

Even as Pound was scolding Ed Dosek, rescuing Paige Fox from her brother's Latinizing, and providing literary tours to Michael Shugrue, honors for her own work continued to pile up. In November 1947 she received the Kiwanis Medal for Distinguished Service in a full-dress ceremony in Lincoln. There was music from the Ethel Owens Trio, solos by Mr. Dale B. Ganz, a printed program with a laudatory essay by Effie Leese Scott reaching back to Pound's Quaker martyr ancestors, a "Tribute" by Dr. Lane W. Lancaster, and "Acceptance and Response" remarks by Pound herself. Two students were cited in Scott's essay. One, described as "advanced," provided a full tribute: "She is so fertile of suggestion of thesis and other subjects that fit the applicant and so ready to suggest a mode of treatment and to watch the accuracy of details that I do not see how her place can be filled." The second is in briefer agreement: "If any able student desired a coveted goal he could count on her support a hundred per cent. She was never known to let a student down."[96]

Here for once Pound was not the "first woman"—at least three had preceded her, including writer Bess Streeter Aldrich—but she joined a distinguished company that included General John J. Pershing and her old editorial antagonist from thirty years before, Addison E. Sheldon. Her wide-ranging accomplishments were summed up in the program under no fewer than six headings—Scholar, Author, Editor, Folklorist, Teacher, Sportswoman—and the whole affair was given extensive coverage in the local press.

Eight years later, in 1955, the "Sportswoman" in Pound came in for special recognition, as she was voted into the Nebraska Sports Hall of Fame at the age of eighty-two. This time she was back in the familiar "first woman" slot—she was the fourteenth honoree, joining thirteen men, including baseball Hall of Famer Grover Cleveland Alexander. The octogenarian Pound was in fine form for yet another round of newspaper stories—she had seen "all the Husker football games for over 30 years," she said, and noted that golf as played in the 1950s "seems to be getting sissier. I see them riding around the course in electric carts now."[97]

Almost simultaneously with the Hall of Fame induction came the news that the Modern Language Association, Percy Long's opposition now removed by his death in 1952, had installed Pound as its first woman president (she was also offered the presidency of the American Name Society in 1956, but turned it down "with regret").[98] Pound covered both events in a single letter to Botkin, noting inaccuracies in the local notices and appearing to take more pleasure in the sports honor than in the scholarly one: "Now comes unexpected election to the Nebraska Sports Hall of Fame. Here I am alongside a celebrated baseball pitcher, a wrestler, two runners, football players, etc., with a real fanfare—and some inaccuracies of course. First woman again—Life has its humors."[99]

But of course this is misleading—the MLA presidency was the crowning honor of Pound's academic career, and she was thrilled with it. An additional first was connected with the presidency beyond the "first woman" title: a "Resolutions Committee" headed by Benjamin Boyce (a Duke professor with Nebraska connections) produced a laudatory statement of congratulation, noting as it did so that no such resolutions had accompanied prior presidents into office. Pound, the statement said, by her "messages of learning," had for many years astonished "a nation of scholars unused to the company of ladies who knew quite as much as they did." Not only her learning but also "her shrewd judgment" had long been recognized "from coast to coast and beyond the seas." Those fortunate enough to know her had "discovered with pleasure that a scholar may be, in addition, a social creature, a wit, and, *mirabile dictum*, a champion in athletic sports." If the MLA, it concluded, had "tarried overlong in electing a woman to highest office," it had distinguished itself in its first choice. This encomium, the "Business Report" noted, was approved "by a standing spontaneous vote."[100]

Pound attended the annual meeting in Chicago in December 1955 to deliver her presidential address in person, opening in her best "Mrs. Throttlebottom" manner with a funny story with herself as the butt of the joke: once, addressing another "learned society," she had noticed "an upright gadget" at the podium and had "with extreme care" spoken directly into it for thirty minutes, "only to find as I went down from the platform that it was a *lamp*."[101] There was a good bit of humor in the body of the address as well, as Pound remembered her days as a graduate student in Germany. Her old mentor Hoops is praised again as "the most helpful of men," in contrast to the situation at Zurich, where Martha Carey Thomas was required "to listen to the professors from behind a curtain," or at Leipzig, where Pound's letter inquiring about admission as a doctoral student elicited a brief "'Nein, *nein*, NEIN!!!' with exclamation points."[102] But her closing paragraph is wholly serious, a ringing affirmation of the credos she had served from her undergraduate days: "I have faith that in a civilized society there will always be some such organization for the promotion of investigation, discussion, and comradely intercourse as our venerable and cherished MLA, with its gatherings at which scholars of distinction may be seen and heard, ideas exchanged, new ones gained, others qualified or discarded, and at which old friendships may be renewed and new ones formed."[103]

Pound's pleasure is evident in a December 1955 letter to Botkin, announcing the frustration of her plans for a grand "finale." The dates conflict, she says, and she will be unable to make the American Folklore Society meeting, but would have made "a good finale to appear on the programs of the 3 societies of which I have been president."[104] If the MLA presidency was a pinnacle honor on the national level, Pound's friends in Lincoln offered up an analogous distinction in 1957, when members of the Wooden Spoon club entertained Louise and Olivia with a series of skits, "These Are Your Spoons," based on events in their own lives and their family history. Dolls named Hallelujah and Hosannah represented Quaker ancestors, while club members acted other parts. A newspaper photograph captioned "A Tale of Two Sisters" shows the seated Louise and Olivia surrounded by the two dolls and costumed participants. Elsie Cather, for example, who is also credited with writing the skits, appears as a bearded male school board member, while Emily Schossberger is costumed as the chancellor of Heidelberg University.[105]

In May 1956, writing to Botkin again, Pound announced an end. She had started in Lincoln, and she would end by circling back after wide traveling from coast to coast and across the Atlantic. She had taken her first steps toward a rewarding life in the academy at Laura Pound's blackboard at 1532 P Street; now, eighty years later, she would return, devote herself again to the family home: "With my presidential effort out and 'More Plural Singulars' in the last issue of *Am. Speech*, and 'Yet Another Joe Bowers' to appear in a coming issue of the *Western Folklore Quarterly* I think I'll stop writing pieces. 1632 L Street needs enough care to keep me busy."[106]

And then, two years later, it was over. At last, as it must even with fortune's most favored, most energetic and strong-willed, the mortal adventure closed. Louise Pound's long life of service and accomplishment ended in a Lincoln hospital on June 28, 1958. The middle child, she was the first of the long-lived siblings to go. (Olivia outlived her sister by almost three years. Roscoe lived the longest, dying in 1964 at ninety-three.) The cause of death was listed as "coronary thrombosis." Louise was not blessed with her father's or her mother's sudden death; she had been in the hospital for three weeks. Local obituaries were fulsome in their praise, though they said nothing that Mencken and Dorothy Canfield Fisher had not already said better (both were quoted), or that Ed Dosek, Frank Hallgren, Paige Fox Namuth, and Michael Shugrue would not improve upon later. "Dr. Louise Pound, Famed NU Educator, Dies at 85" was the *Lincoln Evening Journal*'s front-page headline, over a photograph captioned with a single word, "versatile" (which does seem an inspired, if obvious, choice). The student tributes from the 1947 Kiwanis Medal program were reprinted in full.[107]

The *New York Times* notice, appearing the following day, was briefer and more general, but it managed in its subhead to appoint Pound, as her colleagues and superiors never did, as "Head of the English Department at Nebraska."[108] A memorial service was held on July 2 at which Dr. Edgar Z. Palmer of the Lincoln Religious Society of Friends.[109] Additional memorial notices appeared in *Western Folklore* (in a "Louise Pound Memorial Number" with a tribute written by Botkin), the *Southern Folklore Quarterly* (by Meredith), the *Publications of the American Dialect Society* (by Norman Eliason, Kemp Malone, Allen Walker Read, George P. Wilson, and Meredith), and *Names* (by Malone, Elsdon C. Smith, and Meredith).[110] Meredith, perhaps incompletely familiar with Pound's decades-long trouncing of Gerould, went so far as to call her a "magnanimous victor" in the "ballad war" controversies.[111]

Other notices have appeared in the half century since her death. These range from brief biographical sketches, to conference papers and article-length studies, to a full-length biographical treatment. The biographical sketches include C. Merton Babcock's for *Word Study* in 1962, as part of a "Profiles of Noted Linguists" series; Evelyn Haller's for *Notable American Women, the Modern Period: A Biographical Dictionary* in 1980; Donald R. Hickey's for *Nebraska Moments: Glimpses of Nebraska's Past* in 1992; Elizabeth A. Turner's for *Legacy* in 1992; and Robert Cochran's for *American National Biography* in 1999.[112] Haller's profile includes an especially nice anecdote exhibiting Pound at her best, combining a willingness to be "difficult" in service to a worthwhile cause with her no less characteristic sense of humor. Once in the 1920s, Haller writes, "Pound set up a desk in a hallway outside her classroom to protest her assignment to an office irrationally distant from the site of her teaching."[113]

Two more analytic articles are Evelyn Haller's 1983 conference paper, "Louise Pound and the Taxonomic Rage for Order," and Anne M. Cognard's "Louise Pound: Renaissance Woman," published in 1984. The book-length biography is Marie Krohn's *Louise Pound: The 19th Century Iconoclast Who Forever Changed America's Views about Women, Academics and Sports*. Cognard's primary interest is Pound's writing style—she examines under separate headings the "Diction," the "Structure," and the "Audience Adaptation" of Pound's essays before closing with a description of their "Ethos."[114] Haller's presentation is more sweeping—there is a good bit of biography and a sharply phrased, on-the-money description of Pound's often frustrating attempts to promote the work and careers of her best female students. But her primary focus is on the sources of Pound's habits of thought, of the gift for precise, careful description and enumeration so prominent across the whole range of her work, from her collecting and classifying traditional music to her assembling of Nebraska word lists and slang usages. Haller's argument—that "exposure to botany under Charles Edwin Bessey influenced the course of her work and language and literature"—is wholly persuasive, though surely Laura Pound's enthusiasm for botany and Lucius Sherman's dedication to careful sentence analysis also played important roles.[115]

Krohn's study, first inspired by a family connection, is based on extensive research in Pound's papers; its strengths include a sustained tracing of parallels in the careers of the three Pound siblings. Krohn also provides the first detailed account of Pound's friendship of almost sixty years with Ani Königsberger, plus a careful reading of Pound's will that shows her, even as she contemplates her own end, reaching out to assist her oldest and dearest friends. (Mamie Meredith, Marguerite McPhee—she of the roller-skating/cake-baking contract—and Elsie Cather were named as beneficiaries in the event that Olivia did not outlive her.)[116]

The students cited in the Kiwanis award were right, of course. Pound could not be replaced. But she had done her work diligently and well, and it would last. Hers had been a long life, filled with solid accomplishments and conspicuous service that had been recognized and honored at home and abroad. Little had been left undone. Soon there would be a Pound Hall on the University of Nebraska campus and a Pound Middle School across town. More importantly, her books were on the shelves, her contribution of "one cubic centimeter" secure. Her students had written and were writing their books, and their students would soon enough be adding their own in turn. Generations of women had been sheltered, fed, and encouraged as scholars and writers in the home of Laura Biddlecome Pound and her two daughters. The academy they loved and regarded as their own had been nurtured, and would continue to flourish, continue to enrich the lives of young Nebraskans and send them in turn to enrich the wider world, just as it had sent the Pounds before, in the company of Derrick Lehmer, Alvin Johnson, Dorothy Canfield Fisher, Willa Cather, and the rest of their astonishing generation.

In the largest ideological sense, the whole effort of the Pound family, the ethos they served from the day they crossed the Missouri, might best be understood as a late and more western salient of that "cultural colonization of the Middle West" celebrated in Marilynne Robinson's remarkable essay, "McGuffey and the Abolitionists."[117] Robinson's interest focuses on anti-slavery activists, and certainly at both Laura Biddlecome's Lombard College and Hugh Pound's New York farm there are direct ties to this cause. But her abolitionists are in general a deeply religious folk, with a highly developed sense of a social gospel. They include Congregationalists and Presbyterians and Quakers; they come westward mostly "from New England and New York"; in their passionate devotion to education they found "schools and colleges throughout the Middle West which have greatly affected the cultural development of the region"; and in these "little intellectual communities" they "put into practice their belief in educating women." This same cohort also championed the "universalization of literacy," the "normalization of democratic attitudes and manners," and "the creation of a public school system." They fueled, Robinson concludes, "the greatest period of reform in American history."[118] Stephen Pound and Laura Biddlecome, raised in this tradition, moved its tenets west to Nebraska and raised their children to serve those values. And when Louise Pound in her turn inserts a peppery celebration of the *"consensus gentium"* into a 1924 article, or grows downright waspish on behalf of "Victorian" values in 1942, it is really this credo she is defending, despite the different labels.

Louise Pound is buried in Lincoln's Wyuka Cemetery, established in 1869 as the Nebraska State Cemetery by the same legislative session that created the University of Nebraska. The word "Wyuka" is said (by the cemetery's self-guided tour booklet) to derive from Lakota, and to suggest "rest" or "lying down." It seems an appropriate name—Wyuka is large enough to manage stillness and quiet even today, a haven from the bustle of the surrounding capital city. And Louise Pound is not alone—more than fifty thousand Nebraskans, rich and poor, famous and infamous and unknown, share Wyuka's two hundred acres. The self-guided tour points out the marker of actor and singer Gordon MacRae, but it omits mention of Charles R.

Starkweather, Nebraska's most notorious killer, executed almost exactly one year after Pound's death. He now lies close by, fewer than one hundred yards from Pound's own marker. It is too close for comfort, another deplorable instance of contemporary laxity in such matters, and surely Pound would object if she could to this ongoing apotheosis of the common, yet another impudent Gypsy child on the tennis courts.

But here too, despite the "mud-flats outside," the immediate surroundings are another reassuring "Boston within." Pound is in good company, almost as if the family who lived so many years together at 1632 L Street had simply moved a few blocks and settled down for an even longer stay. Not far away is Mamie Meredith, most loyal of friends, close by even at the last. Closer still, side by side but with separate markers laid flat to the ground, embraced by earth, are Laura and Stephen Pound, loving and encouraging parents, who nearly a century earlier bravely crossed the dangerous ice of the Missouri to make their lives and build a larger world for their splendid, gifted children.

Closest of all, in death as in life, is Olivia Pound, who survived long enough to see to the disposition of her sister's papers, but had to endure, as Louise did not, a final family departure from the cherished home at 1632 L Street. The two sisters share a single flat stone, engraved only with their first and last names, their birth and death years. No granite obelisk stabs the sky, impotently assertive. No middle names, no months or days. A larger stone, also flat, etched only with the family surname in larger letters, lies just to the left. It is all very simple, very plain. Right here, they seem to say. This is sufficient, this quiet bit of Great Plains ground, an inch of which as a young woman Louise Pound prized above all Heidelberg. Like her intrepid mother and dignified father before her, she was always satisfied with Nebraska.

Notes

Abbreviations

ASC-LL Archives and Special Collections, Love Library, University of Nebraska–Lincoln Libraries
LBP   Laura Biddlecome Pound
LP   Louise Pound
NSHS   Nebraska State Historical Society, Lincoln
OP   Olivia Pound
RP   Roscoe Pound

1. "I have always been satisfied with Nebraska"

1. LBP, "Wedding Trip in February 1869," *Lincoln Sunday State Journal*, April 15, 1925, subgroup 1, series 4, subseries 2, folder 1, LBP Papers (RG0910), NSHS.
2. "Who's Who in Lincoln," *Nebraska State Journal*, February 5, 1922, subgroup 1, series 6, box 1, folder 1, LBP Papers, NSHS.
3. LBP, "Wedding Trip."
4. LBP, "Wedding Trip."
5. Paul Sayre, *The Life of Roscoe Pound* (Iowa City: College of Law Committee, State University of Iowa, 1948), 21.

6. Sayre, *Life of Roscoe Pound*, 18.
7. Some biographical sketches claim that Stephen Pound was valedictorian of his class at Union College, but a check of the school's records indicated only graduation with honors. Marlaine DesChamps, e-mail to Robert Cochran, July 27, 2007. I am grateful to Marlaine DesChamps, Archives Specialist at Union College's Shaffer Library, for her assistance.
8. "Some Reminiscences," *Nebraska State Journal*, May 15, 1911, reprint of May 16, 1909, article in the same source, "When S. B. Pound Came to Lincoln," subgroup 2, series 6, box 1, folder 1, LBP Papers, NSHS.
9. Neale Copple, *Tower on the Plains: Lincoln's Centennial History, 1859–1959* (Lincoln: Lincoln Sunday Journal and Star, 1959), 33.
10. Copple, *Tower on the Plains*, 36.
11. Copple, *Tower on the Plains*, 36.
12. Rex R. Schultze, "Judge Stephen B. Pound: First President of the Lancaster County Bar Association," *Lincoln Bar Association Newsletter* 1 (December 1993): 2.
13. OP, "Stephen B. Pound," 3. This eight-page account was written at the request of Paul Sayre, who had undertaken a biography of Roscoe Pound. Subgroup 2, series 1, box 1, folder 1, LBP Papers, NSHS.
14. OP, "Stephen B. Pound," 5.
15. LP, "Wedding Trip," n.p.
16. Copple, *Tower on the Plains*, 41.
17. Copple, *Tower on the Plains*, 60.
18. James C. Olson and Ronald C. Naugle, *History of Nebraska*, 3rd ed. (Lincoln: University of Nebraska Press, 1997), 180.
19. LBP to "Esther," September 15, 1869, subgroup 1, series 3, box 1, folder 2, LBP Papers, NSHS.
20. Mrs. S. B. Pound, "The Lincoln Public Library, 1875–1892," *Transactions and Reports of the Nebraska State Historical Society*, no. 5 (Lincoln: Lincoln Printing Co., 1893), 20, 21.
21. McWatters is named as the leader of the prison uprising in Copple, *Tower on the Plains*, 58.
22. Olson and Naugle, *History of Nebraska*, 177.
23. Mrs. S. B. Pound, "The Lincoln Public Library," 23, 22, 23.
24. Mrs. S. B. Pound, "The Lincoln Public Library," 24, 27, 23.
25. "Some Reminiscences."

26. LBP, "Wedding Trip."
27. Evelyn H. Haller, "Louise Pound," in *Notable American Women: The Modern Period: A Biographical Dictionary*, ed. Barbara Sicherman and Carol Hurd Green (Cambridge: Harvard University Press, 1980), 557.
28. "Who's Who in Lincoln."
29. "Who's Who in Lincoln."
30. "Who's Who in Lincoln."
31. LP to "Dear cousin," August 20, 1881, box 4, file 1, LP Papers RG0912), NSHS.
32. Sayre, *Life of Roscoe Pound*, 38.
33. NEGen Web Project (Lancaster County), Lincoln Women's Club, pp. 2, 3, http://www.rootsweb.com/~nelancas/lwclub/1.htm.
34. LBP, "Wedding Trip."
35. David Wigdor, *Roscoe Pound: Philosopher of Law* (Westport CT: Greenwood Press, 1974), 17.
36. Wigdor, *Roscoe Pound*, 13.
37. Wigdor, *Roscoe Pound*, 14.
38. Robert N. Manley, *Centennial History of the University of Nebraska* (Lincoln: University of Nebraska Press, 1969), 238.
39. Bernice Slote, ed., *The Kingdom of Art: Willa Cather's First Principles and Critical Statements, 1893–1896* (Lincoln: University of Nebraska Press, 1966), 6–7.
40. Haller, "Louise Pound," 557. Haller does not specify the source of this passage. She also includes it in "Louise Pound and the Taxonomic Rage to Order," a paper read at the 1983 Modern Language Association meeting in New York, where she attributes it to Slote's *Kingdom of Art*, 6–7. And that's the problem—the phrasing does not appear there, though the subject does.
41. Robert E. Knoll, *Prairie University: A History of the University of Nebraska* (Lincoln: University of Nebraska Press, 1995), 1, 4.
42. The fullest treatment of the "O.K." debate is the second section (titled "O.K.") of Allen Walker Read, *Milestones in the History of English*, Publications of the American Dialect Society 86 (Durham NC: Duke University Press, 2002), 121–247. Pound discussed "O.K." in two places, suggesting the Greek derivation in "Some Folk-Locutions," published in *American Speech* in 1942, and conceding Read's derivation from an American usage in her PMLA presidential address, published

as "Then and Now" in 1956 (*PMLA* 71 [1956]: 3–13; the reference to "O.K." is on p. 9).
43. RP, "My Sister Louise," *Boston Sunday Globe*, June 30, 1957, 55.
44. "Who's Who in Lincoln."
45. Wigdor, *Roscoe Pound*, 14.
46. OP, "Reading," p. 1, unpublished MS, box 433, Benjamin A. Botkin Collection (MS 66), ASC-LL.
47. OP, "A Day in the Pound Family," p. 5, unpublished MS, box 433, Botkin Collection, ASC-LL.
48. Wigdor, *Roscoe Pound*, 14.
49. "Who's Who in Lincoln."
50. "Who's Who in Lincoln."
51. "Who's Who in Lincoln."
52. "View of Judge S. B. Pound," in *Proceedings and Collections of the Nebraska State Historical Society*, 2nd ser., 2 (Lincoln: State Journal Company, 1898), 154, 155.
53. "View of Judge Pound," 156.
54. "View of Judge Pound," 156, 157.
55. "View of Judge Pound," 157.
56. OP, "A Day in the Pound Family," 2–3.
57. OP, "A Day in the Pound Family," 3.
58. OP, "A Day in the Pound Family," 4.
59. E. S. Sutton, "The Trial and Death of William (Hank) Dodge," *Nebraska History* 63 (1982): 425. Sutton is quoting the *Nebraska City News* of April 9, 1876. In a later passage Sutton describes Judge Pound's sentencing remarks as "lachrymose" (432).
60. OP, "Stephen B. Pound," 7.
61. Wigdor, *Roscoe Pound*, 13.
62. Mrs. Laura B. Pound, "Marking the Site of the Lewis and Clark Council at Fort Calhoun," *Nebraska Pioneer Reminiscences* (Cedar Rapids IA: Torch Press, 1916), 188.
63. LP, "The Ancestry of a 'Negro Spiritual,'" *Modern Language Notes* 33 (1918): 443.
64. OP, "Home Life of the Pound Family," second page of four-page typescript, series 4, box 5, folder 5, RP Papers (RG0911), NSHS.
65. Wigdor, *Roscoe Pound*, 15.

66. RP, "My Sister Louise," 55.
67. OP, "Stephen B. Pound," 8.
68. Nellie Snyder Yost, "Nebraska's Scholarly Athlete: Louise Pound, 1872–1958," *Nebraska History* 64 (1983): 478.

2. "The iridescent glamor of life beginning"

1. LP, "The Class of 1892 . . . Fifty Years After," *Nebraska Alumnus*, May 1942, 4.
2. Louise Pound's papers at NSHS include a memorandum dated March 26, 1895, specifying "Miss Pound's grades for the work which she did with Professor Bennett." Pound apparently collected a number of such transcripts and commendatory letters in preparation for her post-MA studies at the University of Chicago. Box 4, folder 1, LP Papers, NSHS.
3. Edward L. Nichols, "The Scientific Work of Dewitt Bristol Brace," *Physical Review*, 1st ser., 24 (1907): 517, 520. For a more thorough treatment of Brace see David Cahan and M. Eugene Rudd, *Science at the American Frontier: A Biography of DeWitt Bristol Brace* (Lincoln: University of Nebraska Press, 2000). For an extended discussion of physics and astronomy at the University of Nebraska see M. Eugene Rudd, *Science on the Great Plains: A History of Physics and Astronomy at the University of Nebraska–Lincoln*, University of Nebraska Studies, n.s., 71 (Lincoln: University of Nebraska, 1992).
4. For thorough treatments of Bessey and his influence see Ronald C. Tobey's *Saving the Prairies: The Life Cycle of the Founding School of American Plant Ecology* (Berkeley: University of California Press, 1981) and Richard A. Overfield's *Science with Practice: Charles E. Bessey and the Maturing of American Botany* (Ames: Iowa State University Press, 1993).
5. Louise Pound's academic records are preserved in the Archives Special Collections, Love Library, University of Nebraska–Lincoln. For her assistance in retrieving and copying these materials on July 11, 2005, I am grateful to Mary Ellen Ducey.
6. Robert E. Knoll, *Prairie University: A History of the University of Nebraska* (Lincoln: University of Nebraska Press, 1995), 27. Knoll's study is a constant presence in this chapter—I learned about the University of Nebraska and Louise Pound's place in it from other sources as well, but in most instances I was directed to them by Knoll.

7. Knoll, *Prairie University*, 19.
8. Knoll, *Prairie University*, 19, 20.
9. Knoll, *Prairie University*, 22.
10. Robert N. Manley, *Centennial History of the University of Nebraska* (Lincoln: University of Nebraska Press, 1969), 113.
11. Manley, *Centennial History*, 114.
12. Knoll, *Prairie University*, 28.
13. Manley, *Centennial History*, 116. My source for Canfield's course on women is Knoll, *Prairie University*, 28.
14. Knoll, *Prairie University*, 29.
15. Willa Cather, *My Ántonia*, quoted in Knoll, *Prairie University*, 27.
16. Will Owen Jones, quoted in LP, ed., *Semi-Centennial Anniversary Book: The University of Nebraska, 1869–1919* (Lincoln: University of Nebraska, 1919), 46.
17. James A. Canfield and Dorothy Canfield Fisher, "He Saw the Golden Door," *Nebraska Alumnus*, February 1938, 22, quoted in Knoll, *Prairie University*, 27.
18. John D. Hicks, *My Life with History* (Lincoln: University of Nebraska Press, 1968), 139, 131.
19. LP, "The Class of 1892," 4–5.
20. LP, "The Class of 1892," 4. The 1893 date for Edgren's elevation to dean is incorrect; he was the founding dean, but the graduate school was established in 1896. Pound's tone seems wholly straightforward here—her admiration for Edgren is surely genuine—but as a fervent admirer of German culture she was surely aware of the double valence of "Magnificus." This is more than the inherent fatuity of all inflated honorifics, from the Illustrious Grand Potentates of the Shriners, riding tiny motorbikes in red fezzes, to the Imperial Wizards of the semiliterate Klans. "Magnificus" has a long European history. After Faust's inevitable fall, to deploy perhaps the most widely known instance, his former assistant, the obsequious, ambitious Wagner, assuming his mantle, is himself hailed as "Magnificus." Martin Heidegger, coolly betraying his teacher Husserl, is the Nazi-era "Magnificus" at Freiburg. Looking for discussions to substantiate my imprecise sense of the term's ironic dimension, I was helped most by George Steiner's *Lessons of the Master* (Cambridge: Harvard University Press, 2003), especially chapter 3, "Magnificus." In short, though she must

have known the term's ambivalence, Pound appears here to use it entirely as a term of praise and respect.
21. Robert E. Knoll, "The Founders of the Graduate College," in *A Century of Achievement: One Hundred Years of Graduate Education, Research, and Creative Activity at the University of Nebraska*, ed. David Ochsner (Lincoln: University of Nebraska, 2001), 37.
22. A. H. Edgren, April 3, 1895, in box 4, folder 1, LP Papers, NSHS.
23. Annie Prey, "Herbert Bates," *Hesperian*, December 24, 1896, 9.
24. LP, *Semi-Centennial Anniversary Book*, 7–8.
25. Herbert Bates, "The Spirit of the Western University," *Outlook*, February 27, 1897, 604.
26. Bates, "Spirit of the Western University," 605, 606.
27. Alvin Johnson, *Pioneer's Progress: An Autobiography* (New York: Viking, 1952), 92.
28. Johnson, *Pioneer's Progress*, 96.
29. The 1895 *Sombrero* includes her as one of twenty-two assistants in various departments (16); the 1898 number lists "Louise Pound, A.M." as "First Assistant in English Literature" (65); the 1899 edition has her as "Assistant Instructor" (20). Issues of *Sombrero* at located at ASC-LL.
30. L. A. Sherman to F. A. Blackburn, June 26, 1897, in box 4, folder 1, LP Papers, NSHS.
31. Knoll, *Prairie University*, 32, 33.
32. L. A. [Lucius Adelno] Sherman, *Analytics of Literature* (Boston: Ginn, 1893), 13–14, 371, 257–59, 425.
33. *University of Nebraska Catalog, 1888–1889*, 26; *University of Nebraska Catalog, 1889–90*, 13, 26; *University of Nebraska Catalog, 1890–91*, 13, 32; *University of Nebraska Catalog, 1891–92*, 17.
34. LP, "Penthesilea Rediviva," *Sombrero* (1895), 54.
35. LP, "Penthesilea Rediviva," 54, 55.
36. LP, "Penthesilea Rediviva," 55.
37. LP, "Penthesilea Rediviva," 56.
38. LP, "Penthesilea Rediviva," 54.
39. LP, "Organizations," in LP, *Semi-Centennial Anniversary Book*, 59.
40. LP, "Organizations," 59, 60.
41. LP, "Organizations," 60.
42. LP, "Organizations," 62.
43. LP, "The Class of 1892," 5.

44. LP, "The Class of 1892," 5.
45. David Wigdor, *Roscoe Pound: Philosopher of Law* (Westport CT: Greenwood Press, 1974), 16.
46. OP, "Home Life of the Pound Family," [3–4], series 4, box 5, folder 5, RP Papers, NSHS. Derrick Norman Lehmer (1867–1938) was born in Indiana and graduated from the University of Nebraska in 1893. He was a professor of mathematics at the University of California, Berkeley.
47. LP, *Blends: Their Relation to English Word Formation*, Anglistische Forschungen 42 (Heidelberg: Universitäts-Verlags Carl Winter, 1914), 1.
48. Evelyn Simpson, "Louise Pound, Sports Champion . . . and Teacher," *Sunday Omaha World-Herald Magazine*, May 27, 1945, C4.
49. *Hesperian*, November 24, 1892, 20.
50. Yost, "Nebraska's Scholarly Athlete," 484.
51. *Nebraskan*, January 18, 1895, 3.
52. Nellie Snyder Yost, "Nebraska's Scholarly Athlete: Louise Pound, 1872–1958," *Nebraska History* 64 (1983): 486.
53. Simpson, "Louise Pound, Sports Champion," C4.
54. Simpson, "Louise Pound, Sports Champion," C4.
55. *Sombrero* (1892), 46.
56. "The Last Seniors," *Hesperian*, June 15, 1892, 15.
57. "Class Day Exercises," *Hesperian*, June 15, 1892, 12.
58. "University Commencement," *Daily Nebraska State Journal*, June 15, 1892, 1.
59. Matthew Arnold, "Milton," in R. H. Super, ed., *The Complete Prose Works of Matthew Arnold*, vol. 11, *The Last Word* (Ann Arbor: University of Michigan Press, 1977), 328. The eloquent prophet cited by Arnold has never been certainly identified.
60. Arnold, "Milton," 335, 329.
61. LP, "The Apotheosis of the Common," 1, typescript, in box 1, folder 3, LP Papers, NSHS.
62. LP, "Apotheosis of the Common," 1–2.
63. LP, "Apotheosis of the Common," 2, 3.
64. LP, "Apotheosis of the Common," 2, 5.
65. Forty-six years after the publication of Bennett's book, however, in 1997, Loretta Wasserman published Bennett's 1989 account of her 1957 luncheon with Louise and Olivia Pound. Pound had rebuffed

Bennett's earlier attempts to interview her about Cather and the Pounds—"I have done enough for Willa Cather!" she said in response to one telephone query, just before hanging up—but in 1957 she brought a clipping of Cather's column about Roscoe to the luncheon and read it aloud "with a voice trembling with emotion—probably rage." Bennett promptly assured Pound that her reaction to Cather's attack would have echoed Laura Pound's ("Never let that girl darken my door again!"), and the women "were then able to have an excellent conversation." That conversation eventually turned to "the rumor of Miss Cather's being lesbian." "But who was her partner?" asks Pound. Loretta Wassermann and Mildred R. Bennett, "Friends of Willa Cather," *Willa Cather Pioneer Memorial Newsletter* 41 (1997): 5, 6. All this of course proves nothing—Pound could have been disingenuous. But on the face of it she comes across as barely interested in Cather's sexual orientation; her focus, more than half a century after the event, centers still on the insult to her brother and her family.

66. Phyllis C. Robinson, *Willa: The Life of Willa Cather* (Garden City NY: Doubleday, 1983), 58, 59.

67. Sharon O'Brien, *Willa Cather: The Emerging Voice* (New York: Oxford University Press, 1987), 6. A much more extended discussion of the letters came a decade later, in Marilee Lindemann's *Willa Cather: Queering America* (New York: Columbia University Press, 1998). Lindemann's treatment is unusual in its recognition of Pound's work as significant in its own right, rather than understanding her as noteworthy only as the object of Cather's youthful infatuation. On the other hand, Lindemann's discussion of the Cather-to-Pound correspondence demolishes the line between quotation and paraphrase (her transcriptions of entire phrases are not quotations only if quotations are defined as requiring quotation marks). Like other discussions of Cather's overwrought letters (Robinson's excepted), Lindemann's is tendentious, given to overly specific conclusions and stressing passages open to reading from her perspective while omitting others more resistant or more open to alternative readings. To her credit, she is explicit about her own practice, as most others (on both sides) are not, describing her readings as deliberately and happily "perverse" (p. 30). Her conclusions are in general agreement with O'Brien's. Lindemann, even more than O'Brien, seems to take the restrictions of Cather's

will as a personal insult (which may explain her determination to evade them).
68. O'Brien, *Willa Cather*, 137, 209.
69. James Woodress, *Willa Cather: A Literary Life* (Lincoln: University of Nebraska Press, 1987), 85. The point to be stressed is not that either Woodress or O'Brien is correct but that both have their feet firmly planted in the air. It may also be worth noting in passing that Pound (like Cather, for that matter) was conspicuously silent about her sexuality, no doubt regarding it as a private matter. Scholars are adepts at seizing high moral ground in justification of their own interests and agendas—the publication of James Joyce's erotic letters to his wife also sparked widespread debate, with the family appalled and scholars eloquent in their professions of elevated motive. Archaeologists, for their part, now seem (however belatedly) to be at least in some instances ready to recognize some limit to their access to gravesites; it is to be hoped that their literary and cultural colleagues may eventually follow.
70. A trenchant review of these scholarly spats, itself often acerbic in tone and sweeping in its critique of feminist readings, among others (her opponents find it "vicious"), is Joan Acocella's *Willa Cather and the Politics of Criticism* (Lincoln: University of Nebraska Press, 2000), especially 49–60. More recent scholarship has attempted something of a rapprochement between the polemical extremes of the 1980s and 1990s. Janis P. Stout's *Willa Cather: The Writer and Her World* (Charlottesville: University Press of Virginia, 2000), for example, steers between O'Brien's "distorted or overstated judgments" (21) and Woodress's "dismissal of the subject" (55).
71. Woodress, *Willa Cather*, 118.
72. [Willa Cather], "Pastels in Prose," *Hesperian*, March 10, 1894, 4.
73. [Cather], "Pastels in Prose," 4, 5.
74. Joseph Epstein, "Willa Cather: Listing toward Lesbos," *New Criterion*, December 1983, 38. Epstein limits himself to the youthful Roscoe, but Dean Pound's generally positive *American National Biography* notice makes clear that his mature successor could also be a very nasty piece of work. In his own field of legal theory he reacted with hostility to those who developed his ideas into the school that became known as legal realism: "he opposed curricular innovations associated

with the realists, and he became a vocal and tireless critic of both the new politics and the new jurisprudence." Things were even worse in the arena of "practical political life," where in the 1930s Dean Pound "courted anti-Semitic Harvard alumni, made flattering comments about Adolf Hitler, and accepted an honorary degree from The University of Berlin." Richard Warner, "Roscoe Pound," in *American National Biography*, ed. John A. Garraty and Mark C. Carnes (New York: Oxford University Press, 1999), 18:763.

75. Robinson, *Willa*, 60.
76. Woodress, *Willa Cather*, 87.
77. Robinson, *Willa*, 60, 61.
78. Robinson, *Willa*, 61. Other writers have eschewed Robinson's caution. The most cursory inquiry directed to Louise Pound through internet search engines quickly turns up unqualified assertions of a lesbian relationship with Cather. Examples include the Wikipedia entry (http://en.wikipedia.org/wiki/Louise_Pound) and the Answers.com site, which boils it to a single sentence: "She was involved in a lesbian relationship with author Willa Cather" (http://www.answers.com/topic/louise-pound). For a much more impressive examination of the whole matter of "feminine friendship" see Sherrie A. Inness, "Mashes, Smashes, Crushes, and Raves: Woman-to-Woman Relationships in Popular Women's College Fiction, 1895–1915," NWSA *Journal* 6 (1994): 48–68. This piece addresses much more than fiction, and its careful delineation of "the 'right' crush" offers the most fitting description of the Pound/Cather friendship my own investigations encountered. According to Inness, "an acceptable crush socializes outsiders into the community. . . . [S]ome are acceptable, others are not, the most desirable involving a freshman (a student of low status) and a senior (a student of higher ranking)." In addition, the "desirable student is preferably an 'all-around girl,' someone who is actively involved in the student community and maintains a balance between academics and extracurricular activities" (56). Moreover, in the novels of the period the crush often helped the admirer become a more "normal girl": "the freshman goes from writing verse . . . to writing prose and finally, to playing basketball, a sport that invariably identifies the 'best' college girls" (61). Cather, of course, was already writing prose, and lots of it, though she never moved on to basketball, but it is clear that

Pound could have easily played the role of "most desirable" college crush without makeup. Mamie Meredith, in a 1958 letter to Mari Sandoz, uses the term "schoolgirl crush letter" to describe one of Cather's letters to Pound. Meredith to Mari Sandoz, September 9, 1958, box 28, Mari Sandoz Collection (MS 80), ASC-LL. Cather, for all her defiant eccentricity, chose her collegiate crush according to the most approved models. I am grateful to my colleague Susan Marren for directing me to Inness's study.

79. "The Last Seniors," 15.

3. "A genuine Nebraska cyclone"

1. Henry M. Belden, "Autobiographical Notes," in Allen Belden, *A Belden Lineage: 1066–1976* (Washington DC, 1976), 194.
2. *Hesperian*, September 27, 1893, 12.
3. The quotation from the 1895 *Sombrero* is on p. 16.
4. L. A. Sherman to F. A. Blackburn, June 26, 1897. Professor Sherman's note is preserved in box 4, folder 1, LP Papers, NSHS.
5. Evelyn Simpson, "Louise Pound, Sports Champion . . . and Teacher," *Sunday Omaha World-Herald Magazine*, May 27, 1945, C4.
6. LP, *Selected Writings of Louise Pound*, ed. Lowry C. Wimberly (Lincoln: University of Nebraska Press, 1949), 365.
7. *Nebraskan*, November 1892, 18, 24.
8. *Hesperian*, December 22, 1892, 17.
9. "University Dramatic Club: The Play 'A Perjured Padulion' Successfully Presented," *Nebraska State Journal*, December 11, 1892, 2.
10. The "Order of G.O.I." is mentioned in Manley's history of the University of Nebraska's early years, where it is said to date from the late 1880s (*Centennial History*, 241).
11. *Nebraskan*, January 1893, 50.
12. *Hesperian*, December 22, 1892, 7. The "Miss Pound" of this story may refer not to Louise but to Olivia, who was by this time an undergraduate student.
13. Manley, *Centennial History*, 94.
14. LP, "*The Romaunt of the Rose*: Additional Evidence That It Is Chaucer's," *Modern Language Notes* 11 (1896): 97. Pound goes on to note that Skeat, "following certain German scholars," has modified his position some-

what, allowing for the possibility that "a short portion at the beginning may have been and probably was Chaucer's" (97).
15. LP, "The Romaunt of the Rose," 97.
16. LP, "The Romaunt of the Rose," 97, 100.
17. LP, "The Romaunt of the Rose," 100, 101.
18. LP, "The Romaunt of the Rose," 101, 102.
19. LP, "The Romaunt of the Rose," 98.
20. Skeat's *The Chaucer Canon, with a Discussion of the Works Associated with the Name of Geoffrey Chaucer* was published in 1900. Four of its fourteen chapters (5–8) deal explicitly with *The Romaunt of the Rose* (one for each "fragment," and there is also an extended note to chapter 6), but neither Pound's article nor the whole matter of sentence length is discussed.
21. For Waddell's career generally and the reception of *The Wandering Scholars* in particular, see Monica Blackett, *The Mark of the Maker: A Portrait of Helen Waddell* (London: Constable, 1973), especially chapter 8. See Stephanie Trigg, *Congenial Souls: Reading Chaucer from Medieval to Post-modern* (Minneapolis: University of Minnesota Press, 2002), for discussion of studies analyzing "the cozy bonds that hold the masculinized imaginary community of readers together" (223). I am grateful to William Quinn for assistance with Pound's Chaucer study.
22. For example, the introduction to *The Romaunt of the Rose* in the *Riverside Chaucer*, 3rd ed. (Boston: Houghton Mifflin, 1987), concludes: "The 'B' Fragment of *The Romaunt of the Rose* is clearly not Chaucer's; neither are all scholars convinced that either the 'A' or the 'C' Fragments of *The Romaunt of the Rose* are authentic (though most believe that the 'A' Fragment is Chaucer's)" (xxxvi). A recent discussion of Skeat's methods and conclusions is Kathleen Forni's *The Chaucerian Apocrypha: A Counterfeit Canon* (Gainesville: University Press of Florida, 2001); Pound is unmentioned, and Chaucer's sentence length is not discussed.
23. Wigdor, *Roscoe Pound*, 126.
24. LP, "By Homeopathic Treatment," *Nebraska State Journal*, January 27, 1895, 3.
25. LP, "By Homeopathic Treatment," 3.
26. LP, "By Homeopathic Treatment," 3.

27. LP, "Miss Adelaide and Miss Amy," typescript in box 1, file 3, LP Papers, NSHS.
28. LP, "The Passenger from Metropolis," p. 4, typescript in box 1, folder 3, LP Papers, NSHS.
29. LP, "By Homeopathic Treatment," 3; LP, "The Passenger from Metropolis," 1. Descriptions of the constant wind and the juxtaposition of grandiose pretensions with actual ephemerality and insignificance of prairie and Great Plains villages are ubiquitous in such stories. Well-known instances would include the Fort Romper of Stephen Crane's "The Blue Hotel" (1899) and the unnamed village of Cather's "The Sculptor's Funeral" (1905). These could not have served as models or helped form Pound's sense of the "western story," but Hamlin Garland's "Up the Coulee," with its description of the "dull and sleepy and squalid" (55) Wisconsin town, appeared in 1891 as a part of *Main-Traveled Roads* (New York: New American Library, 1962).
30. "This Takes the Championship," *Nebraska State Journal*, April 22, 1894, clipping in box 1, folder 11, LP Papers, NSHS.
31. Maria E. Ward, *Bicycling for Ladies* (New York: Brentano's 1896), 12.
32. "Women, Bike, and History," internet article from Cycling Sisters, a Chicago-area women's cycling group, http://cyclingsisters.org/?q=node/29.
33. Lisa Larrabee, "Women and Cycling: The Early Years," in Frances E. Willard, *How I Learned to Ride the Bicycle* (Sunnyvale CA: Fair Oaks Publishing, 1991), 86, 89. This is a retitled reprint of Willard's 1895 hymn to the "saucy steed" (50), *A Wheel within a Wheel*.
34. The photograph is available online at http://www.newn.cam.ac.uk/about/about_history2.shtml.
35. *Hesperian*, November 24, 1892, 20.
36. Roger Welsch, introduction to LP, *Nebraska Folklore* (1959; Lincoln: University of Nebraska Press, 2006), x.
37. Yost, "Nebraska's Scholarly Athlete," 484.
38. These 1894 tennis tournaments are something of a mystery, with various accounts repeating each other with occasional variations. The earliest general account of Pound's athletic achievements appeared in the *Daily Nebraskan* in 1932 (Gretchen Schrag, "Miss Pound, English Professor, Reveals Tales of Times When She Had Tennis, Bicycle, Golf Titles," *Daily Nebraskan*, February 23, 1932, 1, 3). Next is a 1945 newspa-

per feature by Pound's former student Evelyn Simpson ("Louise Pound, Sports Champion"). Both of these pieces are interview based; neither mentions the 1894 tournaments. The earliest mention located is a newspaper account from 1955, which links Pound's tennis exploits at Nebraska with the 1894 tournaments: "Miss Pound was men's— that's correct—men's tennis champion of the University in 1891. She competed by invitation in many men's tournaments and was winner of second place in the men's intercollegiate tennis tournament in 1894, the same year that she won the intercollegiate doubles with Charles Foster Kent of Wayne County, New York" ("Dr. Louise Pound Named to Journal's Sports Hall of Fame," *Nebraska State Journal*, February 1, 1955, 11). The most plausible conjecture, then, might place the 1894 triumphs in a summer tournament (or tournaments) in New York. Supporting this is a 1932 biographical sketch listing Pound as "men's doubles champion Wayne County, N.Y., 1894, with Charles Foster Kent, of Yale" (*Nebraskana* [Hebron NE: Baldwin, 1932], 963. I located this book through the website of the NEGen Web Project Resource Center's On-Line Library—see http://www.rootsweb.com/%7Eneresour/OLLibrary/index.html).

39. LP, "Then and Now" (presidential address), PMLA 71 (1956): 3–13.
40. LP, University of Chicago Graduate School "Record of Work." I am grateful to the Registrar's Office at the University of Chicago for copying this document, and to Julia Gardner of the Special Collections Research Center, University of Chicago Library, for directing me there.
41. L. A. Sherman to F. A. Blackburn, June 26, 1897.
42. LP, "A List of Strong Verbs and Preterite Present Verbs in Anglo-Saxon" (Chicago: University of Chicago Press, 1898).
43. "West Beats the East," *Chicago Daily Tribune*, September 7, 1897, 5.
44. "West Beats the East," 5.
45. *Nebraska State Journal*, September 10, 1897, clipping in box 1, folder 11, LP Papers, NSHS.
46. Both telegrams are in box 4, folder 1, LP Papers, NSHS.
47. Hal Ryoner, "The New Lochinvar," *Hesperian*, September 17, 1897, 1.
48. *Leslie's Weekly*, October 7, 1897, clipping in box 1, folder 11, LP Papers, NSHS.
49. LP to her family, September [4–5], 1897, box 4, folder 1, LP Papers, NSHS.

50. LP to her family, September [4–5], 1897.
51. LP to her family, September [4–5], 1897.
52. LP to her family, September [4–5], 1897.
53. *Cap and Gown* (1898), 135, 132. I am grateful to Julia Gardner of the Special Collections Research Center, University of Chicago Library, for unstinting aid with queries related to Pound's summers in Chicago.
54. LP to her family, September [4–5], 1897.
55. LP to her family, September [4–5], 1897.
56. LP to her family, October 15, 1899, box 4, folder 1, LP Papers, NSHS.
57. Robert E. Knoll, interview with the author, Lincoln, Nebraska, July 14, 2004.
58. "Miss Pound Is Beaten," *Chicago Tribune*, September 8, 1898, 4.
59. Eleanora Tibbetts Miller, "History of Girls' Basket Ball in the University of Nebraska," in *Girls' Basket Ball in the University of Nebraska* (Lincoln: American School Supply Company, 1906), 9.
60. *Sombrero* (1900), 150.
61. Alice Towne, "Makers of Basket Ball in the University," in *Girls' Basket Ball in the University of Nebraska*, 27.
62. "Girls' Basket Ball Team," *Hesperian*, February 25, 1898, 7.
63. "Girls' Basket Ball Team," 7.
64. "University Girls Victorious," *Hesperian*, March 11, 1898, 7.
65. "University Girls Victorious," 7.
66. "Polly," "In Basket Ball, Athletic Young Women Indulge in a Rough Game, No Weaklings Are Allowed," *Chicago Times-Herald*, August 14, 1898.
67. "In Basket Ball."
68. "In Basket Ball."
69. The passport is preserved in box 1, folder 4, LP Papers, NSHS.
70. Simpson, "Louise Pound, Sports Champion," C4.
71. C. Merton Babcock, "Profiles of Noted Linguists: Louise Pound," *Word Study* 38 (1962): 2. Babcock's source for the "lest it distract the attention of the Herren" remark is Pound's essay/address "Then and Now," 3.
72. LP, *Selected Writings of Louise Pound*, v.
73. Johannes Hoops to LP, November 25, 1947, box 5, folder 16, LP Papers, NSHS.
74. LP to her family, September 26, 1899, box 4, folder 1, LP Papers, NSHS.

75. LP, *The Comparison of Adjectives in English in the XV and XVI Century*, Anglistische Forschungen 7 (Heidelberg: Carl Winter's Universitätsbuchhandlung, 1901), iii, iv, v.
76. LP, *The Comparison of Adjectives*, 1.
77. LP, *The Comparison of Adjectives*, 8–10.
78. LP, *The Comparison of Adjectives*, 13.
79. LP, *The Comparison of Adjectives*, 57.
80. LP, "The Romaunt of the Rose," 102; LP, *The Comparison of Adjectives*, 11.
81. LP, "The Romaunt of the Rose," 98.
82. LP to her family, October 15, 1899.
83. LP to her family, December 24, 1899, box 4, folder 1, LP Papers, NSHS.
84. LP to her family, February [day illegible], 1900, box 4, folder 1, LP Papers, NSHS.
85. LP to her family, March 1, [1900], box 4, folder 1, LP Papers, NSHS. Although this letter is dated March 1, 1899, I have concluded that the year should be 1900. Pound was not in Germany in March 1899, and strong internal evidence supports the year as 1900.
86. LP to her family, September [4–5], 1897.
87. LP to her family, October 15, 1899.
88. LP to her family, December 24, 1899.
89. LP to her family, December 24, 1899. The final term in Pound's "Herren Frei-Kür" phrasing proved puzzling to several native German speakers ("Kür" does not mean "choice" in any usage found in German dictionaries); the translation offered is therefore largely contextual.
90. LP to her family, February [day illegible], 1900.
91. Mellinger E. Henry to LP, January 17, 1900, box 4, folder 2, LP Papers, NSHS.
92. LP to her family, March 26, 1900, box 4, folder 1, LP Papers, NSHS. Everhard Harding, an American from Minnesota, was a chemistry student. For turning up this information, I am grateful to Heidelberg teacher Anna Klamer.
93. LP to her family, December 24, 1899.
94. Königsberger eventually married (in 1919) Max Pfister, a Heidelberg doctor. The couple moved to Shanghai in 1921 and was in China during World War II. After the war Pound was of great help to Ani Pfister, who returned to Europe (Switzerland) following the death of her

husband in November 1945. She was especially diligent in helping Pfister recover and sell some jewels that had been entrusted to an American serviceman in Asia. Pfister outlived her Nebraska friend—a letter of condolence she wrote to OP on July 20, 1958, is in box 6, file 8, LP Papers, NSHS. For digging up information about Königsberger, I am again grateful to Anna Klamer.

95. LP to her family, December 24, 1899.
96. LP to her family, December 24, 1899.
97. In her final (extant) letter from Germany, Pound guesses that her examinations will take place "in about three weeks" and gives her plans for return: "The very earliest steamship I can get is one from London on the Atlantic Transport Line, which sails September 6." LP to her family, July 6, [1900], box 4, folder 1, LP Papers, NSHS.

4. "She's an athlete; she's a scholar"

1. Roscoe married Grace Gerrard in Columbus, Nebraska (her hometown), on June 17, 1899. Their subsequent residence in the Pound home was announced in the *Nebraska State Journal* the following day: "They will be at home at 1632 L Street in this city after July 17." I am grateful to the Lincoln City Library for locating the announcement of Roscoe's marriage. Louise Pound and Grace Gerrard were friends—the *Hesperian* for February 25, 1898, carried the following notice: "Miss Louise Pound gave a skating party in honor of Miss Girrard [sic] '95. About seventy-five guests were present and spent a most enjoyable afternoon" (7).
2. Lynn C. Hattendorf Westney, "Louise Pound (1872–1958)," *Who Was Who in North American Name Study*, website of the American Name Society, http://www.wtsn.binghamton.edu/onoma/Default.htm.
3. Robert Knoll to Ronald R. Butters, June 7, 1983. I am grateful to Mr. Knoll for providing a copy of this letter.
4. James Reidel, *Vanished Act: The Life and Art of Weldon Kees* (Lincoln: University of Nebraska Press, 2003), 136.
5. Weldon Kees, "Every Summer They Came Out," *Selected Short Stories of Weldon Kees* (Lincoln: University of Nebraska Press, 2002), 165.
6. For more on Stepanek see Robert E. Knoll, *Prairie University: A History of the University of Nebraska* (Lincoln: University of Nebraska Press,

1995), 86; for Kees see Reidel, *Vanished Act*, 33–35, 107, 133–34, 186–87, 244–45. Stepanek was correct about the state capitol building's tower—his phrase "phallic symbol" would today seem almost prudishly understated. For the capital's tower is no mere obelisk, but a 400-foot domed spire topped by a 19½-foot bronze statue of "The Sower," a barefoot male figure scattering seed. Rigid vertical tower, seed coming from its tip—this is less symbol than straightforward depiction.

7. Joan Acocella, *Willa Cather and the Politics of Criticism* (Lincoln: University of Nebraska Press, 2000), 48.
8. LP, "The Class of 1892 . . . Fifty Years After," *Nebraska Alumnus*, May 1942, 5.
9. A reasonable observer might understand her hundred-mile bicycle rides as instances of spectacular sublimation. A slightly less reasonable observer might also see diverted libido in her devotion to tennis or basketball, or even in her ambitious studies. But I am not that observer.
10. LP to her family, October 15, 1899, box 4, folder 1, LP Papers, NSHS.
11. LP to her family, July 6, [1900], box 4, folder 1, LP Papers, NSHS.
12. Robert Knoll, telephone interview with the author, July 2, 2007.
13. Alvin Johnson, *Pioneer's Progress: An Autobiography* (New York: Viking, 1952), 96.
14. LP, "Notes on Tennyson's *Lancelot and Elaine*," *Modern Language Notes* 19 (1904): 50–51.
15. LP, "Tennyson's *Lancelot and Elaine*," 50.
16. LP, "Arnold's Sources for *Sahrab and Rustum*," *Modern Language Notes* 21 (1906): 16, 17.
17. LP, "Another Version of the Ballad of *Lord Randal*," *Modern Language Notes* 17 (1902): 6.
18. LP, *Poetic Origins and the Ballad* (New York: Macmillan, 1921), viii.
19. Henry Marvin Belden, "The Study of Folk-Song in America," *Modern Philology* 2 (1905): 573, 577.
20. Henry M. Belden, "Autobiographical Notes," in Allen Belden, *A Belden Lineage: 1066–1976* (Washington DC, 1976), 194–95.
21. LP, "Traditional Ballads in Nebraska," *Journal of American Folklore* 26 (1913): 351.
22. Addison E. Sheldon, "Editor's Preface" to LP, *Folk-Song of Nebraska and*

the Central West: A Syllabus (Lincoln: Nebraska Academy of Sciences, 1915), 2.
23. LP, *Folk-Song of Nebraska*, 4–5.
24. Susan L. Pentlin and Rebecca B. Schroeder, "H. M. Belden, the English Club, and the Missouri Folk-Lore Society," *Missouri Folklore Society Journal* 8–9 (1986–87): 19–20.
25. William Carlos Williams to Charles Sheeler, July 17, 1938, in Joan Shelley Rubin, *Constance Rourke and American Culture* (Chapel Hill: University of North Carolina Press, 2001), xii.
26. LP, "The Pedigree of a 'Western' Song," *Modern Language Notes* 29 (1914): 31.
27. D. K. Wilgus, *Anglo-American Folksong Scholarship since 1898* (New Brunswick NJ: Rutgers University Press, 1959), 149.
28. LP, "Traditional Ballads in Nebraska," 353, 353.
29. LP, *Folk-Song of Nebraska*, 5.
30. C. Alphonso Smith to Arthur Kyle Davis, in Wilgus, *Anglo-American Folksong Scholarship*, 175.
31. LP, *Folk-Song of Nebraska*, 70.
32. LP, *Folk-Song of Nebraska*, 3n. The collection cited is Hubert G. Shearin and Josiah H. Combs, eds., *A Syllabus of Kentucky Folk-Songs* (Lexington KY: Transylvania Printing Company, 1911).
33. Shearin and Combs, *Syllabus of Kentucky Folk-Songs*, 3; LP, "Traditional Ballads in Nebraska," 351; LP, *Folk-Song of Nebraska*, 77.
34. Norm Cohen, "Tin Pan Alley's Contribution to Folk Music," *Western Folklore* 29 (1970): 14.
35. LP, "The Southwestern Cowboy Songs and the English-Scottish Ballads," *Modern Philology* 11 (1913): 195–207.
36. "Minutes of the Twenty-Third Annual Meeting of the Nebraska Ornithologists' Union," *Wilson Bulletin* 34 (June 1922): 121.
37. See, e.g., Tom Isern, "Plains Folk: Native Song," *North Dakota State University Agriculture Communication* (1997), http://www.ext.nodak.edu/extnews/newsrelease/back-issues/000281.txt.
38. B. A. Botkin, "Pound Sterling: Letters from a 'Lady Professor,'" *Prairie Schooner* 33 (1959–60): 22. The excerpted letter is dated January 4, 1929.
39. Sheldon, "Editor's Preface," 2.
40. LP, *Folk-Song of Nebraska*, 22.
41. LP, *Folk-Song of Nebraska*, 5–6n.

42. LP, *Folk-Song of Nebraska*, 6n.
43. Barrett Wendell, introduction to John A. Lomax, *Cowboy Songs and Other Frontier Ballads* (1910; New York: Macmillan, 1929), xvi.
44. John Lomax, "Collector's Note," in Lomax, *Cowboy Songs*, xix.
45. LP, "Southwestern Cowboy Songs," 196.
46. LP, "Southwestern Cowboy Songs," 197, 198.
47. LP, "Southwestern Cowboy Songs," 4–5, 6.
48. LP, "Southwestern Cowboy Songs," 198–99, 200.
49. LP, "Southwestern Cowboy Songs," 201, 202, 206, 201, 207.
50. LP, "Dialect Speech in Nebraska," *Dialect Notes* 3 (1905): 60.
51. LP, "The American Dialect Society: A Historical Sketch," *Publications of the American Dialect Society* 17 (1952): 3–4. This account has several problems, despite its considerable detail and Pound's general reliability as a source. Pound's University of Chicago transcript shows no course in Chaucer, with Hempl or anyone else, and Hempl is not listed as teaching in the summer sessions of 1897 or 1898, the years Pound was enrolled. It is possible that she audited a course taught by Hempl in the summer of 1899, prior to her departure to Gemany—she was in Chicago in May to pick up her transcript. The earliest extant letter from Germany is dated September 26, 1899. Another possibility is that Pound's memory, fifty years after the fact, converted a lecture given by Hempl into a course. Sponsored by the University of Chicago English Club, Hempl gave a lecture titled "The Etymology of 'Pickle'" on July 2, 1897. I am grateful to Julia Gardner, reference/instruction librarian at the Special Collections Research Center in the University of Chicago Library, for locating this reference.
52. LP, *Blends: Their Relation to English Word Formation*, Anglistische Forschungen 42 (Heidelberg: Universitäts-Verlags Carl Winter, 1914), 3, ii, 4.
53. LP, *Blends*, 26, 31–32, 27.
54. LP, *Blends*, 7, 11, 32, 45.
55. LP, "Indefinite Composites and Word-Coinage," *Modern Language Review* 8 (1913): 326, 327.
56. LP, *Blends*, 16, 17.
57. The "Contract" is preserved in box 1, folder 4, LP Papers, NSHS. In 1908 Marguerite McPhee was a newly minted MA (1907) with a long career in the University of Nebraska's English department ahead of

her. Appointed as an assistant professor in 1915, she retired at the same rank in 1944. McPhee died in 1970.

58. LP, "Do You Remember," *Nebraska Alumnus*, November 1954, 13.
59. Major Owen Hatteras [H. L. Mencken], "Dianthus Caryophyllus," *Smart Set*, May 1921, 18.
60. LP, "Do You Remember," 23.
61. LP, "Do You Remember," 23.
62. LP, "Nu Upsilon Tau Tau," letter to editor, *Daily Nebraskan*, [1924], box 28, folder 10, LP Papers, NSHS.
63. *Washington Post*, February 16, 1940, clipping in box 1, folder 11, LP Papers, NSHS.
64. The date and title of the 1901 talk are given in LP's obituary notice in *Names*, the journal of the American Name Society (7 [1959]: 62); the history of ACA/AAUW is available at http://www.aauw.org/museum/history/1920_1929/index.cfm.
65. An even earlier paperback booklet, *Questions on Tennyson's Lancelot and Elaine*, was printed in 1901 by a local Lincoln press. Copies of this volume, as well as the 1905 *Tennyson's Lancelot and Elaine* (also printed in Lincoln), are preserved in the LP Papers (RG12/10/15), ASC-LL.
66. Knoll to Butters, June 7, 1983. Butters was at that time editor of *American Speech*. The *Iliad* edition was published in 1930 by Macmillan.
67. "Dr. Louise Pound" (unsigned poem), *Arrowhead*, March 27, 1901, 174, ASC-LL.
68. "Louise Pound Returns from Holiday Trip," *Lincoln Sunday Star*, November 27, 1927, clipping in box 2, folder 1, LP Papers, NSHS. Dawes practiced law in Lincoln from 1887 to 1894.
69. *Hesperian*, February 25, 1898, 7.
70. Eleanora Tibbetts Miller, "History of Girls' Basket Ball in the University of Nebraska," in *Girls' Basket Ball in the University of Nebraska* (Lincoln: American School Supply Company, 1906), 12.
71. "Nebraska Girls Also Win," *Nebraska State Journal*, November 10, 1901, 9.
72. "Girls Leave for Minnesota," *Nebraska State Journal*, March 24, 1904, 7.
73. "Will Come to Lincoln," *Nebraska State Journal*, April 9, 1904, 7.
74. "Nebraska Girls Victors," *Nebraska State Journal*, April 23, 1904, 3.
75. A. W. B. [Anne Barr], "From the Women's Gymnasium," *Sombrero* (1904), 126.

76. Simpson, "Louise Pound, Sports Champion," C4.
77. Simpson, "Louise Pound, Sports Champion," C4.
78. "Lincoln Enters 'Dark Horse' in Tournament," *Omaha World-Herald*, July 24, 1916.
79. "Two Stars Meet in State Golf Finals," *Omaha World-Herald*, July 28, 1916.
80. "Lincoln Woman Wins a State Golf Title," *Omaha World-Herald*, July 29, 1916. I am grateful to Janet Sullivan of Lincoln for sending me the Omaha newspaper accounts of the 1916 tournament.
81. LP to Klara Collitz, July 28, 1935, Collection MS.015, Special Collections and Archives, Milton S. Eisenhower Library, Johns Hopkins University.

5. "Incapable of orderly thought"

1. D. K. Wilgus, *Anglo-American Folksong Scholarship since 1898* (New Brunswick NJ: Rutgers University Press, 1959), 95, 89.
2. LP, "New World Analogues of the English and Scottish Popular Ballads," *Mid-West Quarterly* 3 (1916): 171.
3. LP, "New World Analogues," 171, 172.
4. LP, "New World Analogues," 178, 174, 178.
5. LP, "New World Analogues," 173.
6. LP, "New World Analogues," 185, 186, 187.
7. LP, "The Beginnings of Poetry," PMLA 32 (1917): 205. The quotations from Gummere's *The Beginnings of Poetry* (New York: Macmillan, 1901) are, in order, from 139, 321 (the word "which" is silently elided from the second element of this quote, and Pound recapitalizes as necesary throughout), 106 (a phrase is also silently elided from this quotation), 212, and 13.
8. LP, "The Beginnings of Poetry," 207, 210, 226–27, 219.
9. LP, "The Beginnings of Poetry," 232.
10. LP, *Poetic Origins and the Ballad* (New York: Macmillan, 1921), viii.
11. For Pound's "review" of an Alexander production in this genre see her "The Pageant in Retrospect," *University Journal*, June 1916, 16–17; previously published in the *Nebraska State Journal*, June 11, 1916.
12. LP, "Hartley Alexander as an Undergraduate," *Prairie Schooner* 22 (1948): 372, 374–75.

13. Hartley Burr Alexander, *Poetry and the Individual* (New York: Putnam, 1906), 30.
14. Hartley Alexander, "Louise Pound," *Nebraska Alumnus*, October 1933, 3, 4; reprinted in condensed form in *Roundup: A Nebraska Reader*, ed. Virginia Faulkner (Lincoln: University of Nebraska Press, 1957), 236–38.
15. LP, "Ballads and the Illiterate," *Mid-West Quarterly* 5 (1918): 274.
16. LP, "Ballads and the Illiterate," 275, 292.
17. LP, "Ballads and the Illiterate," 294.
18. LP, "The Ballad and the Dance," PMLA 34 (1919): 366.
19. LP, "The Ballad and the Dance," 383, 393.
20. LP, "The Ballad and the Dance," 400.
21. LP, "The English Ballads and the Church," PMLA 35 (1920): 163, 172.
22. LP, "English Ballads and the Church," 166, 167.
23. LP, "English Ballads and the Church," 162.
24. LP, "English Ballads and the Church," 187.
25. Sigurd B. Hustvedt, *Ballad Criticism in Scandinavia and Great Britain* (New York: American-Scandinavian Foundation, 1916), 5. This volume does for the initial campaigns of the "ballad wars" (the eighteenth century and before) what Hustvedt's later study, *Ballad Books and Ballad Men* (Cambridge: Harvard University Press, 1930), and Wilgus's *Anglo-American Folksong Scholarship* do for the more recent (nineteenth- and twentieth-century) squabbles.
26. LP to her family, October 15, 1899, box 4, folder 1, LP Papers, NSHS.
27. James C. Olson and Ronald C. Naugle, *History of Nebraska*, 3rd ed. (Lincoln: University of Nebraska Press, 1997), 279, 281.
28. Information about Pound's wartime service comes from several letters from Fisher to Pound and also from the "War Service" section of Mamie Meredith and Ruth Odell's "Bibliography, Professional Activities and Vita," *Selected Writings of Louise Pound*, ed. Lowry C. Wimberly (Lincoln: University of Nebraska Press, 1949), 364. Dorothy Canfield Fisher was herself an enormously impressive figure, in her accomplishments every bit the equal of Pound or Cather. She was a successful author of books for children and adults; as much as any other person, she helped introduce the Montessori method to the United States; she worked tirelessly on behalf of the relocation of Jewish refugees from Nazi Germany to the United States. A study is Ida H. Washington's *Dorothy Canfield Fisher: A Biography* (Shelburne VT: New Eng-

land Press, 1982). Pound is not mentioned. A selection of Fisher's letters, *Keeping Fires Night and Day: Selected Letters of Dorothy Canfield Fisher*, edited by Mark J. Madigan (Columbia: University of Missouri Press, 1993), includes no letters to Pound.
29. Albert H. Tolman, rev. in *Modern Language Notes* 36 (1921): 496.
30. Allen Mawer, rev. in *Modern Language Review* 17 (1922): 299, 297, 298, 297.
31. Gordon Hall Gerould, "The 'Popular' Ballad," *Literary Review*, March 5, 1921, 6.
32. Wilgus, *Anglo-American Folksong Scholarship*, 7.
33. Wilgus, *Anglo-American Folksong Scholarship*, 98. For Jones's review see *Journal of English and Germanic Philology* 22 (1923): 136–41.
34. Norm Cohen, introduction to Gordon Hall Gerould, *The Grateful Dead: The History of a Folk Story* (1908; Urbana: University of Illinois Press, 2000), xii.
35. Alexander, "Louise Pound," 4.
36. H. L. Mencken, "Folk Literature," *Smart Set*, June 1921, 143, 144; reprinted in *A Mencken Chrestomathy* (New York: Knopf, 1956), 471–72.
37. H. L. Mencken to LP, May 11, [1921], LP Papers, Rare Book, Manuscript, and Special Collections Library, Duke University. Quoted by permission.
38. Wilgus, *Anglo-American Folksong Scholarship*, 105, 106, 107, 108, 106–7.
39. LP, "A Recent Theory of Ballad Making," PMLA 44 (1929): 622.
40. LP, "A Recent Theory of Ballad Making," 624, 625.
41. LP, "A Recent Theory of Ballad Making," 630.
42. LP, rev. of Gordon Hall Gerould, *The Ballad of Tradition* (1932), *Modern Language Notes* 48 (1933): 124.
43. LP, rev. of Gerould, *The Ballad of Tradition*, 124, 125.
44. LP, rev. of Gerould, *The Ballad of Tradition*, 125, 126.
45. John Robert Moore to LP, February 5, 1933, box 5, folder 2, LP Papers, NSHS.
46. LP, "Oral Literature," in *The Cambridge History of American Literature* (New York: Putnam and Cambridge University Press, 1921), 503, 512.
47. Kenneth S. Goldstein, foreword to LP, *American Ballads and Songs* (1922; New York: Scribner, 1972), vii–viii.
48. Goldstein, foreword, viii, ix.
49. The folksong survey is "American Folksong: Origins, Texts, and

Modes of Diffusion," *Southern Folklore Quarterly* 17 (1953): 114–21; the three Joe Bowers articles are "'Joe Bowers' Again," *Southern Folklore Quarterly* 1 (1937): 13–15; "More Joe Bowers Lore," *Southern Folklore Quarterly* 2 (1938): 31–33; and "Yet Another Joe Bowers," *Western Folklore* 16 (1957): 111–20.

50. LP, "Literary Anthologies and the Ballad," *Southern Folklore Quarterly* 6 (1942): 128, 129.
51. LP, "Literary Anthologies and the Ballad," 129, 140.
52. LP, "The Term 'Communal,'" PMLA 39 (1924): 440.
53. LP, "The Term 'Communal,'" 444, 445, 446.
54. LP, "The Term 'Communal,'" 445, 446.
55. Wilgus, *Anglo-American Folksong Scholarship*, 90.
56. LP, "The Beginnings of Poetry," 232.
57. LP, "New World Analogues," 178.
58. LP, rev. of George Pullen Jackson, *White and Negro Spirituals: Their Life Span and Kinship*, *American Literature* 16 (1944): 251.
59. LP, "The Ancestry of a 'Negro Spiritual,'" *Modern Language Notes* 33 (1918): 443.
60. LP, rev. of Jackson, *White and Negro Spirituals*, 252.
61. Knoll to Butters, June 7, 1983.

6. "There is always zest"

1. LP, "The Pluralization of Latin Loan-Words in Present-Day American Speech," *Classical Journal* 15 (1919): 163.
2. LP, "Pluralization of Latin Loan-Words," 164.
3. LP to the Williams and Wilkins Company, November 16, 1924, quoted in Connie C. Eble, introduction to "Diamond Anniversary Essays," *American Speech* 75 (2000): 227–28.
4. Arthur G. Kennedy, "Foreword," to *Selected Writings of Louise Pound*, ed. Lowry C. Wimberly (Lincoln: University of Nebraska Press, 1949), x, xi.
5. H. L. Mencken, *The American Language*, abridged ed. (New York: Knopf, 1967), 409, 410.
6. LP, "American English Today," in *Studies for William A. Read*, ed. Nathaniel M. Caffee and Thomas A. Kirby (Baton Rouge: Louisiana: Louisiana State University Press, 1940), 109.

7. Allen Walker Read, "A Life Exhilarated by Language," in *Milestones in the History of English in America*, ed. Richard W. Bailey, Publications of the American Dialect Society 86 (Durham NC: Duke University Press, 2002), 321–22.
8. Mencken, *The American Language*, 61–62.
9. LP, "Notes on the Vernacular," *American Mercury* 3 (1924): 233–37; LP, "Walt Whitman's Neologisms," *American Mercury* 4 (1925): 199–201; LP, "Walt Whitman and Italian Music," *American Mercury* 5 (1925): 58–63. Mencken's "welcome" was not especially "florid"; it appeared in the September issue for 1925 (p. 127), not the December number.
10. H. L. Mencken, "'American Speech,' 1925–1945: The Founders Look Back," *American Speech* 20 (1945): 241, 242, 241.
11. LP to her family, September [4–5], 1897, box 4, folder 1, LP Papers, NSHS.
12. Kemp Malone, "'American Speech,' 1925–1945: The Founders Look Back," *American Speech* 20 (1945): 244.
13. LP, "'American Speech,' 1925–1945: The Founders Look Back," *American Speech* 20 (1945): 242–43.
14. LP, "Chorine," *American Speech* 3 (1928): 368; LP, "Park," *American Speech* 2 (1927): 346.
15. LP, "Curious Club Names," *American Speech* 1 (1926): 268.
16. LP, "The Value of English Linguistics to the Teacher," *American Speech* 1 (1925): 102, 105, 102.
17. LP, "Walt Whitman and the French Language," *American Speech* 1 (1926): 421, 429.
18. LP, "The Dialect of Cooper's Leather-Stocking," *American Speech* 2 (1927): 479, 486, 487.
19. "The Contributors' Column," *American Speech* 1 (1926): 63, 64.
20. "Miscellany," *American Speech* 4 (1929): 257.
21. *Daily Nebraskan*, April 5, 1928, 1, 2.
22. LP to OP, June 18, 1927, box 4, folder 1, LP Papers, NSHS.
23. LP, "The College Woman and Research," *Selected Writings of Louise Pound*, 309; first published in *Journal of the Association of Collegiate Alumnae* 14 (November 1920): 31–34.
24. LP, "The College Woman and Research," 310, 311.
25. LP, "The College Woman and Research," 312–13.
26. LP, "The College Woman and Research," 313.

27. LP, "Graduate Work for Women," *Selected Writings of Louise Pound*, 292, 295.
28. LP, "Graduate Work for Women," 293.
29. LP, "Graduate Work for Women," 294, 297.
30. LP, "Graduate Work for Women," 295, 296–97.
31. LP, "Graduate Work for Women," 300, 299.
32. "Mrs. Laura B. Pound Succumbs to Illness," *Nebraska State Journal*, December 11, 1928, 6.
33. Frank O'Connell, *Farewell to the Farm* (Caldwell ID: Caxton, 1962), 20, 46, 197.
34. Mamie Meredith, "The Pound Family of Lincoln, Nebraska," typescript, p. 2, series 4, box 5, folder 5, RP Papers, NSHS.
35. The "dumb Miss Pound" anecdote comes from Michael Shugrue, telephone interview with the author, December 19, 2006. Shugrue became acquainted with the Pound sisters in 1956, when he was a senior English major at the University of Nebraska.
36. OP, *On the Application of the Principles of Greek Lyric Tragedy in the Classical Dramas of Swinburne*, University of Nebraska Studies in Language, Literature, and Criticism 13 (Lincoln: University of Nebraska, 1913), 341–60.
37. Mabel Lee, *Memories Beyond Bloomers (1924–1954)* (Washington DC: American Alliance for Health, Physical Education, and Recreation, 1978), 45.
38. Lee, *Memories Beyond Bloomers*, 36, 61, 44.
39. Lee, *Memories Beyond Bloomers*, 44, 45.
40. Lee, *Memories Beyond Bloomers*, 45, 44.
41. Lee, *Memories Beyond Bloomers*, 36.
42. Robert E. Knoll, *Prairie University: A History of the University of Nebraska* (Lincoln: University of Nebraska Press, 1995), 197.
43. "Dr. Louise Pound Named to Journal's Sports Hall of Fame," *Lincoln Evening Journal*, February 1, 1955, 11. "No Sissy, She," a condensation of this article, appeared in *Nebraska Alumnus*, March 1955, 24.
44. Lee, *Memories Beyond Bloomers*, 61.
45. Lee, *Memories Beyond Bloomers*, 61–62.
46. Lee, *Memories Beyond Bloomers*, 116, 117.
47. Lee, *Memories Beyond Bloomers*, 118.
48. Kristi Lowenthal, "Mabel Lee and Louise Pound: The University of

Nebraska's Battle over Women's Intercollegiate Athletics" (master's thesis, University of Nebraska, 1999), 106.
49. Lee, *Memories Beyond Bloomers*, 422.
50. Lee, *Memories Beyond Bloomers*, 423, 424, 423.
51. Lowenthal, "Mabel Lee and Louise Pound," 110.
52. Lowenthal, "Mabel Lee and Louise Pound," 110, 6.

7. "First woman again"

1. Robert E. Knoll, *Prairie University: A History of the University of Nebraska* (Lincoln: University of Nebraska Press, 1995), 79. The chancellor quoted is Samuel Avery, speaking in February 1922.
2. B. A. Botkin, "Pound Sterling: Letters from a 'Lady Professor,'" *Prairie Schooner* 33 (1959–60): 29.
3. LP, "On Poe's 'The City in the Sea,'" *American Literature* 6 (1934): 22–27; LP, "Poe's 'City in the Sea' Again," *American Literature* 8 (1936): 70–71. The first had been presented as a paper at the 1932 Modern Language Association meeting in New Haven.
4. LP, "Lowell's 'Breton Legend,'" *American Literature* 12 (1940): 348–50.
5. LP, "Whitman and Bird Poetry," *Selected Writings of Louise Pound*, ed. Lowry C. Wimberly (Lincoln: University of Nebraska Press, 1949), 29.
6. LP, introduction to *Walt Whitman: Specimen Days, Democratic Vistas, and Other Prose* (Garden City NY: Doubleday, Doran, 1935), xli, xlii.
7. LP, academic résumé update, box 1, folder 2, LP Papers, NSHS.
8. Michael Ann Williams, *Staging Tradition: John Lair and Sarah Gertrude Knott* (Urbana: University of Illinois Press, 2006), 22.
9. Williams, *Staging Tradition*, 25–36; Angus K. Gillespie, *Folklorist of the Coal Fields: George Korson's Life and Work* (University Park: Pennsylvania State University Press, 1980), 42–44.
10. Mamie Meredith, "The Pound Family," typescript, p. 1, series 4, box 5, folder 5, RP Papers, NSHS. The quoted letter was written by Ruth Moore (Mrs. Allan Stanley).
11. Mr. Knoll told me the "Breast your cards, Olivia" story several times in conversation, and finally put it in writing in a letter of February 13, 2007.
12. Frank Hallgren, telephone interview with the author, January 9, 2007.
13. Hallgren interview.

14. Dorothy Canfield Fisher to LP, February 16, 1938, box 1, folder 1, LP Papers, ASC-LL.
15. Evelyn Simpson, "Louise Pound, Sports Champion . . . and Teacher," *Sunday Omaha World-Herald Magazine*, May 27, 1945, C5.
16. Botkin, "Pound Sterling," 20. Botkin earned his doctorate at Nebraska in 1931; Pound supervised his dissertation. He expresses gratitude for "the stimulating guidance of Dr. Louise Pound" in its preface (B. A. Botkin, *The American Play-Party Song: With a Collection of Oklahoma Texts and Tunes*, University Studies 37 [Lincoln: University of Nebraska, 1937], viii). Pound continued to promote Botkin and his work, most visibly by her welcoming *American Literature* review of *Folk-Say*, the journal he established and edited. She calls it a "brilliant new venture" and notes that Botkin is already known among folklorists for his "unusually excellent study of 'Play-Party Songs in Oklahoma'" (455–56). LP, "*Folk-Say: A Regional Miscellany*," *American Literature* 1 (1930): 454–56. Pound also wrote for *Folk-Say*, served on its editorial board, and journeyed to Oklahoma in 1932 to speak at a Botkin-organized meeting of the Oklahoma Folklore Society. In 1952, more than twenty years after she had directed his doctoral studies, Pound praised Botkin's *A Treasury of Western Folklore* in *Nebraska History* 33 (1952): 122–24.
17. Lucy Elizabeth Weir, *The Ideas Embodied in the Religious Drama of Calderon*, University of Nebraska Studies in Language, Literature, and Criticism 18 (Lincoln: University of Nebraska, 1940), iii.
18. Maurice O. Johnson, *Walt Whitman as a Critic of Literature*, University of Nebraska Studies in Language, Literature, and Criticism 16 (Lincoln: University of Nebraska, 1938), 3. Johnson went on to a solid academic career, teaching at the University of Pennsylvania and publishing scholarly studies of Swift and Fielding. While studying with Pound in Lincoln he became a good friend of Weldon Kees; their association is presented in some detail in James Reidel's biography of Kees, *Vanished Act: The Life and Art of Weldon Kees* (Lincoln: University of Nebraska Press, 2003). Louise Pound is described (accurately) as a "philologist" and (foolishly) as a "companion of Willa Cather" (38).
19. Clarence Gohdes, untitled review, *Modern Language Notes* 54 (1939): 202. The other thesis was Harriet Rodgers Zink's *Emerson's Use of the Bible*, published as number fourteen in the series in 1935. Zink also thanked Pound in similar terms: "I acknowledge an especial debt to

Professor Louise Pound of the Department of English at the University of Nebraska, who first suggested to me a study of Emerson's use of the Bible, and from whom I had practical suggestions and stimulating advice." Harriet Rodgers Zink, *Emerson's Use of the Bible*, University of Nebraska Studies in Language, Literature, and Criticism 14 (Lincoln: University of Nebraska, 1935), 4.
20. Lilian L. Fitzpatrick, preface, *Nebraska Place-Names* (Lincoln: University of Nebraska Press, 1960), 3.
21. Martin S. Peterson, *Robert Jephson (1736–1803): A Study of His Life and Work*, University of Nebraska Studies in Language, Literature, and Criticism 11 (Lincoln: University of Nebraska, 1930), 3.
22. LP, résumé update, box 1, folder 2, LP Papers, NSHS. Peterson acknowledged Pound's help in the book as well: "The original impulse to investigate Miller came to me from Dr. Louise Pound of the English department of the University of Nebraska, and to her I express my gratitude." Martin Severin Peterson, *Joaquin Miller: Literary Frontiersman* (Stanford: Stanford University Press, 1937), vi.
23. Knoll, *Prairie University*, 85. If Maurice Johnson was Kees's friend, Wimberly was a mentor of sorts; he gets a good bit of attention in Reidel's biography (see note 18 above). In Kees, Mari Sandoz, and Loren Eiseley, *Prairie Schooner* published, according to Rudolph Umland, "three geniuses" in its first decade. Umland's account is unpublished but is quoted in Gale E. Christianson's biography of Eiseley, *Fox at the Wood's Edge* (1990; Lincoln: University of Nebraska Press, 2000), 67. Umland's list omits Dorothy Thomas, another Nebraska writer, whose 1934 *New Yorker* story "The Getaway" was described by editor Harold Ross as the best he had ever published. Thomas also got her start in *Prairie Schooner*—her first publication was the poem "The Beast Room" in 1928.
24. Lowry Charles Wimberly, *Folklore in the English and Scottish Ballads* (Chicago: University of Chicago Press, 1928), viii.
25. Elizabeth Atkins, *The Poet's Poet* (Boston: Marshall Jones, 1922), x. Atkins prepared this study as a PhD dissertation under Pound's direction. Pound's later résumé update notes that "Elizabeth Atkins, Associate Professor of English, University of Minnesota, wished to dedicate her *The Poet's Poet* . . . to me. She took her doctorate under me. I thought she should dedicate it to Dr. H. B. Alexander instead for she

owed much more when dealing with her subject to him than she did to me. And he supervised its publication." LP, résumé update, box 1, folder 2, LP Papers, NSHS.

26. John G. Reid, *Viola Florence Barnes, 1885–1979* (Toronto: University of Toronto Press, 2005), xi, 12, 18–19, 21–22.

27. Reid, *Viola Florence Barnes*, 62, 64, 97, 98.

28. Harry L. Hollingworth, *Leta Stetter Hollingworth: A Biography* (Lincoln: University of Nebraska Press, 1943), 169. Hollingworth's biography was reprinted in 1990 with a foreword by Ludy T. Benjamin and Stephanie Shields (Anker Publishing Company). A more recent biography is Ann G. Klein, *A Forgotten Voice: A Biography of Leta Stetter Hollingworth* (Scottsdale AZ: Great Potential Press, 2002).

29. Ruth Odell, *Helen Hunt Jackson (H.H.)* (New York: D. Appleton-Century, 1939), xi. Pound herself was interested in Jackson and dismayed by the welter of errors that dotted the then-available biographical record—her "Biographical Accuracy and 'H.H.'" appeared in 1931. Odell, whose work was then in progress, is described there (though not named) as "a competent investigator" (421). *American Literature* 2 (1931): 418–21.

30. Knoll, *Prairie University*, 128–29.

31. Odell's studies include "Nebraska Smart Sayings," *Southern Folklore Quarterly* 12 (1948): 185–95; "Mid-Western Saliva Lore," *Southern Folklore Quarterly* 14 (1950): 220–23; "'Goofer Bus,'" *American Speech* 27 (1952): 154. Odell was born in Fullerton, Nebraska, in 1891, and died in 1977. She is pictured in the *Cornhusker* for 1938 (65).

32. Helen Winter Stauffer, *Mari Sandoz: Story Catcher of the Plains* (Lincoln: University of Nebraska Press, 1982), 64. Stauffer also suggests a purely personal influence: "Mari's admiration for her teacher may have extended to other areas as well. Her decision to become a redhead may have stemmed from this acquaintance, for Louise Pound's red-gold braids were famous. . . . Although Louise Pound's traditional costume, a tailored tweed, was considered less than chic on campus, in later years Mari, too, often dressed in tweedy suits" (64–65). Pound is also credited in Laverne Harrell Clark's *Mari Sandoz's Native Nebraska* (Chicago: Arcadia, 2000): Pound "greatly encouraged and endorsed her [Sandoz] both in class and at public literary gatherings. Moreover, Pound became a role model for Sandoz while she struggled to con-

tinue her UNL studies and become a writer" (72). Clark's book is primarily a collection of photographs—Pound is pictured on p. 72, and Mamie Meredith, who also "inspired and encouraged (but never taught) Sandoz," appears on p. 71. Gale E. Christianson's biography of Loren Eiseley also mentions Pound's introductions of young writers (a good list is provided, including Dorothy Thomas and Rudolph Umland) to "Lincoln's better homes." Christianson, *Fox at the Wood's Edge*, 106.

33. Mari Sandoz, *Love Song to the Plains* (Lincoln: University of Nebraska Press, 1961), 238.
34. Christine Pappas, introduction to Dorothy Thomas, *The Getaway and Other Stories* (Lincoln: University of Nebraska Press, 2002), vii. This citation is a very slender reed—Pound's comparison of Thomas to Cather comes from an undated letter written by Thomas herself. Thomas enjoyed great success in the 1930s, publishing two books with Knopf (*Ma Jeeter's Girls* in 1933 and *The Home Place* in 1936) and placing stories in the *New Yorker* and Mencken's *American Mercury*. For more on Thomas, see note 23 above.
35. LP, "Graduate Work for Women," *Selected Writings of Louise Pound*, 295.
36. Knoll, *Prairie University*, 78–79.
37. Botkin, "Pound Sterling," 20.
38. Botkin, "Pound Sterling," 21.
39. Mamie Meredith, "The Nomenclature of American Pioneer Fences," *Southern Folklore Quarterly* 15 (1951): 109–51. In the same year Meredith also published a more general article on pioneer fencing, "The Importance of Fences to the American Pioneer," *Nebraska History* 32 (1951): 94–107. Meredith died in 1966, at seventy-eight. Obituary notices appeared in *American Speech* (41 [1966]: 216) and *New York Folklore Quarterly* (22 [1966]: 298–300), the latter written by Botkin.
40. LP to Melvin Van den Bark, n.d. [1950s?], box 5, file 13, OP Papers (RG0913), NSHS. My own researches overlooked this letter—I was alerted to it by Marie Krohn's biography, which I read in manuscript. See note 105 below.
41. Knoll, *Prairie University*, 123, 124.
42. Knoll, telephone interview, July 2, 2007. Slote's book was *Keats and the Dramatic Principle* (Lincoln: University of Nebraska Press, 1958).

43. Mamie Meredith to Max J. Herzberg, May 9, 1938, box 1, folder 1, LP Papers, ASC-LL.
44. Allen Walker Read, "A Life Exhilarated by Language," in *Milestones in the History of English in America*, ed. Richard W. Bailey, Publications of the American Dialect Society 86 (Durham NC: Duke University Press, 2002), 322; James C. Olson, "Graduate Education in the Humanities," in *A Century of Achievement: One Hundred Years of Graduate Education, Research, and Creative Activity at the University of Nebraska*, ed. David Ochsner (Lincoln: University of Nebraska, 2001), 58.
45. Robert Cochran, *Vance Randolph: An Ozark Life* (Urbana: University of Illinois Press, 1985), 76. Because Randolph's reminiscences sometimes stretch the truth, giving the impression of closer acquaintance with notable figures like Mencken and Pound, there is reason to doubt the Pineville visit. In a 1934 letter to Botkin, Pound asks to be remembered to Randolph and says she would like to meet him. By this time Randolph's Pineville days were mostly behind him; he was living in Galena, Missouri. Botkin, "Pound Sterling," 25.
46. LP to Vance Randolph, August 6, 1927, quoted in Cochran, *Vance Randolph*, 173; review in *American Speech* 7 (1932): 305; the first review of *Ozark Folksongs* appeared in the *New York Herald Tribune Weekly Book Review* on May 25, 1947; the review of volume 2 was published in the same place on August 1, 1948. Both are quoted in Cochran, *Vance Randolph*, 180–81, 260.
47. For the thanks in the folk-song collection see Vance Randolph, *Ozark Folksongs* (Columbia: University of Missouri Press, 1980), 36; for the same in the dialect study see Vance Randolph and George P. Wilson, *Down in the Holler: A Gallery of Ozark Folk Speech* (Norman: University of Oklahoma Press, 1953), vii. The "callipygian folklorist" remark was made to me and Michael Luster as we worked on our bibliography of Randolph's writings, *For Love and for Money: The Writings of Vance Randolph* (Batesville: Arkansas College Monograph Series No. 2, 1979).
48. Botkin, *The American Play-Party Song*, viii.
49. George E. Lankford, ed., *Bearing Witness: Memories of Arkansas Slavery, Narratives from the 1930s* WPA *Collections* (Fayetteville: University of Arkansas Press, 2003), xiv. Botkin is cited twenty-three times, for example, in the most recent book-length study of play parties, Alan L. Spurgeon's *Waltz the Hall* (Jackson: University Press of

Mississippi, 2005). Spurgeon also discusses Botkin as one of five "Prominent Play Party Researchers in the United States" (53–55).
50. Botkin, "Pound Sterling," 31.
51. Jerrold Hirsch, "Folklore in the Making: B. A. Botkin," *Journal of American Folklore* 100 (1987): 10, 15. The reference to Pound is on p. 13.
52. B. A. Botkin, rev. of *Selected Writings of Louise Pound*, *Western Folklore* 11 (1952): 302.
53. Jerrold Hirsch, *Portrait of America: A Cultural History of the Federal Writers' Project* (Chapel Hill: University of North Carolina Press, 2003), 284. The second article is Jerrold Hirsch, "'My Harvard Accent' and 'Indifference'": Notes toward the Biography of B. A. Botkin," *Journal of American Folklore* 109 (1996): 308–19.
54. Hirsch, "Folklore in the Making," 5.
55. Hirsch, *Portrait of America*, 23.
56. Gordon Hall Gerould, "The 'Popular' Ballad," *Literary Review*, March 5, 1921, 6.
57. Other appreciators of Botkin have been less dismissive of Pound. Bruce Jackson's *Journal of American Folklore* obituary, for example, mentions that she supervised his dissertation, while Ellen J. Stekert's notice in *Western Folklore* stresses her more general influence: "Just as his mentor, Louise Pound, he walked directly into the tangled and difficult questions about folklore" (337). Bruce Jackson, "Benjamin A. Botkin (1901–1975)," *Journal of American Folklore* 89 (1976): 1–6; Ellen J. Stekert, "Benjamin Albert Botkin, 1901–1975," *Western Folklore* 34 (1975): 335–38. One reviewer of Jerrold's book noted that his study "virtually ignores women"—see Christine Bold, rev. of Jerrold Hirsch, *Portrait of America: A Cultural History of the Federal Writers' Project*, *Journal of American History* 91 (2004): 1071.
58. Not included, e.g., are dedications from Helen Boettcher Hagstotz (*The Educational Theories of John Ruskin* [Lincoln: University of Nebraska Press, 1942]), who also thanked Ruth Odell, or from V. Royce West, whose *Der Etymologische Ursprung der Neuenglischen Lautgruppe* was published in 1936 as no. 83 in the same series (Anglistische Forschungen) that had issued Pound's dissertation in 1901 (Heidelberg: Carl Winter's Universitätsbuchhandlung, 1936).
59. LP, rev. of Paul G. Brewster, *American Nonsinging Games* (1953), *American Speech* 29 (1954): 56.

60. Botkin, "Pound Sterling," 27–28.
61. Botkin, "Pound Sterling," 29.
62. This anecdote is related on a typescript page, apparently prepared by either Botkin or Olivia Pound. Olivia Pound Correspondence, box 432, Benjamin A. Botkin Collection, ASC-LL.
63. LP, "Nebraska Cave Lore," *Nebraska Folklore* (Lincoln: University of Nebraska Press, 1959), 1.
64. LP, "Nebraska Legends of Lovers' Leaps," *Nebraska Folklore*, 80, 82.
65. LP, "Nebraska Strong Men," *Nebraska Folklore*, 122.
66. LP, "The John G. Maher Hoaxes," *Nebraska Folklore*, 119. There were actually two convicts, Clinton A. Sanders and Joseph W. Blackwell. Several letters from Sanders to Pound, written between 1942 and 1947, are preserved in box 5, LP Pound Papers, NSHS.
67. LP, "The John G. Maher Hoaxes," 117, 119.
68. LP, "Nebraska Legends of Lovers' Leaps," 92. Oksana Kasenkina was a Russian schoolteacher who made a three-story leap from the Soviet consulate in Manhattan in 1942 (she was granted asylum); Jan Masaryk was a Czech foreign minister who either jumped or was pushed to his death in Prague in 1948; Lawrence Duggan was a State Department official (and spy for the Soviets) who jumped to his death from his sixteenth-floor Manhattan office in 1948 (his suicide figures, though his career as a spy is omitted, in the 2005 film *Good Night and Good Luck*); James Forrestal, secretary of the navy from 1944 to 1949, died at Bethesda Naval Hospital on May 22, 1949, following a fall from a sixteenth-floor window. The official ruling of suicide has had doubters ever since (see Cornell Simpson, *The Death of James Forrestal* [Appleton WI: Western Islands, 1966] for details). Pound certainly knew how to pick her examples.
69. Patricia Casey Sutcliffe, rev. of 2006 reissue of LP, *Nebraska Folklore*, *Journal of Folklore Research*, posted online February 15, 2007, http://www.indiana.edu/~jofr/review.php?id=403.
70. LP, "Folklore and Dialect," *Nebraska Folklore*, 217.
71. LP, "Folklore and Dialect," 211, 220, 221.
72. LP, "Nebraska Legends of Lovers' Leaps," 83, 86.
73. LP, "Nebraska Strong Men," 124.
74. LP, rev. of Paul Beath, *Febold Feboldson: Tall Tales from the Great Plains* (1948), *Nebraska History* 30 (1949): 77, 78, 79.

75. Jennie A. Morgan, "Early Reminiscences of Walt Whitman," *American Literature* 13 (1941): 9–17; LP, "Doubtful Whitman Lore," *American Literature* 13 (1942): 411–13; Jennie A. Morgan, "[Early Reminiscences of Walt Whitman]: A Reply," *American Literature* 13 (1942): 414–16.
76. LP, "Doubtful Whitman Lore," 412, 413.
77. Morgan, "A Reply," 415, 414.
78. Read, "A Life Exhilarated by Language," 322. Long, who died in 1952, was president of the Modern Language Association in 1948. Pound became the first woman president in 1956, the year she turned eighty-four.
79. LP, "The American Dialect Society: A Historical Sketch," *Publications of the American Dialect Society* 17 (1952): 26.
80. LP, "The American Dialect Society," 25. Wentworth's *American Dialect Dictionary* was published in 1944 to mixed reviews: George P. Wilson, writing in *American Speech* (19 [1944]: 284–89), dithers a good bit but at last pronounces it "a meritorious work" (289); Raven I. McDavid, in the *South Central Bulletin* (5 [1945]: 7), notes Wentworth's failure to even consult the *Linguistic Atlas* and stresses the absence of a useful "lexical geography," calling it "less a dialect dictionary than an amalgamation of lists."
81. LP, "The American Dialect Society," 26.
82. Pound served as a "consultant in pronunciation" for *Webster's New International Dictionary* in 1935; she was a member of the "editorial and pronunciation committees" for the *Thorndike-Century Senior Dictionary* in 1941, the *Thorndike-Century Junior Dictionary* in 1942, and the *Thorndike-Century Beginning Dictionary* in 1945; in 1944 she was an "informant" for the *Pronouncing Dictionary of American English*; she is a member of the "Advisory Board" for a *German-American Dictionary* listed as "in preparation" by Frederick Ungar. Mamie Meredith and Ruth Odell, "Bibliography, Professional Activities and Vita," *Selected Writings of Louise Pound*, 364.
83. LP, foreword to *The American Thesaurus of Slang*, ed. Lester V. Berrey and Melvin Van den Bark (New York: Thomas Y. Crowell, 1942), v–vii. Van den Bark was Pound's colleague at Nebraska, the author of several *American Speech* articles on Nebraska topics. Berrey and Van den Bark wrote in their acknowledgments: "To Dr. Louise Pound, who en-

couraged us from the inception of the work, we wish to express our indebtedness and sincere thanks" (xiii).
84. LP, "The American Dialect Society," 12, 3.
85. LP, "The American Dialect Society," 13.
86. Percy W. Long, "The American Dialect Dictionary," *American Speech* 1 (1926): 441.
87. This speculative analysis may grossly overstate Pound's understanding of Long's hostility and may be thus overly specific in identifying the sources of her clear defensiveness. Pound's 1956 MLA presidential address makes reference to Long's 1948 address, and his in turn made reference to a witticism of hers from a 1933 Old Guard dinner. Tone is an elusive matter. For the whole series see LP, "Then and Now," *PMLA* 71 (1956): 12.
88. LP, "The American Dialect Society," 26.
89. "Who's Who in Lincoln," *Nebraska State Journal*, February 5, 1922, subgroup 1, series 6, box 1, folder 1, LBP Papers, NSHS.
90. Botkin, "Pound Sterling," 21; Arthur G. Kennedy, "Foreword," to *Selected Writings of Louise Pound*, xi; Read, "A Life Exhilarated by Laguage," 322.
91. For Botkin's review of Pound's *Selected Writings* see *Western Folklore* 11 (1952): 302–4. For the obituary notices by Botkin and Meredith (and others) see note 110 below.
92. Edward Dosek, telephone interview with the author, January 2, 2007. The 1941 University of Nebraska yearbook, the *Cornhusker*, shows Dosek in action as a cheerleader (312).
93. Barbara Fox, telephone interview with the author, December 13, 2006. The Pounds evidently summoned photographers to record family reunions on more than one occasion; an earlier photo (unattributed) of the three siblings at an upstairs window of the Pound home appeared in the *Nebraska State Journal* on October 27, 1949. Benjamin Botkin/Louise Pound, box 433, Botkin Collection, ASC-LL.
94. Paige Fox Namuth, interview with the author, Lincoln, Nebraska, January 4, 2007; Paige Fox Namuth to author, e-mail message, January 7, 2007. Paige Fox Namuth is herself a fine storyteller—and a generous woman; I now cherish one of Louise Pound's golf clubs as my own.
95. Michael Shugrue, telephone interview with the author, December 19,

2006. An immediate rereading of *The Professor's House* revealed no obvious candidate for the passage read to Shugrue, unless it would be the opening-page description of Professor St. Peter's "dismantled" old house: "the stairs that were too steep, the halls that were too cramped, the awkward oak mantles with thick round posts crowned by bumptious wooden balls, over green-tiled fireplaces." Willa Cather, *The Professor's House* (New York: Knopf, 1925), 11. St. Peter loves his old house, but it is not easy to imagine Pound calling attention to anything connected to her family described as "bumptious."

96. Effie Leese Scott, "An Appreciation," Presentation Program for Lincoln Kiwanis Club ceremony, November 14, 1947, box 1, folder 13, LP Papers, ASC-LL.
97. "Dr. Louise Pound Named to Journal's Sports Hall of Fame," *Lincoln Journal*, February 1, 1955, 11.
98. Kemp Malone, Elsdon C. Smith, and Mamie Meredith, "Louise Pound 1872–1958," *Names* 7 (1959): 60.
99. Botkin, "Pound Sterling," 29 (February 6, 1955).
100. PMLA 71 (1956): 44, 43. A typescript of the resolution, without the report of the standing ovation, is preserved in Benjamin Botkin/Louise Pound, box 435, Botkin Collection, ASC-LL.
101. LP, "Then and Now," 3.
102. LP, "Then and Now," 5.
103. LP, "Then and Now," 13.
104. Botkin, "Pound Sterling," 30 (December 23, 1955).
105. My copy of this clipping, which is preserved in box 2, folder 2, LP Papers, NSHS, is undated. The 1957 date comes from Marie Krohn's biographical study, *Louise Pound: The 19th Century Iconoclast Who Forever Changed America's Views about Women, Academics and Sports* (Clearfield UT: American Legacy Media, 2007), which I read in manuscript.
106. Botkin, "Pound Sterling," 30 (May 24, 1956). The 1632 L Street home did not long survive the occupants who loved it, despite a 1958 newspaper story announcing its sale with plans for its preservation as an antique shop. "Pound Home Sold; Longtime Landmark Will Be Preserved Unchanged as Shop," *Lincoln Star*, October 15, 1958, series 4, box 6, folder 6, OP Papers, NSHS. Olivia Pound spent her last years in an apartment at 1631 J Street; she died on April 6, 1961.
107. *Lincoln Evening Journal*, June 28, 1958, 1.

108. "Dr. Louise Pound, Educator, Is Dead," *New York Times*, June 29, 1958, 69.
109. "Services Wednesday for Dr. Pound," *Lincoln Evening Journal*, June 30, 1958, 3.
110. See *Western Folklore* 18 (1959): 200–202; *Southern Folklore Quarterly* 23 (1959): 132–33; *Publications of the American Dialect Society* 31 (1959): 31–33; *Names* 7 (1959): 60–62.
111. Mamie Meredith, "In Memoriam: Louise Pound, 1872–1958," *Southern Folklore Quarterly* 23 (1959): 133.
112. C. Merton Babcock, "Profiles of Noted Linguists: Louise Pound," *Word Study* 38 (1962): 1–3; Evelyn Haller, "Louise Pound," *Notable American Women, the Modern Period: A Biographical Dictionary* (Cambridge: Harvard University Press, 1980), 557–59; Donald R. Hickey, "Louise Pound," *Nebraska Moments: Glimpses of Nebraska's Past* (Lincoln: University of Nebraska Press, 1992), 228–34; Elizabeth A. Turner, "Louise Pound (1872–1958)," *Legacy* 9 (1992): 59–64; Robert Cochran, "Louise Pound," *American National Biography* (Oxford: Oxford University Press, 1999), 17:759–60.
113. Haller, "Louise Pound," 558.
114. Anne M. Cognard, "Louise Pound: Renaissance Woman," in *Perspectives: Women in Nebraska History*, ed. Paul G. Johnson and Rosemary Machacek (Lincoln: Nebraska State Council for the Social Studies, Nebraska Department of Education, 1984), 148–66.
115. Evelyn Haller, typescript of address, "Louise Pound and the Taxonomic Rage to Order," to the 1983 meeting of the Modern Language Association in New York. I am grateful to Robert Knoll for providing a copy of Haller's paper.
116. Krohn, *Louise Pound*, 243–44.
117. Marilynne Robinson, "McGuffey and the Abolitionists," in *The Death of Adam* (New York: Picador, 2005), 137.
118. Robinson, "McGuffey and the Abolitionists," 136, 137, 140, 148–49.

Index

In this index, LP is used for Louise Pound and UN is used for University of Nebraska.

Page numbers in italic refer to illustrations.

African American spirituals, 182–83
Alexander, Grover Cleveland, 258
Alexander, Hartley: folk festival movement, 225; as friend, 121; LP's acknowledgment of, 164–65, 181; review of *Poetic Origins*, 173; as source for Nebraska studies, 244; tribute to Pound, 165–66
Alpha Lamda Delta (educational society), 200
American Association of University Professors (AAUP), 225

American Association of University Women (AAUW), 150–51, 201, 205, 208, 225
American Dialect Dictionary project, 250–53, 303n80
American dialects. *See* dialect studies
American Dialect Society, 142–43, 199, 249–53
American Folklore Society, 142, 199, 260
American Indians, 162, 163, 244–47
American Literature, 200
American Name Society, 258
American Speech: as editor, 148; founding of, 186–87, 189–90; LP's contributions to, 192–97
American Studies, founding of field, 129

Analytics of Literature (Sherman), 46–47, 71
Andrews, Benjamin, 41
Anglistiche Forschungen series: *Blends* in, 146; dissertation in, 119
Anthony, Susan B., and bicycling, 81
Arnold, Matthew, 57, 124
Association of Collegiate Alumnae, 151, 199, 201
athletic costumes: basketball, 80–82, 96–97; bicycling, 80–82, *113*
athletics: during early years as professor, 152–58; at Heidelberg, 105; as sublimation, 285n9; undergraduate, 50, 54–55; at University of Chicago, 90–91, 96; during years of graduate study, 80–82, 84–85. *See also* basketball; bicycling; golf; tennis; women's athletics
Atkins, Elizabeth, 230, 233, 297n25
Atkinson, Juliette: and LP as outsider, 126, 173, 176; rematch with, 93–94; tennis match with, 85–86, 87, 89–90, 91, 104
Avery, Samuel, 209

Babcock, C. Merton, 262
Balfour, Earl, 198
ballad origins controversy: aesthetic response in arguments, 160–61; attacks on communalists, 161, 179–80, 180–82; critical reception of *Poetic Origins and the Ballad*, 170–75; and dance, 162–64, 167; initial foray into, 133, 136–41;

and LP as outsider, 75–76; LP's response to criticism, 250–51; and national identity and character, 168–69; in obituaries of LP, 261–62; sources in aristocratic songs, 166–67, 182; sources in church music, 167–68; sources not in common people, 161
Barnes, Viola Florence, 230–31, 233, 239, 253
Barr, Anne (later Mrs. R. G. Clapp), 94, 155–56
Barry, Phillips, 175, 183–84
basketball: as coach, 153–56; at UN, 94, 95–96, 97
Bates, Herbert, 42, 43–44
Beach, Marie, 96
Beath, Paul R., 247
Belden, Henry Marvin, 126–27, 161, 177, 178, 183–84
Bennett, Charles Edwin, 33, 34, 38, 101
Beowulf, 83
Berrey, Lester V., 303n83
Bessey, Charles E., 33, 35–36, 38–39, 263
bicycling, 54–55, 80–82, 88
bicycling costumes, 80–82, *113*
Biddlecome family (mother's family), 3, 24–25
Black Masque, 141, 231
Blackburn, F. A., 46, 68, 84
blacklisting by DAR, 197–98
Bloomer, Amelia, 82
Bond, Mr. (Chicago tennis player), 91

Botkin, Benjamin: as friend and supporter, 134, 135, 240–42, 253, 254; obituary of LP, 261; as protégé, 228, 233, 235, 296n16, 301n57; as source for Nebraska studies, 244–45
Boyce, Benjamin, 259
Brace, Dewitt Bristol, 33, 34–35, 38
Braune, Wilhelm, 103–4
bridge playing, 226
Bruner, Lawrence, 35–36
Bryan, Mrs. W. J., 95, 155
Bryan, William Jennings, 169
Bumstead, "Lute," 15
Bunyan, Paul, stories about, 247
Burnett, E. A., 212–14
Butler, David, 4

Canfield, Dorothy. *See* Fisher, Dorothy Canfield
Canfield, Flavia, 63
Canfield, James H., 39–40, 41, 51, 70
Carmer, Carl, 247
Carroll, Lewis, 53–54, 144
Carroll Club, 52–53
Cassidy, Frederic, 250
Cather, Elsie, 128, 260, 263
Cather, Willa, *112*; attack on Roscoe Pound, 63–64; comparison with Ani Königsberger, 108; description of LP's house, 257, 305n95; influence on LP's fiction, 77; relationship with LP, 45–46, 60–65, 70, 120, 215, 275n67; as undergraduate, 40, 46–47, 51, 62, 69–70, 263; writings, 43
Chaucer studies: article on, 71–74, 102, 125, 279n22; LP ignored by Chaucer scholars, 129
Chi Delta Phi (literary society), 200
Child, Francis James, 129–30, 166, 171, 242
Child ballads, 137, 140, 161
Clapp, Anne Barr, 94, 155–56
Class Day oration "The Apotheosis of the Common" (LP), 56–60, 161, 169
Clements, Frederic, 36, 119
Clenen, Nettie, 48–49
Cochran, Robert, 262
coeducation. *See* women students
Cognard, Anne M., 262
College English, 200
College Equal Suffrage League, 231
Combs, Josiah H., 131–32, 134
common people: in ballad origins controversy, 161; and Class Day oration, 56–60, 161, 169
"communal" theory of ballad origins: LP's criticism of, 160, 246; in LP's early work, 137; in "The Term 'Communal'" (LP), 180–82. *See also* Harvard school of ballad origins
community of scholars, 45, 123–24, 263
consensus gentium, 181, 182, 264
Cook, Harriet, 96
Cooper, James Fenimore, 194
Copper Kettle Club (social-literary club), 200, 226
Coulton, G. G., 75
Covel, Miss, 70
cowboy songs, 133, 137–41, 160

Craigie, W. A., 198, 252
Craven, Jennie, 85, 87, 89
croquet, LP's skill at, 26
Crowell Publishing Company, 250–51
crushes, schoolgirl, 277n78

dance as origin of poetry, 162–64, 167
Daughters of the American Revolution (DAR): and Laura Pound, 7, 24, 119, 198, 206; and LP, 42, 93, 147, 200; LP blacklisted by, 197–98
Dawes, Charles G., 153
Delta Kappa Gamma (educational society), 200
Delta Omicron (musical society), 200
dialect studies: American English as subject for scholarship, 188; and *American Speech*, 191–93; early work in, 123, 141–42, 143, 145–47, 189; return to, 183–86, 188, 190, 193, 194, 261; and students, 239
dictionary projects, 251, 303n82
Dorsey, George A., 247
Dosek, Edward, 254–55, 261, 304n92
dramatic productions: LP in, 69–70; theater-going in Heidelberg, 106
Dumbbells, 149–50

Edgren, August Hjalmar, 38, 42, 71, 272n20
Eliason, Norman, 261
English school of ballad origins, 138, 141. *See also* Henderson, T. F.; Ker, W. P.

Feboldson, Febold, stories about, 247
figure skating, 55, 88, 105
Fisher, Dorothy Canfield: friendship with LP, 55, 121, 170, 227, 290n28; obituaries for LP, 261; at UN, 41, 263
Fitzpatrick, Lilian Linder, 229, 233, 245
Fletcher, Alice, 247
folk festival movement, 225–26
folklore and folk music research: African American spirituals, 182–83; cowboy songs, 133, 137–41, 160; early work on, 123, 125–26, 129–31, 132, 180; folklore as scholarly discipline, 246; *Folk-song of Nebraska and the Central West* (LP), 127–28, 136–41; "Joe Bowers" series, 179, 261, 291n49; return to study of, 177–80
Folk-Say, 200, 296n16
Food for France Committee, 170
footracing at tennis dinner, 89
Forward, Kenneth, 122
Fossler, Laurence, 122
Fox, Paige, 255–57, 261
French studies by LP, 42–43, 56, 70, 125, 144, 181, 193, 224
Furnas, Robert W., 10–11

Ganz, Mrs. Dale B., 257
Gardner, James P., 89
Gardner, Mary, 89
Gardner, Sarah, 89
Geisthardt, S. L., 54
Gere, Charles H., 7, 39–40

Gere, Mrs. Charles H., 63, 95
Gere, Muriel, 63
Germans, attitude toward, in WWI, 170
Gerould, Gordon Hall: attacks on LP, 242; gives up communalist views, 174–75; and LP as outsider/insider, 93, 176; LP's critiques of, 161, 175–77, 179–80; response to *Poetic Origins*, 171–73
Gerrard, Grace (Roscoe's wife), 119, 284n1
Gerwig, W. S., 74
ghost dance religion, 245
G.O.G. (Go Out Girls)/G.O.I. (Go Out Independents), 51, 70, 278n10
Goldsmith, Oliver, 151
golf, 157–58, 195, 217, 256, 258
Gray, Asa, 16, 35
Greet, William Cabell, 192
Grimm brothers, 169
Grinnell, George Bird, 247
Grundtvig, Svend, 168, 169
Guggenheim Foundation advisory council, 197, 231
Guilmette, Mr., 70
Gummere, Francis B.: as communalist, 138; defended by Gerould, 171, 172; and disregard of LP as scholar, 242; LP's attacks on, 161, 162–63, 246, 289n7; on oral tradition, 166. *See also* Harvard school of ballad origins
Gustavson, Reuben, 215

Hagstotz, Helen Boettcher, 301n58
Haller, Evelyn, 262

Hallgren, Frank, 226–27, 257, 261
Hapgood, Norman, 197
Harding, Everhard, 107, 120, 283n92
Hardy, Emory, 54
Hargreaves, Mr. and Mrs. A. E., 155
Harvard school of ballad origins, 138, 161, 162–63. *See also* "communal" theory of ballad origins; Gummere, Francis B.; Kittredge, George Lyman
Harwood, Mrs. N. S., 86
Hempl, George, 142
Henderson, T. F., 138
Henry, Mellinger E., 107, 132, 179
Herder, Johann Gottfried von, 169
Hickey, Donald R., 262
Hicks, John D., 41
Hicks, Lewis, 38
Hirsch, Jerrold, 241–42
Hollingworth, Leta Stetter, 231–32, 239
Holloway, Emory, 248–49
Hoops, Johannes, 98, 103, 104, 165, 170, 259
House, H. C., 125
Hudson, Sadie, 89

individualism: in composition of songs, 182; importance of to LP, 59–60, 65, 170
"Infantry Drill" course, 48–49, 55
infatuations, schoolgirl, 277n78
International Council for English, 197, 198–99

Jackson, Bruce, 301n57

James, Henry, 188
"Joe Bowers" song, 179, 261, 291n49
Johnson, Alvin, 45–46, 109, 123, 255, 263
Johnson, Herbert, 152
Johnson, Maurice O., 121, 228–29, 239, 296n18
Jones, H. S. V., 172
Jones, Will Owen, 41

Kappa Kappa Gamma (social club), 200, 231
Kees, Weldon, 120–21, 296n18
Kennedy, Arthur G., 187–88, 189–90, 233, 239–40, 254
Kent, Charles Foster, 83
Kentucky folk songs, 131–32
Ker, W. P., 138
Kittredge, George Lyman: annotated LP's first major article, 129; as communalist, 138, 171; and disregard of LP as scholar, 242; as editor, 130, 134, 135; LP's attack on, 161; on oral tradition, 166. *See also* Harvard school of ballad origins
Kiwanis Medal for Distinguished Service, 257–58, 261
Knoll, Robert, 92, 122–23, 151–52, 183–84
Knott, Sarah Gertrude, 225
Königsberger, Ani. *See* Pfister, Ani Königsberger
Krapp, George Philip, 198
Krohn, Marie, 262, 263

La Fleche, Francis, 247

Lancaster, Lane W., 257
Latin School, 33–36
Lee, Mabel and controversy over women's athletics, 209–15
Lehmer, Derrick Norman, 51–52, 53, 263, 273n46
Leipzig (Leipzic), University of, rejected application to, 98, 242, 260
Le Rossignol, J. E., 181
Lincoln Country Club, 200
Lincoln NE: in 1870s, 7–11; elite society in, 17–18; founding of, 4; position of LP in, 227; response to LP's tennis victory, 86–87
Lincoln Public Library, 10
Lincoln University Club, 200
Lincoln Women's Club, 16
literary criticism: *Beowulf*, 83; dissertation, 98–104, 123; in early career, 123, 124–25; editing of school texts, 151–52, 288n65; Lowell and Poe, 224; *The Romaunt of the Rose*, 71–74; Whitman studies, 190, 193, 224–25, 248–49
literary societies at UN, 50–51
Lloyd, Rachel, 38, 237
Lomax, John, 129, 135, 137–38, 160–61, 169
Long, Percy W., 249, 251–53, 303n78, 304n87
Lord Randal, article on, 125, 141
"Louise Pound Alumni Association," 228, 240, 241
Loundsbury, Thomas Raynesford, 72
Lowell, James Russell, 224
Lowes, John Livingston, 198

MacLean, Chancellor, 95
MacLean, Mrs., 95
Malone, Kemp, 187, 189, 191, 197, 261
Manatt, J. Irving, 37–38, 41
mass communication and folk songs, 131–32, 136, 143, 160, 179, 182
Matthews, M. M., 250
McDonald, J. B., 86
McPhee, Marguerite, 147–48, 263, 287n57
Mencken, H. L.: on American English, 188; and *American Speech*, 186; on LP, 184, 189–91, 261; publishes LP spoof, 149; review of *Poetic Origins*, 173–74
Meredith, George: *Modern Love*, 127
Meredith, Mamie J., *218*; acknowledgment of by LP, 191, 245; burial of, 265; on Cather, 277n78; obituaries, 261–62; as protégé, 240, 253, 263; vita, 68, 127, 254; as woman scholar, 236–37, 238–39, 299n39
Middle West, 264. *See also* Nebraska and Nebraska studies
Miller, Jim, 122–23, 238
Mitchald, Mrs. A. R., 86
Modern Language Association (MLA): first paper presented at, 83; Long prevents presidency of LP, 249, 303n78; presidency of, 142, 199, 258–59
Molbech, Christian, 168
Moore, John Robert, 177
Morgan, Jennie, 248–49
Motherwell, William, 169

music: opera loving, 153, 208, 243, 244; piano playing by LP, 15–16, 47
music research. *See* folklore and folk music research

Namuth, Paige Fox, 255–57, 261
National Association of Deans of Women, 203–5
national identity and character in ballad origins controversy, 168–69
National League for Women's Service, 170
Nebraska, University of. *See* University of Nebraska
Nebraska Academy of Sciences, 127
Nebraska and Nebraska studies: in early career, 127; *Folk-song of Nebraska and the Central West* (LP), 127–28, 131–33, 136–41; importance to LP, 13, 151, 177, 191, 192; in later career, 243, 244–48, 302n66; *Nebraska Folklore* (LP), 228, 244–47; state capitol building, 121, 164–65, 285n6; and University of Nebraska Press, 228
Nebraska Ethnology and Folk Lore series, 134
Nebraska Sports Hall of Fame, 157, 216, 258–59
Nebraska Women's Golf Association, 157
Nebraska Writers Guild, 200
Neel, Mr. (Chicago tennis player), 91
Neely, Carrie (tennis player), 91, 92, 153

New England Quarterly, 200
Nu Upsilon Tau Tau (Nutts), 150

O'Connell, Frank, 206–7
Odell, Ruth, *218*; acknowledgment of, 245; assembled vita for LP, 68, 254; as protégé, 238, 240, 253; as woman scholar, 232–33, 235, 237, 298n29, 298n31
"O.K.," LP's studies of, 18, 269n42
Old English: dissertation on, 98–104; knowledge of in dialect studies, 145; LP's interest in, 186; teaching of, 152, 187, 226, 233
Olson, James C., 239
"Oral Literature," *Cambridge History of American Literature* (LP), 177–78
Order of the Golden Fleece, 148–49
Owens, Ethel, 257

Paine, Mrs. C. S., 198
Palmer, Edgar Z., 261
Percy, Thomas, 168
Peterson, Martin S., 229, 297n23
Pfister, Ani Königsberger, 107–9, *116*, 121, 170, 215, 283n94
Phi Beta Kappa (PBK): activities in, 184, 189; LP's election to, 18, 56, 67, *114*; spoof of, 150; UN chapter of, 199, 200, 239
Pi Gamma Mu (sociological society), 200
play in Pound children's education, 20, 25
Poe, Edgar Allan, 224
poetry, theories of origin: in aristocratic song, 164; in dance, 162–64, 167
Poppleton, Andrew J., 3–4
popular songs and folk songs, 131–32, 136, 143, 160, 179, 182
Pound, Laura Biddlecome (mother), 27; arrival in Nebraska, 1–2, 5–6; basketball patroness, 154; as cultural colonist, 264; death of, 206–7, 265; influence on LP, 147, 253, 263; language studies, 16–17; in Lincoln, 6–7, 9; retirement, 119; sense of humor, 2, 24; as source for Nebraska studies, 244; student at UN, 42; as teacher, 14–20, 25
Pound, Louise: as advocate for women, 13, 205, 263; aesthetic response in, 102, 123, 125, 138, 160–61, 224; as assistant to Sherman, 46, 273n29; as athlete, 13, 26, 258 (*see also* athletics); birth, 14; as bridge player, 226; burial of, 264–65; competitiveness of, 90, 104, 106, 134, 166, 210, 226; cultural politics of, 80–82, 169, 245; dancing at Heidelberg, 105–6, 120, 134; death of, response to, 261–64; decisiveness of, 253–54; described as cold-hearted, 56, 109, 120; described as difficult, 136, 234, 238, 262; disregard of in scholarly community, 241–42; dissertation of, 98–104, 123; in drama productions, 60; drawing skills, 77; driving skills, 152, 227; and early education, 18, 19, 25; as

editor, 199, 200, 258; elitist attitudes in, 56–60, 92, 135, 139–41, 161, 169, 182, 265; friendships of, 98, 107–9; and graduate studies, 83; and honorary societies, 42, 148–50; honors received, 257–58, 262; and individualism, 59–60, 65, 170, 182; as insider/elite, 17, 67, 91–93, 135; insider/outsider oscillation, 75, 91–93, 126, 135, 173, 176, 235; literary societies, 56; as mentor, 226, 228–34, 238–39, 254, 258; national reputation of, 125–26, 199–200, 262–63; as Nebraskan and westerner, 13, 177, 191, 192; as opera lover, 153, 208, 243–44; organizational skills of, 15, 102, 144, 262–63; personality of, 165–66; Phi Beta Kappa membership, 18, 56, 67, 114, 184, 189; and prep school, 33–37; professional activities, 198–99, 200; Quakerism of, 242, 257, 261; relationship with Cather, 45–46, 60–65, 70, 120, 215, 275n67; response to criticism, 215, 250–51; scholarship of, 76, 101–2, 109–10, 123, 185–86, 258, 264; self-deprecation (Mrs. Throttlebottom remarks), 151, 176, 182, 198, 259; sense of humor of, 49–50, 146–50, 184, 194–97; sexuality of, 61, 109, 120–21, 274n65, 276n69, 277n78, 285n9; short stories by, 77–80; as speaker, 83, 151, 225–26; as teacher, 68–69, 122, 152, 179–80, 187, 193, 255, 258; as undergraduate, 42, 55–56; and undergraduate studies, 43, 46–48; on UN golden era, 41–42; as winner, 55–56, 182; writing style of, 125, 147, 148, 205, 262

Pound, Louise, portraits: in bicycling costume, *113*; as golf champion, *217*; with Mari Sandoz, *221*; as mature woman, *222*; as preparatory school student, *30*; with siblings, *220*; signing copies of *Selected Writings*, *219*; as tennis champion (1897), *115*; as UN student, *114*; with Willa Cather, *112*; as young child, *29*; as young instructor, *117*

Pound, Louise, publications: *American Ballads and Songs*, 178–79; *Blends: Their Relation to English Word Formation*, 143–45; book reviews, 243–44; first fifteen years of professional career, summary, 151–52; first publication, 71–74; *Folk-song of Nebraska and the Central West*, 127–28, 131–33, 136–41; *Nebraska Folklore*, 228, 244–47; "Oral Literature," *Cambridge History of American Literature*, 177–78; *Poetic Origins and the Ballad*, 125–26, 141, 161, 170–75; "Weeping Mary" article, 24–25, 182–83

Pound, Olivia (sister), *219*, *220*; as basketball enthusiast, 154; birth and childhood, 14, 18–19, 25; burial of, 265; in dramatic productions, 69; as educator, 119, 128, 208–9; relationship with LP, 120–21, 208, 243–44; tribute to,

Pound, Olivia (sister) (*continued*) 260; writings for *American Speech*, 192–93

Pound, Roscoe (brother), *220*; assistance to LP, 181; blacklisting of, 198; Cather's attack on, 63–64, 274n65, 276n74; childhood, 13–14, 16–17, 19–20, 24, 25; controversial positions of, 76; marriage of, 119, 284n1; move to Harvard, 158; politics of, 169; and raid on sporting club, 82; relationship with sisters, 227; at UN, 36, 38, 41, 46, 53; in visit home, 255–56

Pound, Stephen B. (father), *28*; background of, 2–3, 5–6, 12, 268n7; as baseball fan, 26; burial of, 265; as cultural colonist, 264; death of, 158; influence on LP, 59–60; as judge, 6, 23, 270n59; retirement of, 119; sense of humor of, 20–22, 148; as source for Nebraska studies, 244; as teacher, 17, 19

Pound family home (1632 L Street), 6, 17, *31*, 119; sale of, 305n106

Pound Middle School, 18–19, 263

prairie villages setting in LP's fiction, 79–80, 280n29

Prey, Annie, 43

"primitive" music and beginnings of poetry, 162

Quakers: ancestors as, 2, 169, 260, 264; LP as, 242, 257, 261

Randolph, Vance, 239, 240, 253, 300nn45–46

Raymond, Donald, 54
Raysor, Thomas M., 232–33, 235, 237
Read, Allen Walker, 188–89, 239, 249, 250, 254, 261
Ritson, Joseph, 168
Robinson, Marilynne, 264
Robinson, Seth, 4
romanticism in nineteenth-century scholarship, 161, 169, 180–81
Roosevelt, Theodore, 161
Rourke, Constance, 129
Ryoner, Hal, 87

Sandoz, Mari, *221*, 233–34, 240, 244, 297n23, 298n32

scholarly investigation, nature of: arguments in, 181–82; disagreements and Gerould, 172–73; humor in, 195; in LP article in *Mid-West Quarterly*, 160; position of women in, 201–5, 235; resolution of disagreements, 174–75; vitriolic criticism in, 168

school texts: LP's criticism of, 180; LP's editing of, 151

Schossberger, Emily, 237, 260
Schwab, Mrs. S., 86
Scott, Effie Leese, 257
Scott, Walter, 169
Shakespeare, William, 62, 151
Sharp, Cecil, 175
Shaw, George Bernard, 198, 199
Shearin, Humbert G., 131–32, 134
Sheldon, Addison E., 128, 133–34, 245
Sherman, Lucius A., *111*; hires LP as adjunct professor, 110, 122; influ-

ence on LP, 46–47, 263; MA thesis written under, 71; recommendation to Blackburn, 68, 84
Sherwood, Lyman H., 3
Shugrue, Michael, 257, 261
Sigma Tau Delta (literary society), 200
Skeat, W. W., 71–72, 93, 146, 173, 278n14, 279n20
Slote, Bernice, 237–38
Smith, C. Alphonso, 131, 132
Smith College, honorary doctorate from, 197
sounds, unconscious symbolism of, 146–47
Southern Folklore Quarterly, 200
stamp collecting, 14, 102
Stanton, Elizabeth Cady and bloomers, 82
Stepanek, Orin, 120–21, 285n6
Stetter, Leta, 231–32, 239
Stewart, Mrs. J. T., 157–58
Studies in Language, Literature, and Criticism, 199, 200, 228, 240
Sweet, James, 7–8

tatting, 166
tennis: during early years as professor, 152–53; during graduate study years, 82–83, 84–87, 280n38; at Heidelberg, 94, 105; portrait of LP as player, 87, *115*; street children on courts, 92, 182, 265; during undergraduate years, 50, 54; visit to Wimbledon, 198; Women's Western Championship (1897), 85–90, 94, 191, 235. *See also* Atkinson, Juliette
Tennyson, Alfred, studies of, 124, 151
textbooks, 84, 214
Theta Sigma Pi (journalism society), 200
Thomas, Dorothy, 234, 297n23, 298n32, 298n34
Thomas, Jean, 226
Thomas, Martha Carey, 259–60
Thompson, Stith, 246
Thompson, T. J., 255
Throttlebottom, Mrs., 151, 176, 182, 198, 259
Tilton, Clara, 97
Turner, Elizabeth A., 262

Umland, Rudolph, 298n32
Union Literary Society, 50–51, 60
University Dramatic Club, 69–70
University of California visiting professorship, 197
University of Chicago: athletics at, 90–91, 96; and Hempl, 142, 287n51; studies at, 83–84, 97; LP as visiting professor at, 197
University of Heidelberg: dancing at, 105–6, 120, 134; LP as outsider, 93, 173, 235; recreational activities at, 105–10; studies at, 98–105; tennis victory, 94, 105
University of Minnesota, 154–55
University of Missouri: basketball, 154; song collecting at, 128–29
University of Nebraska: Alexander at, 164; Andrews Hall as English

University of Nebraska (*continued*)
department at, 122; basketball at, 94–95, 153–56; coeducation at, 40, 45, 51, 127; and controversy over women's athletics, 209–15; disregarded by eastern establishment, 242; in education of Pound children, 26; football team, 254–55, 258; founding and early years, 1, 7, 11, 18; golden era of, 37–43; graduate studies curriculum, 71; literary societies, 50–51, 60; LP as outsider at, 235–36; LP in Department of English, 121–22; LP's commitment to, 41–42, 110; mother's studies at, 16–17; and Populists, 169; Pound Hall at, 263; praise for, 43–44; shift of emphasis at, 232–33; *Studies in Language, Literature, and Criticism*, 199, 200, 228, 240; University Hall as English department, 122; women faculty at, 237

University of Nebraska Press, 228, 237

Van den Bark, Melvin, 191, 237, 303n83
Van Doren, Carl, 178
Victorian period, LP's defense of, 52–53, 60, 264

Waddell, Helen, 75
Ward, Maria, and bicycling, 81
"Weeping Mary" article (LP), 24–25, 182–83
Weir, Lucy Elizabeth, 296n7

Wendell, Barrett, 137
Wentworth, Harold, 250–51, 252
West, V. Royce, 301n58
Western Folklore Conference, 208, 243–44
Western Kentucky Folklore Archive, 132
Whitman, Walt, 190, 193, 224–25, 228–29, 248–49
Who's Who in America, 199–200
Wilson, George P., 261
Wimberly, Lowry Charles, 191, 229–30, 233, 240, 253, 254
Wimer, M. E., 85, 87, 88, 91
women: "The College Woman and Research" (LP), 201–4; friendships between, 277n78; "Graduate Work for Women" (LP), 203–5, 235; LP's relationships with, 121; mentoring of, 230–34; as song collectors, 128–29, 142
women scholars, 13, 38, 201–5, 235, 237, 263
women students: as boarders with Pounds, 207–8; coeducation at UN, 36, 40, 45, 49, 51, 70, 127; at Heidelberg, 102, 103; LP and, 49, 262; and need for male escorts, 51, 70
Women's Athletic Association, 210
women's athletics: controversy at University of Nebraska, 209–15; costumes for, 80–82, 96–97; delicacy of men in audience, 95; LP's support for, 205, 216
Women's Committee of the State Council of Defense, 170

women's gymnasium, controversy over, 212–14
women's rights: bicycling as political statement, 80–82; in LP's fiction, 77–78, 80
Wooden Spoon (social professional club), 200, 226, 260

World War I, LP's service during, 169–70
wrestling at tennis dinner, 89

Yale, visiting professorship, 197

Zink, Harriet Rodgers, 296n19